JAMIE'S

AMERICA

HYPERION

NEW YORK

Also by Jamie Oliver

The Naked Chef
The Naked Chef Takes Off
Happy Days with the Naked Chef
Jamie's Kitchen
Jamie's Dinners
Jamie's Italy
Cook with Jamie
Jamie at Home
Jamie's Food Revolution

JAMIE'S AMERICA
JAMIE OLIVER

Photography and collages
by David Loftus

Published by arrangement with Michael Joseph / The Penguin Group

www.penguin.com
www.jamieoliver.com

Copyright © Jamie Oliver, 2009, 2010
Photography and collages copyright © David Loftus, 2009, 2010
Illustration on page 8: Shepard Fairey/Press Association Images

Note to Reader: Cup measures are spooned and leveled unless specified otherwise.

ISBN: 978-1-4013-2360-8

Hyperion books are available for special promotions and premiums. For details contact the HarperCollins Special Markets Department in the New York office at 212-207-7528, fax 212-207-7222, or email spsales@harpercollins.com.

First U.S. Edition

10 9 8 7 6 5 4 3 2 1

jamieoliver.com

FRANCESCO "NONNO" CONTALDO
14 NOVEMBER 1912 – 29 MAY 2009

This book is dedicated to my mentor's mentor –
Gennaro's father, Nonno – who was still cooking delicious
food for himself every day at the ripe old age of ninety-six.

A great man, a great cook, and a great father.
Rest in peace, Nonno.

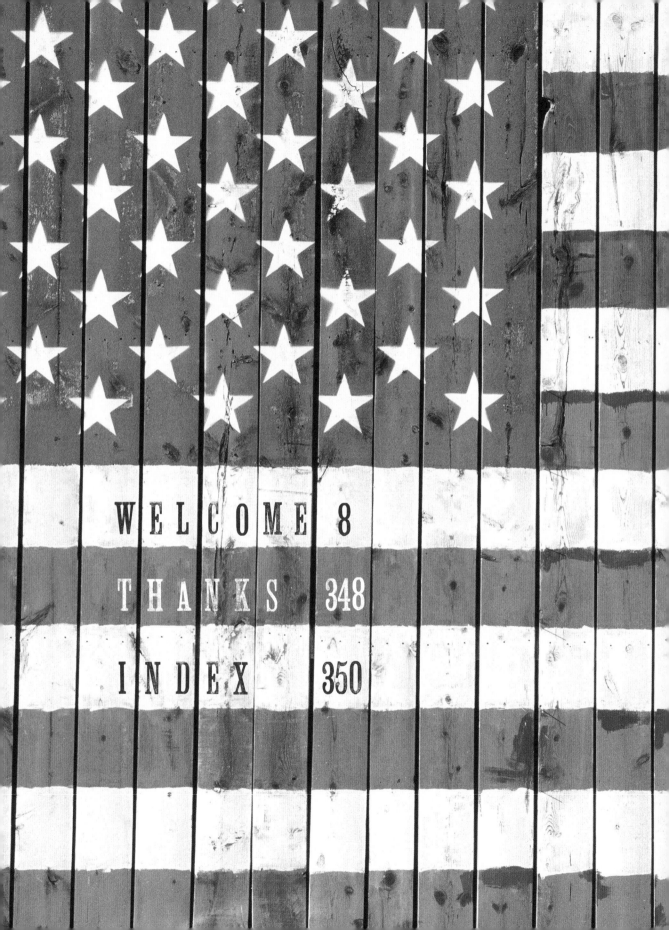

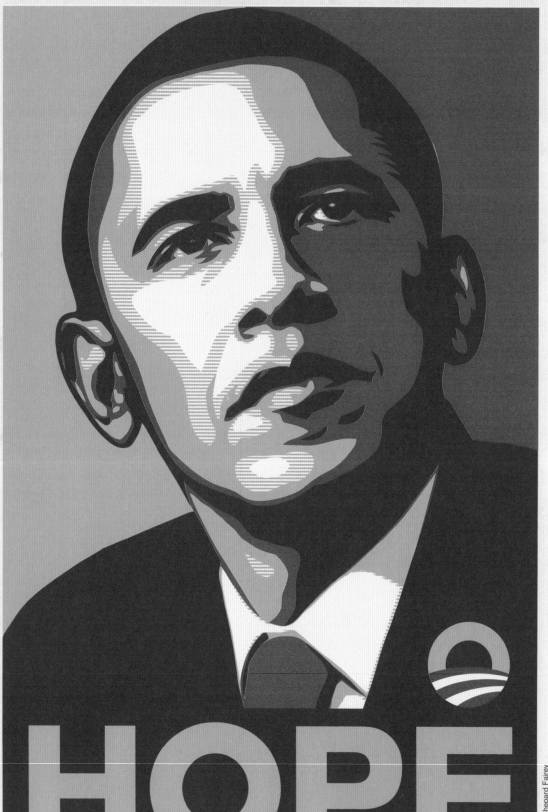

HOPE

★ ★ WELCOME TO ★ ★
JAMIE'S AMERICA!

Wow! What a year. Originally this book was my chance to get out and satisfy my lifelong curiosity about America: the people, the country, and, of course, the food. You guys might know what the real story is, but for those of us in other countries, America is still a bit of a mystery. We've all watched at least a bit of *The Jerry Springer Show* ... but what is *real* American family life like? We've all heard about the American dream ... but what is the American reality? We're all familiar with the clichés of American food: junk food and supersizing ... but what is *real* American food all about? I wanted to get under the skin of the country, find the answers to these questions, and, most importantly, bring the best of what I learned there home for my family, my friends, and you guys.

So as you can see, the idea for this book came from a really personal and curious place; but fast-forward eighteen months and the world that most of us live in has definitely changed, especially for Americans. A kick-ass world recession that seemed to come overnight, and the election of America's first black president, Barack Obama, who stormed to victory with his inspirational words and promise of change, have turned America upside down and made it an even more fascinating place. Incredibly, just one week before sitting down to write this introduction, I cooked the state dinner for the G20 London Summit on the global financial crisis, which President Obama and his wife, Michelle, attended. They were such a lovely couple. Never when I started this journey did I imagine I'd be chatting with them before the end of it!

When I told people I was writing a book about American food, all the familiar jokes about junk food would come up. But that didn't put me off in the slightest, because if there's one thing I know it's that we are all guilty of clinging to a cliché. I've spent ten years of my career defending British food against the perception that it's nothing but slop, so I feel a bit sympathetic toward America when that junk food label gets slapped over *all* American cooking. It's true that their fast-food culture and huge portions have led to massive health problems. But anyone with half a brain knows that how people feed their families is where the real story is. Everywhere I went it seemed people were focusing on the simpler things and family life. Instead of being shown glitzy, flamboyant food, I was being welcomed into homes and seeing sides of America I'd never dreamed existed. Because of that, I've been able to pick up on new and innovative ways of cooking, as well as learn more about the old-school, accessible, and affordable comfort classics that make the country tick. The recipes in this book reflect my take on those much-loved classics, as well as things I made up as I went along. I hope you enjoy all of them.

Maybe it was the recession, maybe it was Obama-fever, but everyone I met on my travels seemed to be in an open and humble frame of mind: it felt like America laid open. Times are really tough for most of the people I met. At a soul food restaurant in Savannah, Georgia, I asked a group of people having lunch how they were adapting their home cooking to cope with the credit crunch. They told me, "It doesn't matter; we always cook like we're in a recession!" They already had frugal cooking nailed, and that just made the recipes I picked up on the way even more relevant, so there couldn't have been a better time to dip into American cooking. It felt pretty special to be a fly on the wall in a lot of lovely family homes during this reflective time. Alongside all the wonderful food I found, I think the

warmth of those people (many of whom you'll see in the photos) and their "can do" attitude will be the longest-lasting memory for me.

Without sounding too pleased with myself, I'm really proud of this cookbook. I'm proud of what I've written and of what I'm now able to share with you. Although the dishes here are just the tip of the iceberg, this book is a true snapshot of the diverse and delicious food that's being cooked in homes across America. I've deliberately gone off the beaten track, away from the predictably foodie places, to get you the real thing, and have had a lot of funny (sometimes odd and even slightly scary!) but mostly inspiring moments because of that.

Although I would have loved to visit every state, a man with a pregnant wife and two kids can only do so much, so I pinpointed six places I hoped would kick-start my voyage of discovery. I started with two cities I already knew pretty well: New York and Los Angeles. This time, though, I explored their gritty underbellies and discovered things even my friends who live there had never heard of.

The cultural mix of Louisiana, along with the incredible spirit of the people who live there, made that state another must for me. I arrived just two weeks after the second major hurricane in four years had hit, and left with a huge respect and admiration for all the resilient people I met. Because the South in general fascinated me, the next trip I planned was through

Georgia, Martin Luther King's home state. That incredible journey gave me a chance to get my head around the emotional inspiration behind the legendary type of cooking that is soul food, not to mention learn something about what it means to be an African-American today.

To properly get to grips with American food, I felt I had to get back to the original landlords of the country: the Native Americans. In the wilderness of the Arizona desert I found a completely different, but incredible side of America, one that helped give this book a really solid food foundation.

In Wyoming, I saddled up a horse and experienced a big part of American life: ranching. Cowboy life, even today, is all about back-to-basics living and hard work, the kind where you need to have your wits about you. I absolutely loved it, and found the history of the pioneers who settled the West brave and inspiring.

Like a lot of other "young" countries in the world (it's weird to think my house is twice as old), the U.S. is built on wave upon wave of immigration. More than three hundred languages are spoken there, and I just knew that if I kept my eyes open those gems of influence would come shining through in the food. If you were to take away any form of immigrant cooking, not only would it be a huge shame, but you wouldn't have those wonderful dishes that have evolved to the point that they now symbolize America. The fact that this new country isn't bound up in cooking tradition the way so many other parts of the world are makes it really interesting to me from a food perspective.

Don't get me wrong, there's plenty to get excited about in countries like France, Spain, and Italy, but – to my mind anyway – the U.S. is a metaphor for the rest of the world. The incredible diversity in American cooking was the real revelation to me. So although I went looking for "quintessential American food," my conclusion is that there is no such thing; instead there's a huge wealth of seriously exciting dishes.

Every single recipe in this book is something I love and have enjoyed on my travels. As in every cookbook I've written, there's food here to be eaten with gusto! Loads of these recipes are light and fresh and can play an exciting part in your daily routine. But I couldn't edit out the classic American showstoppers, like the fantastic fried chicken (page 270), the stupidly delicious bread pudding (page 116), and the beautiful deep-pan pizza (page 32). Many of these recipes are my own expressions of America's classic or well-known dishes, which I've freshened up and adjusted to be "less excessive" in the sugar and fat department, without losing the whole point of the dish in the first place. Even so, I've tried to signpost the naughtier recipes for you pretty clearly in their introductions, so use those as a guide and just be sensible about mixing it up.

The America I see in my head now is definitely a more true and honest one than the one I saw at the age of ten in Disneyland. It is a country of extremes, and that is definitely reflected in the cooking that goes on there. Without a doubt, this experience will change the way I holiday there from now on. There's so much to be said for just hiring a car and getting going. My only advice would be to remember to look beyond what's right in front of you, because that will only lead you back to the junk. Talk to the locals, be adventurous, and you'll discover the places, characters, and food that make this country so incredible. I hope you enjoy this book and that it inspires you to take a bit of the best of America home with you. I know it has me.

Jamie O xx

PS: My very good mate David Gleave of the UK wine supplier Liberty Wines (www.libertywines.co.uk) knows just about everything there is to know about wine. I was thrilled when he very kindly agreed to suggest wines for a load of the recipes here. Use his advice. I do, and it never lets me down. (Cheers, David!)

I've been making trips to New York for more than ten years now, although admittedly they have usually been for work rather than just to hang out. When I'm working hard I want to eat in great places, meet local chefs, and be inspired, and the Big Apple never lets me down. However, I hadn't really ever ventured out of Manhattan, so this time I wanted to explore the diversity of the food and the communities in the city.

New York has just about every type of nationality, food, and ethnic mix you can imagine. Many different communities live side by side in Manhattan and the surrounding boroughs, and I wanted to find out a bit more about them, their recipes, and what brought them to this amazing city. I'm not talking just about the Dutch, British, Irish, Germans, and Italians that historically settled in New York; I'm talking about the more recent immigrants from South America, Africa, China, and the Middle East. I knew I was in for some great food, and I'm happy to say I wasn't disappointed.

New York is an animal of a city, and if you don't run at it and jump in with two feet, you're going to get eaten up and spat out. I imagine it takes a lot of guts to make the move, but many people in all kinds of different situations have taken the plunge and started afresh there. More than anything, it represents a place where immigrants who might hate each other in their hometowns or countries can get along.

Alex, a Ukrainian Jew who runs Yonah Schimmel's bakery in the Lower East Side of Manhattan, summed things up when he said that immigrants arrive in a country looking for freedom and a better life with opportunities. Two days later, I was sitting in a cab and my driver was a perfect example of that. Sallie had come to New York from the war-torn region of Darfur in the Sudan. He'd come on his own to find a job and a place to live, and to lay down some foundations for his family. He was waiting for his pregnant wife's paperwork to come through so they could start their new lives together in New York. His first child will undoubtedly be born a New Yorker and an American, and Sallie hopes the family will be able to enjoy the American

dream: peace and access to education, health, and opportunity. I certainly hope they get all those things and more.

I'd never imagined there was all this crazy, amazing, authentic food from across the world being served literally two miles away from where I'd been eating in posh restaurants and visiting TV studios for all those years. A few of my New York friends weren't even aware that some of the places I went to existed – like the supper clubs or illegal restaurants being run in people's homes or the incredible food markets selling food for a dollar a hit. Hopefully in this chapter I've managed to get across some of the excitement and attitude of the food I found. I think it's fair to say that a country's immigrants always bring color, energy, and value with them. If there is any one thing that can help people in a new place feel at home, it is being able to eat the food they are used to, with all its comforting rituals around the table.

The city is like a cocktail with lots of layers that haven't been stirred yet, and for me this is one of the things that makes New York hum and keeps it vibrant, interesting, exciting, and unpredictable.

BURGERS & SLIDERS

I couldn't possibly leave the great American burger out of this book. Sadly, the classic burger has gone from humble beginnings (as something brought over by German immigrants) to becoming a symbol of fast food and junk. But when made at home with quality ingredients, it's an absolute joy. So, introducing my great American burger, and its little cousin, the "slider," or mini burger . . . Have fun with your toppings and flavor combos and enjoy.

Serves 6

★　　　★　　　★　　　★　　　★　　　★

For the burger mix
olive oil
2 medium red onions, peeled and finely chopped
4 slices of bread, crusts removed
1¼ lbs good-quality lean ground beef
1 teaspoon kosher salt
1 heaped teaspoon freshly ground black pepper
1 large egg, preferably free-range or organic, beaten
a handful of freshly grated Parmesan cheese

For the spicy mayo
4 teaspoons mayonnaise
1 teaspoon ketchup
a good pinch of smoked paprika or cayenne pepper
juice of ½ lemon

To serve
12 slices of smoked bacon, the best quality you can afford
6 large or 8 small burger buns
1 butterhead lettuce, leaves washed and spun dry
4 tomatoes, sliced
6 gherkins, sliced
a few pickled chiles

You can make these burgers or sliders in an oven at full whack, on the grill, or in a hot pan. If you're using the oven or grill, preheat it now.

Put a splash of olive oil into a large frying pan on a low heat and add your chopped onions. Fry for 10 minutes or until the onions have softened, then put to one side and let cool completely. Blitz your bread in a food processor until you get a fine consistency. Oil a clean sheet pan and put aside. Put the cooled onions into a large bowl with the rest of the burger ingredients. Use clean hands to scrunch the mixture together really well, then divide into 6 equal balls for burgers and 18 equal balls for sliders. Wet your hands and roll the balls into burger-shaped patties about ¾ inch thick. Put your burgers or sliders on the oiled sheet pan and pat with a little olive oil. Cover them with plastic wrap and put the pan into the refrigerator for at least an hour, or until the patties firm up. This is a good time to make your spicy mayo, so put all the ingredients into a bowl, mix well, and put to one side.

If using a frying pan or grill pan, put it on a high heat now and let it get really hot. However you decide to cook your burgers, they'll want around 3 or 4 minutes per side – you may have to cook them in batches if your pan isn't big enough. When your burgers or sliders are nearly cooked on one side, add the slices of bacon – whichever way you're cooking them – then flip the burgers and cook the bacon until golden and crisp. When the burgers are cooked to your liking and it's all looking really good, halve your burger buns and warm them through. Put the bacon on a plate lined with paper towels to drain.

When everything comes together pop your burgers or sliders onto their buns, add all your lovely toppings and your spicy mayo (you know how to put a burger together!), then tuck in with a lovely fresh salad and baked potatoes or potato wedges.

WALDORF SALAD MY WAY

Serves 4

4 large handfuls of interesting green salad leaves (such as frisée, romaine, Belgian endive, arugula, and watercress), washed and spun dry
2 large handfuls of seedless or seeded green or red grapes, halved
3 medium celery stalks, trimmed
2 large handfuls of walnuts (approx. 4 oz), roughly crumbled
a small bunch of fresh Italian parsley
1 red apple
6 oz blue cheese, such as dolcelatte

For the dressing
1 heaped teaspoon Dijon mustard
2 tablespoons white or red wine vinegar
good-quality extra virgin olive oil
1 heaped tablespoon natural yogurt
sea salt and freshly ground black pepper

Wine suggestion:
French white – a Vouvray demi-sec

Although everyone seems to agree that this salad was created in 1893, there's still a little bit of debate over who came up with it. It's commonly thought to have been Oscar Tschirky, the maître d'hôtel of the Waldorf-Astoria in New York City. If someone served a nice Waldorf salad on a platter for lunch, I'd say they were obviously a pretty confident person: it's a dead simple salad to make, but it gives you a great combination of flavors and really is a laid-back and cool thing to dish up. To make it really great you need to get hold of some very good, sweet grapes to go with the saltiness of the blue cheese and the crunch of the lettuce. Although most Waldorf salads are made with mayo, I love to freshen mine up with yogurt.

★　　★　　★　　★　　★　　★

In a large bowl, toss together your salad leaves and grapes. Using a speed peeler, carefully remove the stringy bits from the outside of the celery. I like to do it this way as it's a bit more delicate and you don't lose too much of the celery. Finely slice it at an angle, then toss the pieces in with your leaves and grapes.

Get a dry frying pan over a medium heat and toast your walnuts. Give them a shake every 25 seconds or so – you want to heat them through but you don't want them to color too much.

Discard the tougher ends of the parsley stalks and finely chop the rest of the stalks. Put to one side, then chop the leaves and add these to the bowl of salad leaves. Put your chopped parsley stalks into a clean screw-top jar with your mustard and vinegar, then pour in 3 times as much extra virgin olive oil. You want the dressing to be fresh and creamy, so add the yogurt and a good pinch of salt and pepper. Whack the lid on and give it a really good shake. Dip your finger in for a quick taste and balance the flavor with a little more vinegar, oil, or yogurt.

Drizzle over enough dressing to just cover your leaves. Finely slice your apple into lovely matchsticks and scatter these over the top. Tip over the toasted walnuts, and use your hands to dress and toss everything together. Transfer your salad to a large platter, piling all the grapes and walnuts on top of the leaves.

Use a knife to break off little pats of blue cheese and scatter these over the salad. Drizzle over a little extra virgin olive oil and you're done!

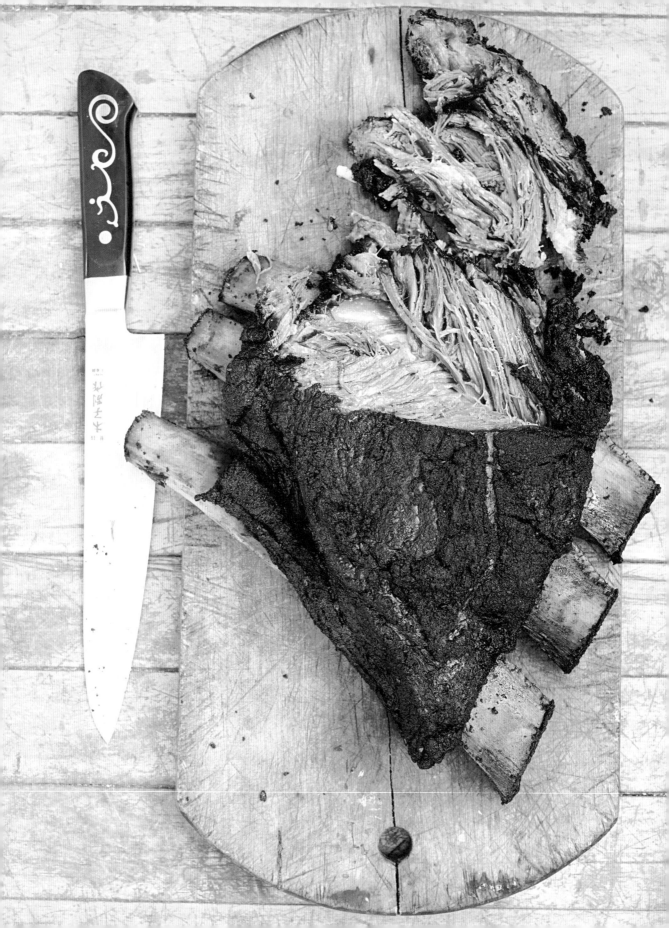

My very good friend Adam Perry Lang owns a restaurant in NYC called Daisy May's BBQ. It's the coolest pared-back restaurant, with an incredible barbecue. I've eaten there a number of times and I can tell you from experience that Adam's ribs are the absolute business.

Adam barbecues all his meat using wood like pecan, oak, hickory, and hardwoods to add all sorts of insane smoky sexy flavors. I've slightly adapted his recipe so you can make it at home in your oven, but the principles are still the same and the result is wonderful, fall-off-the-bone meat. In Britain people often cook pork ribs but never give a thought to beef ones, which is too bad – they're economical and will blow your mind. You may need to order a whole slab of ribs in advance from your butcher.

DAISY MAY'S BBQ RIBS

Serves 4

Preheat your oven to 250°F. Rub your mustard all over the meat. Mix all the rub ingredients together in a bowl, then pour over your ribs and rub the mix in with your hands, making sure every last bit of meat is evenly coated. You want the meat to develop a nice even crust, so don't put it on too thickly. Place the ribs in a roasting pan, bone side down, and cook in the oven for 5 hours.

About 10 minutes before the time is up, crack on with your marinade. Put all the marinade ingredients into a saucepan over a medium heat. Add a tablespoon or two of water and cook until combined, stirring the mixture as the butter melts to help it along.

Get yourself a large sheet of heavy-duty aluminum foil. Pour your marinade over the sheet and spread it out with a brush, then put your ribs on top, meat side down. Bring the foil edges together so you have a closed foil parcel, and wrap it in a second sheet of foil. Place the foil parcel in the roasting pan so that the meat side is facing down, and cook for another hour.

After this time, remove the ribs from the oven and turn the temperature up to 275°F. Unwrap the foil and carefully pour away the marinade and juices. Lay the ribs meat side up in the roasting tray and return them to the oven for a further 35 to 40 minutes. Remove from the oven and let the meat rest on a board for at least 10 minutes before slicing into ¼ inch slices, or shred with forks, against the bone.

Brush the cut side of the meat with any lovely juices left on the board, and sprinkle each slice with sea salt – the flavor will blow you away.

5 tablespoons yellow mustard
1 x 4-bone rack of beef
short ribs (approx. 4½ lbs)

For the rub
¼ cup smoked paprika
1 tablespoon mild chili powder
½ tablespoon freshly
ground black pepper
½ tablespoon sea salt,
plus extra to serve
2 tablespoons vegetable oil

For the marinade
¼ cup light brown sugar
2½ tablespoons honey
a large pat of unsalted butter
1 beef bouillon cube, preferably
organic, crumbled
1½ tablespoons water

Wine suggestion:
Australian red – a Grenache
from McLaren Vale

This is not just any old omelet; it's my twist on an Omelet Arnold Bennett. Arnold Bennett was a writer who wrote a whole novel while staying at the Savoy Hotel. The chefs there perfected the recipe for him and word has it that he requested this omelet everywhere he traveled from then on (talk about demanding!).

Traditionally, this omelet is made with haddock, but I've mixed things up a bit here and recommend using mackerel or trout instead. It's brilliant served with a bowl of lemony-dressed salad greens and some fresh warm bread.

★　　★　　★　　★　　★　　★

Put a large nonstick frying pan on a medium to low heat and add a drizzle of olive oil. Add the sliced scallions, then flake in the fish so you get different-sized chunks. Add your pats of butter and shake the pan a bit to get everything coated in the butter and oil. Finely grate in the zest of half your lemon and a pinch of black pepper. Cook for about 3 to 4 minutes, until the scallions have softened but not colored.

Turn the heat down so it's quite low. In a bowl, beat your eggs well and add the grated Parmesan and a small pinch of salt and black pepper. Make sure your scallions and fish are nicely distributed across the pan, then pour in your eggs. Use a wooden spoon to slowly move everything around so the raw egg settles into the gaps you've left. Keep everything in a nice flat layer as you go, and use your instincts – when you've run out of wet egg, stop spooning stuff around and turn the heat down really low.

Use a spatula to gently lift the edges of the omelet and make sure it isn't overcooking. When the liquid egg on top has just set and turned opaque, slide the omelet onto a serving plate. I like to serve this omelet open so you can see all the scallions and fish. Sprinkle over your chopped chives and take it straight to the table with a hunk of warm bread and a little Parmesan for sprinkling over. For lunch it's really nice with a watercress salad on the side. Cut your remaining lemon half into wedges to squeeze over the top and tuck in.

OMELET GORDON BENNETT

Serves 2

olive oil
4 scallions, trimmed and finely sliced
7 oz smoked fish (mackerel or trout), skin and bones removed
2 small pats of butter
1 lemon
sea salt and freshly ground black pepper
5 large eggs, preferably free-range or organic
1 heaping tablespoon freshly grated Parmesan cheese, plus extra to serve
a small bunch of fresh chives, finely chopped

Wine suggestion:
French white – an oaked Chardonnay from Burgundy

CANDIED BACON GREEN SALAD

Serves 4

★   ★   ★   ★   ★   ★

For the creamy French dressing
⅓ cup good-quality extra virgin olive oil
3 tablespoons white wine vinegar
1 heaping teaspoon Dijon mustard
1 heaping tablespoon natural yogurt
sea salt and freshly ground black pepper

For the salad
12 slices of smoked bacon, the best quality you can afford
1 clove garlic, peeled
3 slices of fresh white bread
olive oil
freshly ground black pepper
2 heaped teaspoons turbinado sugar
3 clementines
5 large handfuls of mixed salad leaves, washed and spun dry
1 pomegranate
a small bunch of fresh mint, leaves picked

Wine suggestion:
Californian white – a Fumé Blanc

This salad was inspired by two of the loveliest girls, Tamara and Zora, who regularly host an anti-restaurant supper club in Queens. Supper clubs are becoming quite popular in New York, and I think the idea behind them is quite cool. By opening up their homes and serving food at decent prices, people are sort of rebelling against the crowded, overpriced, and rushed service of established city restaurants. This is a great twist on your standard warm salad, and although I'm not crazy about ultra-sweet things, it was cleverly done because the candied layer goes so well with the crispy smoked bacon. Add a good green salad and some seasonal fruit and you're on to a winning combo.

Depending on the season, you can vary the lettuces and salad leaves, and the fruit too: apples, pears, peaches, figs, grapes, and strawberries would all be great, so use your imagination. Thanks for the inspiration, girls!

To make your dressing, put all the ingredients into a large serving bowl, whisk together, and season to taste. You want it to be slightly too acidic, so add a splash more vinegar if you think it needs it. Put to one side.

Get a large frying pan on a medium heat, add the bacon and cook until lightly golden (but not really crispy), turning it every so often. Remove the bacon to a plate. Squash your garlic clove and add it to the pan, then turn the heat up a little and tear your bread into medium-sized chunks. Drop them into the pan so they suck up all the flavors and become crispy. If your bacon didn't release a lot of fat and you think the bread needs a little help to crisp up, simply add a lug or two of olive oil. Add a pinch of black pepper and shake the bread around until crispy and golden, then remove to the plate with your bacon.

Wipe the pan clean with paper towels, then put the bacon back in with the sugar or honey and the juice of 1 clementine. Concentrate on what you're doing, and make sure you don't touch or taste anything at any point because it will burn you. Stir everything around in the pan so the syrup starts to stick to the bacon. As soon as the bacon slices are perfectly caramelized and sticky, use tongs to carefully move them to an oiled plate and leave to cool down for a minute. Whatever shape you leave the bacon in at this point is how it will set, so give the slices a bend or a twist. Peel the remaining clementines and slice them into rounds.

Grab your bowl of dressing and add your salad leaves. Halve the pomegranate and use a spoon to knock the back of each half and pop the seeds over the salad. Add your mint leaves, then use your hands to toss and dress everything thoroughly. Lightly toss your croutons through the salad and lay your candied bacon on top. Place your clementine rounds on top of the salad, then pass the bowl around the table and let everyone serve themselves.

DEEP-PAN PIZZA

Serves 10–12

★　★　★　★　★　★

For the dough
Scant 2¾ cups lukewarm water
1 x ¼-oz envelope active dry yeast
1 tablespoon sugar
1 level teaspoon salt
8 cups white bread flour,
plus extra for dusting

For the tomato sauce
a swig of white wine vinegar
1 clove garlic, peeled
a handful of fresh basil leaves
1 x 14-oz can diced tomatoes
sea salt and freshly ground black pepper

For the toppings
olive oil
3 red onions, peeled and finely sliced
a few sprigs of fresh
thyme, leaves picked
4 pork sausages, the best
quality you can afford
1 dried red chile
1 teaspoon fennel seeds
a good pinch of dried oregano
¼ lb fresh buffalo mozzarella
a handful of fresh basil leaves
2 fresh red chiles, finely sliced
2 large handfuls of freshly
grated Parmesan cheese
12 slices bacon

This isn't really so much a "New York Pizza" as it is my own version of an America-style pizza that I *ate* in New York. I've always looked at pizza with thicker dough as a slightly greedy way of bulking out crusts and toppings. I hadn't realized Italian immigrants had cleverly adapted their Old World recipes to suit New World coal-fired ovens. Making pizza in a tin to protect the base from the soot of the oven makes perfect sense to me now. Delicious.

To make your dough, pour your lukewarm water into a large bowl and use a fork to stir in the yeast and sugar. Let stand for a few minutes then add your salt and flour, bit by bit, until it comes together. You want smooth, springy dough, so keep adding a bit more flour if necessary. Dust a clean surface with flour, then knead the dough with your hands. When you're happy with the consistency, pop it into a flour-dusted bowl, cover with a damp cloth, and leave in a warm room until the dough has almost doubled in size.

Meanwhile, put a lug of olive oil into a large frying pan on a medium heat. Add your sliced onions and thyme leaves and cook for 15 minutes, or until softened and golden. Take the pan off the heat and put aside. Put all the tomato sauce ingredients into a food processor or liquidizer with a good pinch of salt and pepper and blitz to a purée. Have a taste and season carefully, adding a bit more salt and pepper if it needs it.

Slit the sausages open and squeeze the meat into a bowl. Bash up the dried chile and fennel seeds in a pestle and mortar, add these to the meat with the dried oregano, and mix well with a fork.

Preheat your oven to 400°F. Divide the dough in half and oil 2 quarter sheet pans (about 9 × 13 inches) with olive oil. Use a rolling pin or clean hands to flatten and stretch the dough out. Roll or push the dough around each tray and really push it into the corners so you get a chubby crust and a base about ½ inch thick.

Divide your blitzed tomato sauce between the pizzas and spread around. Scatter over the caramelized onions and dot small pinches of the sausage mixture around the top of each pizza. Tear up the mozzarella and dot the pieces over the sausage, then sprinkle over the fresh basil leaves, sliced fresh chiles, a good pinch of salt and pepper, and the grated Parmesan. Finally let your slices of bacon sort of fall onto the pizzas so they curl and crisp up as they cook. Place in the bottom of the oven for about 20 minutes so the base gets nice and crispy while the top is cooking. Once your pizzas are beautifully cooked, serve right away with a fresh green lemony salad.

It seemed as though New Yorkers were really into their Bibb lettuce, which is also known as butterhead lettuce, or Boston lettuce. In Britain, we call this a round lettuce. It's soft and crunchy, and even though it's one of the cheapest lettuces you can buy, there's something so simple and delicious about it. It's one of my favorites, and kids tend to like it better than other types of lettuce because it has a mild flavor. The outer floppy leaves are great for using in sandwiches or cooking with fresh boiled peas. The inner leaves are delicious in salads.

I've used thyme to flavor the mushrooms but you could also add chopped chives, tarragon, oregano, or rosemary if you fancy. The warm, meaty mushrooms mixed with the lovely lettuce leaves and crispy garlic make this absolutely delicious.

★ ★ ★ ★ ★ ★

Get rid of any tatty outer leaves on your lettuces and gently wash the rest of the leaves. Spin them dry in a salad spinner or wrap them in a clean dish towel and swing it around your head like a lunatic to get rid of any excess water. It's really important that the leaves are dry because that helps the dressing to stick to them. Mix the oil, vinegar, mustard, and a good pinch of salt and pepper in a large bowl and put aside.

Put a large frying pan on a medium heat and add 2 good lugs of olive oil. Let it heat up for a minute or two, then sprinkle in your slices of garlic. Keep spooning them around so they don't stick, and tilt the pan on a slight angle every few seconds so the garlic deep-fries a bit.

Once they are golden (but not too dark!), spoon the garlic chips onto a paper towel to drain and turn the heat up to high. Tear or slice your mushrooms into bite-sized pieces and drop them into the pan. Toss them around for a few minutes, and when they start to take on a little color add the butter, thyme leaves, and a good pinch of salt and pepper. Add a splash of water to stop them drying out, and continue to fry until delicious and golden. Have a taste and add a bit more salt and pepper if the mushrooms need it. Spoon them over a large platter or plate, and drizzle over any lovely juices left behind in the pan.

Use your hands to lightly toss your lettuce leaves in a large bowl with your dressing. When each leaf is lightly coated, lay them over the mushrooms. Sprinkle over your garlic chips and dive in!

BIBB SALAD & PAN-FRIED MUSHROOMS

Serves 4–6

2 Bibb lettuces or butterhead lettuces
olive oil
8 cloves garlic, peeled and thinly sliced
1¼ lbs mixed mushrooms, brushed clean
2 large pats of butter
2 sprigs of fresh thyme, leaves picked
sea salt and freshly ground black pepper

For the French dressing
9 tablespoons extra virgin olive oil
3 tablespoons white wine vinegar
3 teaspoons Dijon mustard
sea salt and freshly ground black pepper

Wine suggestion:
Italian rosé – a light, dry Valpolicella
(or a cold beer)

Cheesecake and New York go hand-in-hand, so I just had to include this. I've been working on the recipe for quite a while, and finally perfected it during this trip. I've swapped regular cream cheese for a reduced-fat version to make my cheesecake *slightly* less calorific. A word of warning, though: use reduced-fat cream cheese rather than fat-free as the fat-free version will behave differently and won't give the results you're looking for.

★   ★   ★   ★   ★   ★

Preheat the oven to 310°F and grease a 10-inch springform cake pan. Put your crackers into a food processor and whiz until you've got really fine crumbs, then mix in your melted butter. If you don't have a food processor, just wrap your crackers in a dish towel and bash them up with a rolling pin until fine. Spread the crumb mixture around the base of your greased pan, making sure you get it right to the edges, then press it with your hands to pack it down. Place the pan on a cookie sheet and pop it into the refrigerator while you make the filling.

Whiz the cream cheese in a food processor until smooth, then gradually add the sugar. Add the eggs one at a time, mixing well after each one. Pour in the lime juice and whiz again until just combined. Again, if you don't have a food processor, just do this by hand. Don't worry if the mixture seems too thin – it's supposed to be like that. Tip it over your chilled crumb base, spread it out evenly, and bake in the oven for 45 to 55 minutes – you want the cheesecake to still have a slight loose wobble. Remove from the oven and set aside for 15 minutes to cool slightly. Turn the oven up to 425°F.

To make the meringue topping, put your egg whites into a clean bowl and beat until they form soft peaks – an electric mixer is quite handy here. Gradually add the sugar and beat until thick and glossy. Finally, fold in the coconut. Spoon this meringue mixture onto the middle of the cooled cheesecake and spread it to the edges, using the back of a spoon, so it just covers the filling. It should be about ¾ inch thick. I like to make a few ripples and peaks in the top so it looks impressive. Bake in the oven for 5 minutes, or until the meringue is starting to turn golden in color and is crisp to touch.

Let it cool down, then place it in the refrigerator for a few hours (this is important) to chill before serving. Carefully remove it from the pan, transfer it to a nice platter, and sprinkle over the lime zest. Really nice served with mango, strawberries, and raspberries when they're in season.

MY NYC CHEESECAKE

Serves 10–14

22 sheets graham crackers
9 tablespoons butter
4 x 8-oz bars reduced-fat cream cheese
¾ cup superfine sugar
5 large eggs, preferably free-range or organic
juice of 6 limes (approx. ½ cup)
finely grated zest of ½ lime

For the meringue topping
3 large egg whites, preferably free-range or organic (the yolks can be used for making scambled eggs)
heaping ½ cup superfine sugar
½ cup unsweetened shredded coconut

Wine suggestion:
Sweet German white – a Riesling Auslese

VELVET CUPCAKES

Makes 12 cupcakes

½ stick (¼ cup) unsalted butter,
at room temperature
¾ cup superfine sugar
1 large egg, preferably free-range
or organic
sea salt
1 teaspoon good-quality vanilla extract
optional: 3 tablespoons natural
red food coloring
2 heaping tablespoons
unsweetened cocoa powder
1¼ cups all-purpose flour
½ cup buttermilk
½ teaspoon baking soda
1½ teaspoons white wine vinegar

For the frosting
¾ × 8-oz bar cream cheese,
at room temperature
½ stick (¼ cup) unsalted butter,
at room temperature
1 cup confectioners' sugar
½ teaspoon vanilla extract
zest and juice of 1 lemon

Manhattan bakeries churn out the most outrageously pretty and delicate cakes. Red velvet cake is not only beautiful thanks to its dramatic color, but also light, fluffy, and such a treat. Its vibrant red color is usually achieved through artificial food dye. I've gone for a natural food coloring here, but have made it optional in the recipe because these cupcakes are gorgeous no matter what color they are. But if it's drama you're after, go for it.

★   ★   ★   ★   ★   ★

Preheat the oven to 350°F and line a 12-hole muffin pan with paper liners.

Using an electric mixer, or by hand, cream your butter and sugar together until light and fluffy. Gently beat in the egg, a pinch of salt, the vanilla extract, and, if using, the red food coloring. In a separate bowl, whisk together the cocoa and flour and fold half of it into your butter mix, followed by half the buttermilk. Repeat with the remaining flour and buttermilk until you have a gorgeous smooth mixture.

In a small bowl mix your baking soda and white wine vinegar together so it fizzes up, and stir this into your cake mix.

Divide the mixture between your paper liners and bake in the oven for 20 to 25 minutes. To check they're cooked through, insert a skewer into the center of a cake – if it comes out clean, they're perfect, if not, just pop them back into the oven for another couple of minutes. Let them to cool for 5 minutes in the pan, then transfer to a wire rack to cool completely while you make your frosting.

Put all your frosting ingredients into a bowl and mix together until smooth and creamy. Spoon this creamy frosting onto your cupcakes once they have cooled down, and serve.

CHINATOWN

A friend of mine told me that if I wanted to experience some serious Chinese food in New York, I had to visit an area in Queens called Flushing. So I decided to make my way over there – in a cab it's about forty minutes from Manhattan via the Midtown Tunnel, or you can jump on the subway to Flushing Main Street, the terminus of the number 7 train line – it's known locally as the "Immigration Express."

You can tell when you're approaching the area: suddenly everything changes and everywhere there are neon signs with Chinese symbols and everyone is speaking Mandarin or Cantonese. It's such a buzzy place, and a large part of that is down to the food stalls that line the streets. Even if you only have $1 in your pocket, there will be a stall or a counter where you can buy yourself dinner. If you've got $5 you'll be able to fill up on a fantastic Chinese feast! On the street, you can choose from lamb skewers, chicken cooked over charcoal flavored with lots of different spices, fish balls, or a whole selection of noodle dishes and filled dumplings.

If I'm being completely honest, I didn't really expect to be blown away by this kind of street food. Quite often I've found that food served in this way is made by people who don't care about food; they know they're just cooking things for gullible tourists. However, I quickly realized that this area really only exists for the local Chinese community and, of course, they're not going to put up with any old rubbish – they're going to want the real, authentic tastes of home. When I watched the quality of the cooking being done, I knew I was around proper Chinese cooks.

I went to three or four food courts and fish markets, tasting and chatting to people. It was just the coolest thing to do. Every single person I spoke with was so lovely and welcoming. So please, if you're in New York and you've got a few hours to hang out and just wander around, get yourself out to Flushing, and don't have a meal first – grab a couple of beers and just go and graze. You'll have a great time – I couldn't recommend it more.

FIERY DAN DAN NOODLES

In the western Szechuan province of China they make this dish in massive buckets, which they carry on poles over their shoulders. In China, *dan* means "pole," so these are quite literally "pole pole noodles." It's a very simple dish, full of soft, silky noodles, lovely veg, some great crispy meat, and a wonderful hum from the raw garlic. So there are a load of punchy flavors here, and then of course you've got the Szechuan pepper and the wonderful chiles ... I absolutely love chiles, but this dish is right on the edge of my tolerance. Personally I think that's the beauty of it, and you've kinda just got to go for it. But by all means feel free to halve or even quarter the amount of chiles in the oil if you want a slightly mellower dish.

Serves 4   ★   ★   ★   ★   ★   ★

1 beef or chicken bouillon cube, preferably organic
1¼ lb ground beef
2 tablespoons honey
10 oz Chinese wheat noodles
4 handfuls of mixed green veg (Napa cabbage, broccolini, bok choy, spinach)
4 cloves garlic, peeled and minced
3 tablespoons dark soy sauce
2 teaspoons freshly ground Szechuan pepper
5 tablespoons good-quality chile oil (see PS below)
2 scallions, trimmed and thinly sliced
1 lime, quartered, to serve

Wine suggestion:
New Zealand white
– a Sauvignon Blanc
(or a cold beer)

Crumble your bouillon cube into a large saucepan of water and get it on the heat.

Add the beef to a dry frying pan and, on a medium to high heat, keep moving it around until it's golden and crunchy, which will take about 10 to 15 minutes. Pour away any excess fat, then add the honey and toss until all the beef is nicely coated. Cook for about 30 seconds, then take the pan off the heat.

Stir your noodles into the boiling broth and move them about a bit so they don't stick together. Cook following the package instructions. Shred your cabbage into ½ inch strips, quarter your bok choy, and snap up the broccolini spears. When the noodles have 1 minute to go, throw in the prepared greens to blanch them. Drain the whole lot in a colander, reserving a mugful of the cooking water. Tip your noodles, veggies, and the mugful of water back into the hot pan.

Add your garlic, soy sauce, Szechuan pepper, and chile oil. Give it all a good mix with tongs and divide between 4 bowls. Sprinkle over the crunchy beef (you can reheat this at the last minute if you like), finish with a scattering of scallions, and serve each dish with a lime quarter to squeeze over. A serious noodle dish!

PS You can buy good chile oil, or you can make your own simply by getting a handful of mixed dried chiles (use as many as you like), toasting them in the oven to bring the flavor out, whacking them in a food processor with a bottle of peanut oil, and pouring it back into the bottle. This will keep well in your cupboard for a year.

QUICK & PUNCHY KIMCHI

Makes a 1 quart jar

5 tablespoons sesame oil
3 medium dried red chiles,
stalks removed, sliced
2 star anise
1 teaspoon Szechuan peppercorns
1 Napa or white cabbage
(approx. 1¼–1½ lbs)
sea salt
2 heaping tablespoons sugar
5 tablespoons white wine
or rice wine vinegar
2–3 cloves garlic, peeled
a thumb-sized piece of
ginger root, peeled

Kimchi (or kimchee) is a classic Korean cabbage pickle. Traditionally, it's fermented over the course of days or weeks; my version here is faster and a bit coarser, but still delicious. I've eaten kimchi in so many ways: in delicious buns stuffed with slow-cooked pork, with lovely grilled meat, in burgers, and even in noodle dishes. It's hot, spicy, fresh, cold, and zingy and delicious with a cold beer.

Even though there are three dried chiles in this, it's a lot milder than you might expect. It will keep happily in a sterilized jar for a few days, so you should have plenty of opportunities to find ways of eating it up.

★　　★　　★　　★　　★　　★

Place a frying pan on a low heat and add the sesame oil, chiles, star anise, and Szechuan peppercorns – you don't want to cook the chiles and spices or brown them, you just want to gently heat them and bring out their flavors. This will take 5 minutes. Take the pan off the heat.

Remove any tatty leaves from the cabbage, trim off the base, and slice the cabbage about ½ to ¾ inch thick in any way you like. Bring a large saucepan of salted water to a boil, add the cabbage, and cook for about 1 minute with the lid on. Drain in a colander, then scatter it over a sheet pan so it steams dry but keeps its moisture as it cools.

After about 10 minutes the cabbage should have cooled down, so pop it into a bowl and add the flavored sesame oil, sugar, and vinegar. Grate in the garlic and ginger and add a really good pinch of salt. Use your hands to lightly scrunch everything together, then cover the bowl and put it into the refrigerator, where it will keep for a good 3 to 4 days.

Lamb Liver Kabob
$1.00

Ox Liver Kabob
$1.00

Shurpa (Lamb Soup)
$3.99

Baked Samsa
$1.00 Each

Eyili Style Salad
$1.99

Fried Samsa
$1.00 Each

Baked
$1.00

Get down to the Roosevelt
Food Court and have an
absolute feast - $10
goes a long way

SMALL STEAMED BUN 4/$1.25

SCALLION PANCAKE $ 1.00

Sher ping translates as "pan-cooked filled pancake," and they are one of the best things I've eaten in ages. A lovely lady from the north of China taught me how to make them at her food counter in the Roosevelt Food Court. It sounds like a cheat to explain how to make these pancakes, but it's well worth mastering, because you can swap the pork for other delicious fillings like chicken or seafood.

Make the dough by mixing the flour, water, vegetable oil, a bit of pepper, and a pinch of salt with a fork. Then use your hands to knead it until smooth and elastic. Cover it with plastic wrap and let it rest for a couple of hours.

When you're ready to make your pancakes, mix all your filling ingredients together in a large bowl. Use your hands to really scrunch everything together, and season well with a good pinch of salt and Szechuan pepper.

Dust a clean surface with flour and cut the dough into 8. Divide your filling into 8 even piles. Oil a sheet pan and your hands. Pick up a piece of dough and create a patty like a mini pizza about 4¾ inches across and ½ inch thick.

Take one of your piles of filling and pop it into the middle of the dough. Pat it flat with your fingers, then slowly stretch the edges of the dough out, folding them back in over the pork mixture (see the photos). Do this all the way around and, once closed, press down on the stuffed pancake with your hand. It should be about 1 inch thick and 3¼ inches across.

Do the same with the other 7 pancakes, then lay them on your oiled sheet pan and put them into the refrigerator for about 20 minutes or so. After that, get a large dry frying pan on a medium heat. Add a tiny drizzle of vegetable oil and lay each pancake, folded side down, in the pan. Gently push down on them with a spatula slice to flatten them slightly. Keep doing this until they're about ½ inch thick and about 4 inches wide. Be careful that the pan's not too hot, though, otherwise your pancakes will brown before they're properly cooked through.

After about 4 minutes you'll have a nice golden color happening, so turn the pancakes over, push them down lightly, and cook them for 4 minutes on the other side. Only push down once on this side. When they're golden and crisp, the meat should be perfectly cooked, but you can always break one open to check.

To serve, pour some chile sauce into one bowl and some soy sauce into another. Pop a few wedges of lime on the side for squeezing over, and dunk away in your sauces. These pancakes hit all the right spots!

SHER PING PANCAKES

Serves 4 (makes 8 pancakes)

For the dough
3¾ cups white bread flour,
plus extra for dusting
scant 1 cup water
¼ cup vegetable oil
sea salt and freshly ground black pepper

For the filling
14 oz ground pork, the best
quality you can afford
a handful of finely grated white cabbage
a small bunch of fresh cilantro,
leaves and stalks finely chopped
a thumb-sized piece of root ginger
peeled and finely grated
4 scallions, trimmed and finely chopped
1 clove garlic, peeled and finely grated
sea salt
freshly ground Szechuan pepper

To serve
sweet chile or hot chile sauce
soy sauce
2 limes, cut into wedges

Wine suggestion:
New Zealand red –
a Marlborough Pinot Noir

I'm sure every Jewish family has its own version of this absolutely classic feel-better soup. "Schmaltz" is the Yiddish word for chicken fat, which makes the matzo balls in the soup so special. Traditionally the chicken fat would be rendered separately, but I think skimming the fat works just as well. If someone around you is feeling a bit under the weather, make a big batch of this for them and you'll be their favorite person.

★　　★　　★　　★　　★　　★

Rinse your chicken in cold water, pat it dry with paper towels, and put it into your biggest saucepan. Cover with cold water to come about 3 to 4 inches above the chicken. Bring to a boil, then turn the heat down and simmer for 30 minutes. Skim the froth off the top of the chicken.

Add the chopped vegetables, garlic cloves, bay leaves, and thyme sprigs, and season with a good pinch of salt. Bring everything back to a boil, then turn the heat down and leave it to simmer for 1 hour. Carry on skimming the broth, reserving ¼ cup of this fat for your matzo balls.

To make your matzo balls, beat the eggs in a large bowl and add 5 tablespoons of cold water, your cooled chicken fat, and the salt and pepper. Beat again, then slowly stir in your matzo meal until well blended. Leave, covered with plastic wrap, in the refrigerator for 30 minutes, then wet your hands with cold water and roll the dough into about 20 small balls. Don't roll them too big because they'll double in size when you cook them.

When the soup has had its hour and a half, use tongs to carefully transfer the chicken to a roasting pan. Let cool, uncovered, for a few minutes. Remove the soup from the heat and strain it through your biggest sieve or colander. Pull out the decent-looking bits of vegetables and put these back into the soup, getting rid of anything else. Put the pan back on a medium heat and bring back to a boil, then add your matzo balls. Put a lid on the pan, turn the heat down a bit, and simmer for 20 minutes, until the balls are light and puffy. Halfway through the 20 minutes, add your noodles to the pan and cook gently for the final 10 minutes.

When your chicken has cooled enough to handle, either use two forks or pop on a pair of rubber gloves and use your hands to shred the meat off the bone. Pile it onto a plate and get rid of the skin and bones. Pick the leaves from your parsley and roughly chop them with the dill. Add all your shredded chicken meat to the soup, along with the chopped herbs, and warm through for 3 minutes. Have a taste, and season with salt and pepper. I'd usually serve soup with a nice crusty bread roll, but to be honest, this is a meal in itself and perfectly delicious and nourishing on its own.

JEWISH PENICILLIN

Serves 10–12

1 x 5–6 lb chicken, preferably free-range or organic
3 medium onions, peeled and roughly chopped
3 carrots, peeled and roughly chopped
3 celery stalks, trimmed and roughly chopped
4 cloves garlic, peeled
4 fresh bay leaves
a few sprigs of fresh thyme
sea salt and freshly ground black pepper
2 handfuls of Jewish fine egg noodles or spaghetti, broken into bits
1 small bunch of fresh Italian parsley
1 small bunch of fresh dill

For the matzo balls
4 large eggs, preferably free-range or organic
¼ cup chicken fat
1 teaspoon sea salt
½ teaspoon freshly ground black pepper
1 cup matzo meal (or matzo crackers, blitzed to a fine powder)

Wine suggestion:
a Spanish fino sherry

POTATO LATKE BREAKFAST

Serves 4

1lb potatoes, peeled and coarsely grated
1 onion, peeled, halved, and very
thinly sliced
sea salt and freshly ground black pepper
6 large eggs, preferably free-range
or organic
1 tablespoon self-rising flour
a splash of white wine vinegar
vegetable oil
4 fillets of smoked mackerel or whitefish
a pat of butter
a large handful of watercress, to serve

New Yorkers really know how to do breakfast. Latkes are Jewish potato pancakes, traditionally eaten at Hanukkah, and they are just delicious, especially the ones I tried at Yonah Schimmel's bakery. The smoked fish I used was from a fantastic Jewish deli called Russ & Daughters on the Lower East Side – they have amazing subtle smoked mackerel and whitefish as well as their famous lox. There are loads of little smokeries all around the country, but if you don't know of one near you, you can check out www.russanddaughters.com.

Latkes are usually deep-fried, but you can easily shallow fry them in just a little oil as I've done here.

★　　　★　　　★　　　★　　　★　　　★

Preheat your oven to 350°F. Mix your grated potato and sliced onion in a bowl with a good pinch of salt. Leave for a few minutes to allow most of the water to drain out of the vegetables, then really squeeze the mixture with your hands and pour away any excess liquid. Beat 2 of your eggs, add these to the bowl, and mix well. Stir in the flour and a pinch of pepper and put to one side.

Fill a wide, deep saucepan with water, add a splash of vinegar and a good pinch of salt and pepper, and bring to a boil. Meanwhile, heat a large frying pan or skillet on a medium heat. Add a splash of vegetable oil and spoon in 1 heaping tablespoonful of the potato latke batter at a time. This mixture should make 8 latkes. Press each one down into a little pancake with the back of your spoon as you put them into the pan. Depending on the size of your pan, you may have to make these in batches. After a couple of minutes the latkes should be lovely and golden underneath, so flip each one over and fry for another couple of minutes until cooked through. Transfer them to a cookie sheet and pop them into the oven for 10 minutes while you get everything else ready.

Wipe out your frying pan with paper towels and add the fish. Pour 1 inch of water into the pan and add a pat of butter. Bring everything to a boil, then turn the heat down and simmer for 5 minutes to warm the fish through.

Add a pinch of salt to your saucepan of boiling water and turn down to a simmer. Crack in your remaining 4 eggs and let them poach – a soft-poached egg should take 2 to 3 minutes, a firmer one 4 minutes. Meanwhile, take your latkes out of the oven and put 2 on each plate. Use a perforated spoon to take the fish out of the frying pan, drain, then pop the fillets on top of the latkes. Take an egg out of the water with a perforated spoon and touch it with your finger to check how soft or hard it is. You know how you like your eggs, so use your instincts.

As soon as your eggs are ready, spoon one onto each plate and finish with a few sprigs of watercress and some black pepper. Breakfast heaven.

Italian immigrants brought this dish to America, and since then veal parmigiana has become a classic New York dish, and rightly so. I love it when it's layered up like this, with the tomato sauce and cheese, then baked in the oven to gratinate. Feel free to swap veal for pork leg or even chicken that's been battered out. If you want to spike this with a bit of extra flavor you could also add a few capers or olives to the tomato sauce.

★　　★　　★　　★　　★　　★

Preheat your oven to 400°F. Pick the leaves off the sprigs of basil and put them into a small bowl of water to keep them fresh. Finely chop the tender stalks. Put a frying pan on a medium heat and add a splash of olive oil, the chopped basil stalks, garlic, and anchovies and cook for a few minutes. Prick the chile a few times and add it to the pan. Allow everything to sizzle for a minute or so, then pour in the canned tomatoes. Bring to a boil, then turn the heat down and simmer for 20 minutes. Season to taste with salt and pepper.

Meanwhile, prepare your escalopes. Mix the bread crumbs in a bowl with the thyme leaves and Parmesan. Finely grate your lemon zest into the bread crumbs, mix again, then lay out three plates in front of you. Put the flour on one and season it with salt and pepper, pour the eggs onto the next plate, and put the herby bread crumbs on the third. Dip the escalopes, one at a time, into the flour until well coated. Shake off any excess, then dip into the egg. Let the extra egg drip off, then lay the escalope in the bread crumb mixture. Sprinkle a handful of crumbs over the top and press them down. Make a real point of getting bread crumbs onto every part of the escalope.

Heat a large nonstick frying pan over a medium heat and add a good splash of olive oil. Let it heat up a bit, then add your escalopes. If your pan isn't big enough, you may have to cook them in batches, adding a little extra oil if needed. Cook for a few minutes on each side until lightly golden, then transfer to a plate lined with paper towels to drain. Get yourself a snug-fitting, appropriately sized baking dish (approx. 12 x 8 inches) and spread the tomato sauce in the dish. Lay your escalopes on top, side by side. Tear the buffalo mozzarella into pieces and dot these over the dish with a few basil leaves.

Bake in the oven for 20 minutes until golden, bubbling, and deliciously cooked. Sprinkle the rest of the basil leaves over. Perfect with a crunchy zingy salad, but you may also like to serve it with things like spaghetti, rice, mashed potatoes, polenta, or crusty bread.

VEAL PARMIGIANA

Serves 4

a few sprigs of fresh basil
olive oil
3 cloves garlic, peeled and thinly sliced
3 anchovies
1 fresh red chile
2 x 14-oz cans diced tomatoes
sea salt and freshly ground black pepper
4 cups fresh bread crumbs
a few sprigs of fresh thyme, leaves picked
a handful of freshly grated Parmesan cheese
1 lemon
1¼ cups all-purpose flour
2 large eggs, preferably free-range
or organic, beaten
4 x 7 oz veal or pork leg escalopes,
flattened to a thickness of ¾ inch
¼ lb buffalo mozzarella cheese

Wine suggestion:
Italian red – an Aglianico from
Campania or Basilicata

NYC VODKA ARRABBIATA

Adding vodka to tomato sauce is an Italian-American twist that I really love. Here I have added it to an incredible spicy and delicious arrabbiata sauce that really benefits from the freshness the vodka gives it. Before you go thinking you can't serve this to kids, I have to tell you that the alcohol in this is going to burn off, leaving a wonderful flavor and fragrance behind. Fresh herbs and lemon zest add exceptional flavor.

Serves 4

★　　★　　★　　★　　★　　★

4 fresh red chiles
⅓ cup olive oil
4 cloves garlic, peeled and thinly sliced
a small bunch of fresh Italian parsley, leaves picked, stalks finely chopped
4 anchovy fillets
1 x 14-oz can diced tomatoes
sea salt and freshly ground black pepper
3 shots of vodka
1lb spaghetti
1 lemon
optional: extra virgin olive oil

Wine suggestion:
Italian white – a Fiano di Avellino

Prick the chiles 6 to 8 times with a small, sharp knife. Put a large frying pan over a medium heat, add the olive oil and chiles, and let them cook slowly for 5 minutes. Turn the heat up to full whack and add the garlic, parsley stalks, and anchovies. Keep moving everything around the pan, and when the garlic starts to take on some color, add the canned tomatoes and season with salt and pepper. Bring this mixture to a boil, add the vodka, and turn the heat down so the sauce simmers. Gently bash up your chiles with a wooden spoon to release more of their great flavor into the sauce.

Add your pasta to a saucepan of boiling salted water and cook following the package instructions. Drain in a colander, then immediately toss the pasta in the sauce.

Divide between bowls or serve on a big platter. Roughly chop the reserved parsley leaves and sprinkle them over your pasta. Finely grate the lemon zest over the top, then squeeze in the juice, making sure you catch any pips in your hands. Drizzle with a little extra virgin olive oil to finish it off, and serve immediately with a fresh green salad.

A KILLER MAC 'N' CHEESE

"Mac 'n' cheese" is a classic American pasta dish – everyone loves it. Sometimes it's done so badly in the convenience area, it's almost become famous for being horrible, but when you do it properly, trust me, it's an absolute killer. Feel free to use any tubular pasta you want. I've made this dish my own by lightening it with sweet tomatoes and given it some crunch with delicious bread crumbs. Just you wait till you try it!

This dish isn't going to win any prizes in the nutrition department, but you can, and should, balance it with a nice salad. If you only have it once in a while as a special treat, it'll do you no harm.

★　　★　　★　　★　　★　　★

Serves 8–10

sea salt and freshly
ground black pepper
3 tablespoons butter
3 heaping tablespoons all-purpose flour
10 cloves garlic, peeled and
thinly sliced
6 fresh bay leaves
1 quart reduced-fat (2%) milk
4 cups elbow macaroni
8 tomatoes
1½ cups grated Cheddar cheese
1 cup freshly grated Parmesan cheese
a few sprigs of fresh
thyme, leaves picked
optional: a couple of splashes
of Worcestershire sauce,
such as Lea & Perrins
optional: a grating of nutmeg
3 big handfuls of fresh bread crumbs
olive oil

Wine suggestion:
dry Italian white – a good Pinot Grigio

Get a large saucepan of salted water on to boil. Melt the butter in a large ovenproof saucepan, or Dutch oven, over a low heat, then add the flour and turn the heat up to medium, stirring all the time, until you get a paste – this is your roux. Add all the sliced garlic – don't worry about the amount, because each slice will caramelize like toffee in the roux. Keep cooking and stirring until golden and the garlic is nice and sticky. Add the bay leaves and slowly whisk in the milk a little at a time to ensure you get a nice smooth sauce. Bring the mixture to a boil, then leave it on a low heat to simmer and tick away, stirring occasionally. Preheat your oven to 425°F.

Add the pasta to the pan of boiling salted water and cook following the package instructions. Meanwhile, roughly chop the tomatoes on a board and season them well with salt and pepper. Drain the pasta and add it immediately to the sauce. Give it a good stir and take the pan off the heat. Stir in your grated cheeses, chopped tomatoes, and some of the thyme leaves. A little Worcestershire sauce added now is nice, and so is a little grating or two of nutmeg. Now work on the flavor – taste it and season it until it's hitting the right spot. You want it to be slightly too wet because it will thicken up again in the oven, so add a splash of water if needed.

If you've made your sauce in a Dutch oven, leave everything in there; if not, transfer it to a deep earthenware dish. Bake it for 30 minutes in the oven, until golden, bubbling, crispy, and delicious.

While it's cooking, put your bread crumbs and remaining thyme into a frying pan with a few drizzles of olive oil over a medium heat. Stir and toss the crumbs around until crunchy and golden all over. Remove from the heat and tip into a nice bowl. Serve your macaroni and chese in the center of the table, with your bowl of crispy bread crumbs for sprinkling over, and a lovely green salad.

Peruvian café was brilliant - restaurants don't offer home-cooked food like this

PERUVIAN CEVICHE

Serves 4 as a starter

14 oz sea bass, flounder, sole, or
snapper, pinboned, skinned, and filleted
1 red or yellow bell pepper,
seeded and finely chopped
2 scallions, trimmed and finely sliced
juice of 3 lemons
1 teaspoon sea salt
1–2 fresh red chiles, seeded and
finely chopped
8 sprigs of fresh mint, leaves picked
8 sprigs of fresh cilantro, leaves picked
large handful mustard cress or alfalfa
optional: a few fennel tops, leaves picked
extra virgin olive oil
freshly ground black pepper

Wine suggestion:
Spanish white – an Albariño

During my time in New York I got to visit all sorts of wonderful and fascinating places, and on one occasion I was lucky enough to be taken to a fantastic Peruvian restaurant – it was great fun. This ceviche was on the menu that night. Ceviche is a lovely little appetizer of fresh fish marinated in citrus juices. As long as you've got mega fresh fish, it's an absolute dream and delight to make and eat.

★　　　★　　　★　　　★　　　★　　　★

Cut your fish fillets into ½-inch cubes. Put these into a bowl with your chopped bell peppers and scallions, then cover and place in the refrigerator until you need them. In a separate bowl or a screw-top jar, mix together the lemon juice, salt, and chiles, then pop the lid on and put in the refrigerator to chill too. This may seem like a lot of salt but most of it gets drained off.

Finally, wash and dry your herbs and cress and put them into the refrigerator as well.

You can assemble the ceviche just before your guests are ready to eat. It's important that you don't leave the fish marinating for too long – you don't want the acids in the juices to cook the fish. Pour the lemon dressing over the fish mixture and immediately mix it up. Leave it to sit for about 2½ minutes while you lay out the plates.

Throw most of your herb mixture into the bowl with the fish and very quickly toss it together – I'm talking no more than 10 seconds here. Divide the ceviche between your 4 plates, gently spoon over a little of the dressing (discarding the rest), and sprinkle with the rest of the herbs. Drizzle over some good-quality extra virgin olive oil from a height, sprinkle with some freshly ground black pepper, and enjoy.

THE EGYPTIAN CONNECTION

The Astoria neighborhood in Queens is one of my favorites. It's traditionally a Greek neighborhood but is fantastically diverse now. It has a large Egyptian community, and there I met Ali El Sayed at his restaurant, Kabab Café, a renowned Egyptian hangout. It's a small, intimate, and rustic kind of place, with an open-plan kitchen that rattles out really tasty food. Ali is definitely a character, and he passed on lots of information to me about his culture's food history.

Egyptian cooking is one of the oldest cuisines in the world. It makes wonderful use of fresh meat, slow cooking, quick cooking, spices, dried and fresh fruit, wild herbs, and flatbreads ... all of which are absolutely delicious. After Ali and I bonded over the food, he took me shopping for meat at a slaughterhouse ... right in the middle of Queens! This was where the halal slaughter was done. Honestly, it felt as though I'd walked right out the back door and into the Egyptian desert. But to me this was brilliant, because it was exactly the sort of experience I was after – a side of New York I had never seen.

When we got back to Ali's, I felt inspired by the things I'd seen, so I cooked him the spicy duck recipe on page 70, which he loved. We then played checkers and smoked hookah pipes, which are sort of like smoking a regular pipe through a bong of water. Up until this point, the only bongs I'd heard of were illegal! Everyone around us was speaking Arabic and the whole atmosphere was just really cool. I had to keep reminding myself that I was in New York. How wonderful when a neighborhood can make you feel like you're on the other side of the world.

P.S. Egyptian cooking often uses a sweet and sour berry called sumac and a spice mixture called zahtar (or za'atar). You should be able to find both of these in decent ethnic food stores and gourmet stores; otherwise go online and look at www.deandeluca.com.

Ali made his version of this wonderfully delicious soup for me. There are two spices here that really make it incredible: sumac, which is a sweet and sour berry, and zahtar, which is a mixture of sesame seeds, thyme, and sumac berries. There are enough lovely ingredients here for it still to be delicious and tasty without these two spices, but if you see them in a deli they're worth getting hold of.

★　　★　　★　　★　　★　　★

Cook your bulghur wheat following the package instructions, until tender, then drain and put to one side.

Put your diced onion, bell peppers, and minced garlic into a large saucepan with a few lugs of olive oil and a good pinch of salt and pepper, and cook on the highest heat for about 3 minutes, stirring occasionally. Add your spices and cook for another minute.

Next, add your cooked bulghur wheat, fresh and canned tomatoes, and broth. Slowly bring to a boil, then reduce the heat and simmer for 10 minutes. After that, check the seasoning and preheat the oven to 350°F.

Rub your tortillas with a little olive oil, then dust over a little sumac and zahtar. Lay them flat on a cookie sheet and warm them in the oven for a couple of minutes until the edges crisp up.

Serve your tortillas on the side for dipping, or pop them into the bowls before pouring over the gorgeous soup. Sprinkle over a little extra sumac, zahtar, and cumin, scatter over your torn-up mint leaves, and you're done. Serve with lime wedges for squeezing over.

MY ASTORIA SOUP

Serves 6

heaping ⅓ cup bulghur wheat
1 red onion, peeled and diced
1 red bell pepper, seeded and diced
1 yellow bell pepper, seeded and diced
1 green bell pepper, seeded and diced
4 cloves garlic, peeled and minced
olive oil
sea salt and freshly ground black pepper
2 tablespoons sumac (see page 66), plus a little extra for sprinkling over
2 tablespoons zahtar (see page 66), plus a little extra for sprinkling over
1 teaspoon ground cumin, plus a little extra for sprinkling over
1 teaspoon smoked paprika
12 cherry or grape tomatoes, halved
1 x 14-oz can diced tomatoes
1¼ quarts duck, chicken, or vegetable broth
6 flour tortillas
a small handful of fresh mint leaves, picked and roughly torn
1 lime, cut into wedges, to serve

Wine suggestion:
Austrian white – from the Grüner Veltline grape

ALI'S DUCK WRAP

Serves 4–6 as an appetizer

1 x 4½ lb duck
olive oil
½ teaspoon ground cumin
1 level tablespoon sumac (see page 66), plus a little extra for sprinkling over
1 level tablespoon zahtar (see page 66), plus a little extra for sprinkling over
½ teaspoon chile powder or paprika
a good pinch of sea salt and freshly ground black pepper
a small bunch of fresh mint
a small bunch of fresh cilantro
seeds from 1 pomegranate
2 iceberg lettuces
a small jar of hoisin sauce

For the onion and radish pickle
1 small red onion
10 large radishes
a good pinch of sea salt
juice of 2 limes
1 fresh red chile, seeded and finely sliced

Wine suggestion:
Australian red – a Pinot Noir from the Yarra Valley

Seeing all the great stuff Ali was cooking at his Kabab Café restaurant got my creative juices going, so I came up with this spiced duck dish for him. It's a bit of a mix of influences: spiced Egyptian duck, with hoisin sauce in an iceberg lettuce wrap, but it worked so well that Ali loved it. When I was there with him I named this *eid a mania*, which is Egyptian for "a handful of Ali"!

★　　★　　★　　★　　★　　★

Preheat the oven to 350°F. Rub the duck with a little olive oil, then mix up your spices, salt, and pepper in a small bowl. Rub this spice mix into the duck. Pop it into a roasting pan and put in the oven to cook for around 2 hours, basting occasionally. Halfway through, drain away the fat from the bird. Pour the fat through a strainer into a jar, then store it in the refrigerator for up to a couple of months and use it for roasting potatoes.

Cut your onion and radishes into really thin slices. Hit them with a good pinch of salt, your lime juice, and the sliced chile. Mix it all up with a spoon and put it into the refrigerator.

When the duck skin is nice and crispy and the meat shreds easily, it's ready. Put some clean rubber gloves on and strip the meat and crispy skin from the bones, making sure you get all those lovely sweet bits of meat from the bottom of the carcass too. What's quite nice here is to put all the meat into a dish, with the skin at the top, and just pop that back into the oven to get crispy and hot for 5 minutes. Don't throw away the duck carcass – boil it up with a few vegetables and some water to make a nice broth that you can freeze for later use.

Squeeze all the moisture from your onion pickle and pour these extra juices away. Transfer the pickle to a nice bowl. Slice about 1 inch off the stalk end of your icebergs (you can save this for a salad another time) and click off nice cup-sized leaves. Twelve leaves is about right for 4 to 6 people. Put these on a platter on your table, with the onion pickle, pomegranate seeds, a bowl of your mint and coriander leaves, and a bowl of hoisin sauce.

Get your crispy shredded duck from the oven, sprinkle a little more sumac and zahtar on top to give it a real perfume, and let everyone tuck in. I say the best way to assemble the wraps is to grab a lettuce leaf, dollop on a teaspoon of hoisin sauce, followed by a good bit of duck and crispy skin, some pickle and herbs, and top with a few pomegranate seeds. Roll it up like a pancake and eat it – absolute heaven.

THIS WAS MY FIRST TIME SMOKING A HOOKAH PIPE AND IT WAS QUITE RELAXING! I HAD TO KEEP REMINDING MYSELF I WAS IN NEW YORK

My new Egyptian friend, Ali, made a version of this dish using leftover lamb. It really reminded me of a quesadilla in Mexican cooking – but an Egyptian version. I thought it was absolutely delicious and I'll definitely be making it again. It's great for using up all those scruffy bits of lamb you have left over after doing a big roast, and if you ask me, slow-cooked shoulder works best. Leftover chicken, pork, or beef also work well. If you can't get flatbreads, just use tortillas instead – they'll work brilliantly too. Sometimes when friends come around, it's nice to knock up a few of these flatbreads, slice them on a board, and serve like rustic-style canapés.

★　　★　　★　　★　　★　　★

Preheat your oven to full whack. Spread your leftover meat on a board and, with a large knife, chop it all up into rough little chunks and pieces. Put it into a large bowl with your lemon zest, then halve the lemon and squeeze over the juice from one half. Add all your spices, the eggs, a pinch of salt and pepper, and most of your scallions. Mix everything up with a spoon.

Lay out your flatbreads. You're going to fold them in half, so just cover half of them with the filling, leaving a ½ inch gap around the edge. Use a spoon to spread the lamb mixture out, then fold over your flatbreads and gently press the two halves together so you have a half-moon shape.

Get two big sheet pans roughly the same size and lightly rub one of them with olive oil. Lay your flatbreads on the oiled pan, then lightly rub the underside of your second pan with oil and pop this on top of your flatbreads. If your pans aren't big enough you may need to do this in two batches. Whack the trays into your preheated oven and cook for 6 to 8 minutes. Using the two pans this way ensures that your flatbreads get lovely and crisp on both sides.

Cut the flatbreads up into slices and arrange them around a big cutting board or on a large serving platter. Dollop your hummus next to them, making a small well in the center of it so it's like a little dish, and drizzle in some extra virgin olive oil.

Scatter over your reserved scallions and sprinkle everything with a little cumin and zahtar. Mix your yogurt up with some chopped mint, a good squeeze of lemon juice, and a pinch of salt. Have a little taste, and add an extra squeeze of lemon if it needs it. Spoon this over, and tuck in!

EGYPTIAN STUFFED FLATBREAD

Serves 4 as a snack or appetizer

4 cups (approx. 10 oz) shredded cooked lamb, beef, pork, or chicken
1 lemon, finely zested
1 tablespoon sumac (see page 66)
1 tablespoon zahtar (see page 66)
1 tablespoon cumin seeds, toasted
1 teaspoon paprika
2 large eggs, preferably free-range or organic, beaten
sea salt and freshly ground black pepper
4 scallions, trimmed and thinly sliced
4 large flatbreads or flour tortillas
olive oil
heaping ¼ cup hummus
good-quality extra virgin olive oil
¼ cup natural yogurt
a small handful of fresh mint, leaves picked

Wine suggestion:
Chilean red – a Carmenère

LOUISIANA

Forget partridge and rabbit; out here 'local game' means something completely different!

It's quite difficult to visit America without having some preconceptions about it, whether from movies, the news, or hearing people talk about it. My friends had raved about New Orleans for years, so I expected great things. But I still wasn't prepared for either the color and noise or the incredibly potent mix of people and cultures a few hours outside the city, in Cajun country. It was an experience I shall never forget.

I kicked off my trip in New Orleans – a truly special place. The way the locals have picked themselves up after the devastation of Hurricanes Katrina and Gustav is completely inspiring. The music, the art, the pace of life, the chaos, the architecture, the food … it's as good as it gets. And there is such a positive atmosphere everywhere. All the people I met during my time in Louisiana couldn't have been friendlier. They really opened up to me and were incredibly generous with their time and their cooking stories.

Because a lot of what I'd heard about Louisiana had been through news stories about the hurricanes that pass through the area, I'd always ask myself, "Why would you bother living somewhere where Mother Nature gives you a kicking on a regular basis? Wouldn't you just move somewhere calmer and safer?" So, during my trip, I asked every person I met why they stayed … and they all replied with Dorothy's famous line from *The Wizard of Oz*: "There's no place like home!" And you know what? They're right. When you've been brought up somewhere, it doesn't matter what Mother Nature hurls at you. It's your home.

Outside New Orleans the landscape is really lush, beautiful, and charming. Leaving the city, I headed west in my pick-up truck along Highway 10, toward the little town of Breaux Bridge, past the state capital of Baton Rouge and over the Mississippi River. Almost the whole way (a two-hour drive) the highway was elevated on huge stone columns, and as far as I could see, there were watery swamps below. An incredible feat of engineering, especially as this area is full of alligators …

The people I met at Breaux Bridge and the surrounding area were so patriotic, not only about their country but about their underlying culture. The two main cultures here are Creole and Cajun. Creole food is a complete blend of influences: you've got Spanish, French, and German cooking mixed with the herbs and ingredients of the Native Americans as well as those of the West Indian and African slaves, who put their own special spin on things as they stirred the pots in those Louisiana kitchens.

The Cajuns were the French Acadians who settled around the bayous and swamps after they'd been kicked out of Canada by the Brits. Their cooking style was influenced by the fact that the men came down long before the women – so it was all about big bold flavors and one-pot cooking. They made friends with the Native Americans, who showed them how to make use of wild game, seafood, and anything else the bayou had to offer.

You'll find dishes inspired by both these cultures on the following pages, and I hope you give them a go. If you fancy visiting Louisiana, I'd absolutely recommend banging out three or four days in New Orleans, then hiring a car and taking yourself out to Cajun country for a week. The people are warm and friendly, the beer is great, the seafood rocks, and the local game (yes, I'm talking alligator!) is amazing.

LOUISIANA

SOUTHERN RED BEANS & PORK

This is a great one-pot comfort dish, full of robust flavors. With the exception of the much-loved baked bean, beans tend to get overlooked, but if you put some love into cooking them you can make a delicious, cheap dish that is wonderfully satisfying to eat. Traditionally, kidney beans are used in this dish, but you can use any type, or a mixture, as long as you keep in mind that different beans take different times to cook. It's worth remembering that the beans and pork will keep for a few days in the refrigerator and can also be frozen, so you'll be able to put any leftovers to good use (a spoonful in a soup or stew rocks!).

Serves 8

★　　★　　★　　★　　★　　★

2¾ cups dry kidney beans
1 head of garlic
1 smoked ham hock (approx. 4½ lbs), the best quality you can afford
4 celery stalks, trimmed and roughly chopped
2 large onions, peeled and roughly chopped
4 fresh bay leaves
8 sprigs of fresh thyme
1 tablespoon dried oregano
1 tablespoon sweet paprika
½ teaspoon cayenne pepper
1 tablespoon ground black pepper
2 x 14-oz cans whole peeled plum tomatoes
sea salt and freshly ground black pepper
apple cider vinegar
extra virgin olive oil

Wine suggestion:
French red – a young and gutsy Côtes du Rhône

It's best using dried kidney beans here, but if you plan on using canned beans, don't add them until the ham hock is cooked and remember to drain them first! Soak the dried beans overnight in cold water. The next day, drain them and put them into a large saucepan covered with at least 1 quart of fresh cold water.

Halve your head of garlic across the middle so you cut across all the cloves, then add it to the beans and water along with the ham hock, chopped vegetables, herbs, spices, and canned tomatoes. Bring everything to a boil and cook briskly for 5 minutes, then reduce to a gentle simmer and cook for around 2 hours with the lid on. If you try to rush cooking dried beans like this, they'll split. The exact cooking time will depend on the size of your beans, and how long they've been dried for, so check on them every so often, and when you're happy that they're tender and creamy on the inside, they're ready. At this point your meat should be nice and soft and falling away from the bone.

Remove the ham hock, garlic, and any sprigs of herbs from the pan. Discard the herbs and put the garlic aside. Pull the rind from the ham and throw it away, then shred the meat from the hock with a fork, discarding the bones. Pile the meat onto a plate or board.

Spoon about a quarter of the beans and veggies into a bowl and squeeze in the pulp from the cooked garlic head, discarding the skin. Use a potato masher to mash the garlic into the beans and veggies until you get a nice creamy consistency. Stir these mashed beans and veggies back through the stew, along with all the shredded meat. Have a taste and season carefully with salt, pepper, and a small swig of apple cider vinegar. I like to drizzle over a little extra virgin olive oil because I think it works well here. Keep the beans warm while you cook some rice, then tuck in!

I first tried this dish in New Orleans, on a food crawl through the city. I love it because it's rustic, hearty, and full of good flavors. This kind of food isn't about state-of-the-art stainless steel, it's all about cast-iron pots and rough kitchens, and I love that. If you can't get hold of tasso, which is an American smoked ham, then by all means improvise with another smoked meat like bacon, pancetta, or chorizo.

This "working man's dish" is respectful of the fact that every dish needs a good flavor base. If people didn't have enough money to buy all the flash cuts of meat, they had to add flavor from somewhere. That's where chicken livers come in. For some reason, people don't seem to buy them much these days, but they're delicious, so please use them. Once you put them with the vegetables and fresh herbs here, you'll be amazed by the depth of flavor they'll give you.

DOWN 'N' DIRTY CAJUN RICE

★ ★ ★ ★ ★ ★

Cook your rice following the package instructions. Drain it, then rinse it well under cold water – this will prevent it overcooking. Put to one side.

Put a large saucepan over a fairly high heat and add your smoked meat. Frying it will allow the fat to render out, give the meat a nice color, and help give the dish a better overall flavor. Let it get a bit crispy, then add your bay leaves. Toss it all around and add a lug of olive oil to help it along. Once the meat is nice and golden, add your onion, bell pepper, and celery, and season with a pinch of salt and pepper and the cayenne. Keep everything moving around in the pan for about 10 minutes, until your veggies have softened, then add the minced garlic and all your thyme leaves.

Put your trimmed chicken livers into a small bowl with a good splash of milk to rinse them. After a few minutes, pour away the milk and roughly chop the livers. Keep stirring the vegetable mixture, and once you've got a lovely deep color and flavor going, add your chopped chicken livers and kidney beans. Fry for 3 to 4 minutes, then add your drained, cooked rice, stirring and scraping the goodness from the pan as you go. Cook until the rice is piping hot, then add a shake or two of Tabasco (just to be polite to my friends in Louisiana, where Tabasco is made).

To get a bit of freshness in there, stir in the chopped scallions and parsley along with a good squeeze of lemon. Serve on a lovely big platter so everyone can dig in. This dish can be eaten cold, but is best when hot.

Serves 4–6

2 cups long-grain rice
¼ lb tasso, thick-cut smoked bacon (the best quality you can afford), or pancetta, chopped into ½-inch cubes
4 fresh bay leaves
olive oil
1 onion, peeled and diced
1 green bell pepper, seeded and diced
2 celery stalks, trimmed and diced
sea salt and freshly ground black pepper
1 teaspoon cayenne pepper
6 cloves garlic, peeled and minced
a small bunch of fresh thyme, leaves picked
7 oz chicken livers, trimmed
milk, for rinsing
1 x 15-oz can of red kidney beans, drained
Tabasco sauce
6 scallions, trimmed and roughly chopped
a small bunch of fresh curly parsley, roughly chopped
1 lemon, to serve

Wine suggestion:
Italian red – a young Valpolicella

AMAZING PORK CRACKLINGS

Serves 10 for nibbles

1¾ lbs good-quality pork skin, preferably
organic, the best quality you can afford

olive oil

sea salt

½ teaspoon cayenne pepper

ground cinnamon

3 or 4 cloves garlic, peeled
and thinly sliced

2 tablespoons honey

Pork rinds, or "cracklings" as they call them in Louisiana, are a fantastic snack with cold local beers. Usually they're deep fried at 300°F, taken out of the pan while the oil is turned up to 350°F, then fried again so that they puff up and get wonderfully crispy. Although this method gives great results, it does involve a lot of hot oil, so you have to be careful.

But rather than deep frying them, I'm cooking mine in a frying pan first, then hitting them with a bit of cinnamon, cayenne, and honey and roasting them in the oven until they're puffy and golden brown. You should be able to buy the pork skin from a good butcher.

★　　★　　★　　★　　★　　★

Preheat your oven to 400°F. Chop your pork skin into nice bitesized pieces – I find the best way to do this is with scissors or a very sharp knife. Heat a small lug of olive oil in a large frying pan over a low to medium heat. In batches, fry your pieces of skin, stirring every few minutes, until they crackle and turn a light golden brown. Using tongs, transfer them to a roasting pan and pop them into the preheated oven to roast for 20 to 30 minutes, or until puffed up and deep golden.

Remove the pan from the oven and drain away any excess fat (any fat that drips off can be poured into a jar and saved in the refrigerator, ready to be used the next time you want to make roast potatoes, braise greens, or even fry some fillets of fish). Sprinkle over a couple of pinches of sea salt, your cayenne, a pinch of cinnamon, and the sliced garlic. Add the honey and mix it all up well, then pop the pan back into the oven for another 5 to 7 minutes, but please, please, keep your eyes peeled. You don't want the cracklings to burn after all the care you've given them. Serve and enjoy!

Jambalaya is a French word that means "jumbled" or "mixed up," and I have no doubt that the philosophy and heart of this recipe come from a similar place to paella, kedgeree, and risotto.

Originally, any Louisiana "critter" unlucky enough to get caught would have gone into this: rabbit, duck, squirrel, frog, alligator . . . you name it! And similarly, you can adapt it to whatever your local butcher or fishmonger happens to have. Go cheaper by using things like frozen shrimp and chicken livers, or more expensive by including lobster or crab. I used an incredible local smoked sausage called andouille, but fresh chorizo or any other smoked sausage would work just as well.

This dish makes me happy every time I eat it. And if more people than expected turn up for dinner just add a bit of extra rice.

★　　★　　★　　★　　★　　★

Season the chicken with salt, pepper, and a pinch of cayenne. Pour a couple of lugs of oil into a large Dutch oven and brown the chicken pieces and sliced sausage over a medium heat. After 5 minutes, once the meat is nicely browned on all sides, add your onion, bell peppers, and celery as well as your bay, thyme, and a pinch of salt and pepper. Stir, then fry on a medium heat for 10 to 12 minutes, stirring every now and again. It's important to control the heat of the pan: you don't want it to be so slow nothing's happening, or so fast that things are catching and burning. You want a steady, solid heat.

Once the veggies have softened, add your garlic and chiles, stir around for a minute, then stir in the canned tomatoes and chicken broth.

Bring everything to a boil, then turn the heat down, pop the lid on the pan, and simmer for 25 to 30 minutes. When you can pull the meat from the bone and shred it easily, the chicken's ready. Feel free to remove the chicken bones at this point if you like, then add your rice. Give it all a good stir, then put the lid on. Give it a stir every few minutes, scraping the goodness from the bottom of the pan as you go. Let it cook for about 15 to 20 minutes, until the rice is perfectly cooked. Stir in the shrimp, and if it needs it, add enough water to make it a kind of oatmeal consistency (look at the pictures). Pop the lid back on and cook for another 3 to 4 minutes while you chop your parsley. Stir the parsley through and serve on a lovely big platter. I absolutely love this with a lemony green salad.

CHICKEN, SAUSAGE & SHRIMP JAMBALAYA

Serves 8–10

4 chicken thighs, skin on, preferably free-range or organic
4 chicken drumsticks, skin on, preferably free-range or organic
sea salt and freshly ground black pepper
cayenne pepper
olive oil
¾ lb smoked sausage, such as andouille or fresh chorizo, skin removed, cut into ½-inch-thick slices
1 large onion, peeled and roughly chopped
1 green bell pepper, seeded and roughly chopped
1 red bell pepper, seeded and roughly chopped
4 celery stalks, trimmed and roughly chopped
4 fresh bay leaves
4 sprigs of fresh thyme
6 cloves garlic, peeled and sliced
1–2 fresh red chiles, seeded and minced
1 x 14-oz can diced tomatoes
1½ quarts chicken broth, preferably organic
3½ cups long-grain rice
16–20 large raw shrimps, shell-off and cleaned
a handful of fresh curly parsley

Wine suggestion:
American Pinot Noir – try one from Oregon

In the UK, we love our bangers and mash, and to me this dish felt fairly similar to that but with rice and Louisiana gravy. It pushes similar buttons, and it has the added advantage of having extra spices, and it also reminds me of a kinda Italian peperonata. But, let's be honest, beautiful sausages in a lovely stew are a winning combo in any country.

In the spirit of Cajun cooking, this is a simple one-pan dish, perfect whether you're at home or cooking outdoors. Give this a try and you'll love it.

★　　★　　★　　★　　★　　★

Put a splash of olive oil in a large saucepan and let it get hot. Add your sausages and let them cook away so they brown nicely on all sides. Once golden and crisp, take them out of the pan and put them on a plate to rest. Depending on your sausages, there may be a lot of fat left behind in the pan. You only want to keep about ¼ cup of it in the pan, so carefully pour any extra away. If you don't have enough, just add a splash more olive oil.

Add your onion, bell peppers, and celery to the fat and fry on a medium heat for 10 to 12 minutes, stirring occasionally, until softened. Stir in your garlic, chiles, thyme, and spices and fry for another minute or two. Stir in your flour and vinegar, and after a couple of minutes add your browned sausages, chicken broth, and canned tomatoes, using a wooden spoon to break them up a little. Season with a nice big pinch of salt and pepper, stir, then bring to a boil and let it tick away for 15 minutes or so, until you have a thick and delicious gravy.

Serve with a hearty spoonful of rice on the side and sprinkle over some sliced scallions, chopped parsley, and any reserved celery leaves. Really tasty stuff!

PS: I've also stirred chopped up pieces of cooked chicken, quail, and smoky bacon through this with great results!

SOUTHERN SAUSAGE STEW

Serves 6

olive oil
good-quality sausages (2 or 3 per person)
1 onion, peeled and roughly chopped
1 red bell pepper, seeded and roughly chopped
1 green bell pepper, seeded and roughly chopped
1 yellow bell pepper, seeded and roughly chopped
2 celery stalks, trimmed and roughly chopped, yellow leaves reserved
4 cloves garlic, peeled and chopped
1–2 fresh red chiles, seeded and finely chopped
10 sprigs of fresh thyme, leaves picked
1 heaping teaspoon paprika
1 heaping teaspoon cayenne pepper
2–3 heaping tablespoons all-purpose flour
1 tablespoon white wine or apple cider vinegar
generous 3 cups chicken broth, preferably organic
1 x 14-oz can diced tomatoes
sea salt and freshly ground black pepper
cooked long-grain rice, to serve
3 scallions, trimmed and thinly sliced
a small bunch of fresh curly parsley, roughly chopped

Wine suggestion:
Argentinian red – a Malbec from Mendoza

Soft-shell crab, shrimp, okra, and sweet potato are all incredible cooked in batter this way. Fresh soft-shell crabs are a wonderful delicacy but are only really available for about six weeks of the year, when they shed their old shells and hide under rocks until their new ones firm up. You'll often find pretty good frozen ones in Asian supermarkets, or you can ask a good fishmonger to order them for you.

Soft-shell crabs have long, gray, frilly gills underneath the shell – these are usually called "dead man's fingers." Remove them before cooking by simply lifting up the soft shell and then pulling them off. If you're buying the crabs frozen or from a fishmonger, they may well have been removed already so you won't need to worry.

★   ★   ★   ★   ★   ★

First make your tartar sauce. Spoon the mayonnaise into a bowl with the chopped gherkins, parsley, onion, capers, and lemon juice and mix well. Taste, season with salt and pepper, and set aside.

Pour your oil into a large saucepan and heat it to about 350°F. If you don't have a thermometer, use a little piece of sweet potato as your gauge. When it rises to the top and turns golden, the oil is about hot enough and you can turn the heat down until you're ready to fry. Keep an eye on the pan and be careful, though – hot oil can burn very badly.

Put your flour into a large mixing bowl and stir in a few good sprinkles of salt and pepper and half the cayenne. Crack your eggs into another large bowl and add your baking powder, 2 good sprinkles of sea salt, the rest of your cayenne, a good splash of white wine vinegar, the beer, and the mustard. It will foam up instantly, so get your whisk in there and mix it up. Toss your whole crabs, shrimp, sweet potatoes, and okra in the seasoned flour until completely coated. Shake off any extra flour, then dip each of the floured ingredients into the batter until completely coated. Put back in the seasoned flour one more time. It's best to do this in batches. This double-dipping will give you the most brilliant crunchy coating.

Always fry your ingredients in smallish mixed batches so you get plates of perfect, hot, crispy food rather than a whole load of soggy food, which is what happens if you overload the pan. Lower a mixed batch of battered food slowly into the hot oil. Fry the crab for about 4 to 5 minutes, and the shrimp, okra, and sweet potato for 3 to 4 minutes. By this time the food will be golden, crisp, and floating at the top of the oil. Use a perforated spoon to transfer the fried bits to some paper towels to drain. Sprinkle with a little sea salt and serve straight away, with lemon halves for squeezing over, your tartar sauce, and a nice cold drink. Delicious!

LOUISIANA FRY & TARTAR SAUCE

Serves 6

2 quarts vegetable or corn oil
2½ cups all-purpose flour
sea salt and freshly ground black or white pepper
3 tablespoons cayenne pepper
3 large eggs, preferably free-range or organic
1 tablespoon baking powder
a good splash of white wine vinegar
1 cup beer (lager)
2 tablespoons whole-grain mustard
6 small soft-shell crabs, gray gills removed (see introduction)
6 large raw shrimp, shell-off but heads and tails left on
3 sweet potatoes, scrubbed and thinly sliced
12 whole okra, halved lengthways
3 lemons, halved

For the tartar sauce
¾ cup mayonnaise
2 large gherkins, diced
a small bunch of fresh Italian parsley, finely chopped
½ small red onion, diced
1 tablespoon capers
juice of ½ lemon
sea salt and freshly ground black pepper

Wine suggestion:
Italian white – a good Soave Classico

GUMBO

The day after I arrived in New Orleans I was lucky enough to meet a fantastic woman called Leah Chase. She's been cooking her famous food for the locals at her restaurant, Dooky Chase, since the 1950s and is known as the "Queen of Creole Cuisine," so I was learning about gumbo from the best! The word "gumbo" comes from the African word for okra, which is a vegetable introduced to America by African slaves. They smuggled seeds over in their ears, hair, and even bellybuttons to make sure they had food wherever it was they were going. Once in America, they planted those seeds and started using okra in this feast of a dish.

Gumbo is basically a stew-cum-soup (or, as Rachael Ray would refer to it, "stoup"!), to which you can add lots of ingredients to take it in different directions. However, the two things that all gumbos have in common are that they are always made from a "roux" of fat and flour or with okra, which is a natural thickener, and always include a vegetable mixture of onions, bell peppers, and celery known everywhere in Louisiana as the "holy trinity." People in Louisiana are big on cooking and stirring their roux until it's as dark as they can get it. Some people do this for an hour, and as a color guide, they'll use all sorts of things, from a jar of peanut butter to the color of their skin (like Leah does), to help them decide when it's at the right stage.

The two gumbos that follow are the ones I served up at the second line – a New Orleans tradition which is basically a big brilliant street party. During old-style jazz funerals the brass band and funeral procession would walk through the streets in a "first line." Eventually the rest of the neighborhood would join in and dance at the back, forming a "second line." I wasn't sure what to expect but I loved it. The neighborhood was filled with music and dancing and the musicians dressed up in incredible outfits, sometimes wearing masks, and they'd take their turns to come out of a long building playing their music and dancing through the surrounding streets. Check out the photos on pages 94–5 and you'll see how amazing the whole thing was. Without a doubt music and dancing is what makes a second line procession, but food is a huge part of the party, with food stands and stalls lining both sides of the street.

Second line street parties give the locals
an excuse to dress up, eat, drink and
dance. That's New Orleans for you

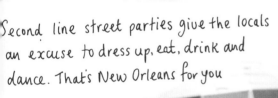

If there's one thing I've learned from the people I met in New Orleans, it's that everyone has their own take on gumbo. It's definitely more of a philosophy than a recipe. As long as you don't mess with the roux of fat and flour or the "holy trinity" of onions, bell peppers, and celery that you'll find in so many of Louisiana's recipes, you can add all sorts of tasty stuff.

I used chicken, a lovely local smoked sausage called andouille, and sweet potato for this. Although they told me they never use sweet potato in gumbo, it went down a treat with the lovely people at the second line street procession. And that was a real test!

SPICY MEAT GUMBO

Serves 6–8

★   ★   ★   ★   ★   ★

Season your chicken with salt, pepper, paprika, and cayenne. Put a large saucepan on a high heat, add a little olive oil, and fry your chicken, sausage, and bacon for around 15 minutes, or until it is all golden brown and crispy. Remove the browned pieces of meat to a dish, leaving the flavorful fat in the pan, as you'll be using this to make that all-important roux.

Turn the heat down and add your holy trinity of onion, bell peppers, and celery. Slowly stir and fry for 10 minutes, until softened, then stir in the flour. This is the time to dedicate a bit of love to your roux, so keep stirring the vegetables and flour so the mixture cooks evenly and gets nice and dark. It might take around 10 minutes to get it to the right darkness. Peanut butter color is a good starting point, but you can take it even darker if you prefer by stirring and cooking it for another 20 to 30 minutes.

At this point, add your garlic, sweet potatoes, browned meats, thyme, and bay leaves and stir and fry for a further minute. Pour in the hot chicken broth, bring everything to a boil, then turn the heat down and simmer on a medium heat for 45 minutes, or until the chicken pulls apart easily. The fantastic flavors will mix together and the sweet potato will break down and help thicken the gumbo.

Before serving, I like to scoop the chicken pieces out, shred the meat from the bone with a fork, and put all the meat back into the pan, discarding the bones and skin.

Taste the gumbo and season if necessary. Seasoning is important to the folk from New Orleans, so work it, baby! Roughly chop your parsley and stir it in, then divide your gumbo into bowls over some fluffy rice. Scatter over some sliced scallions and enjoy.

4 chicken thighs, skin on, preferably free-range or organic
4 chicken drumsticks, skin on, preferably free-range or organic
sea salt and freshly ground black pepper
1 teaspoon paprika
1 teaspoon cayenne pepper
olive oil
14 oz smoked sausage, such as andouille or fresh chorizo, thickly sliced
4 slices of smoked bacon, the best quality you can afford, roughly chopped
1 large onion, peeled and diced
1 green bell pepper, seeded and chopped
1 yellow bell pepper, seeded and chopped
4 celery stalks, trimmed and diced
3 heaping tablespoons all-purpose flour
6 cloves garlic, peeled and minced
2¼ lbs sweet potatoes, peeled and roughly chopped
6 sprigs of fresh thyme, leaves picked
4 fresh bay leaves
1½ quarts hot chicken broth, preferably organic
a small bunch of fresh curly parsley
4 scallions, trimmed and finely sliced

Wine suggestion:
Italian red – a Barbera d'Alba or d'Asti

SURF & TURF GUMBO

This is my own expression of gumbo and it's a bit like the people of New Orleans: gregarious and out there. I loved what Leah Chase said to me when we made gumbo together: "Dishing up a portion of gumbo is like going fishing ... you get what you get."

I used beautiful blue crabs for this dish, but you can use prepared crabmeat. Make sure you make a nice dark roux and get the "holy trinity" base of onions, bell peppers, and celery really going, and you can then substitute shrimp with crayfish or fish, and use any other type of cured sausage you like. It's the principle of the dish that counts, and swapping ingredients is just fine – in fact, that's sort of the point!

Serves 8–10

★   ★   ★   ★   ★   ★

16–20 large, raw shrimp preferably shell-on
olive oil
1¼ lbs spicy cured sausage, sliced into ½-inch rounds
3 quarts chicken broth, preferably organic
5 heaping tablespoons all-purpose flour
1 large onion, peeled and diced
2 large green bell peppers, seeded and diced
3 celery stalks, trimmed and diced
5 fresh bay leaves
a small bunch of fresh thyme, leaves picked
8 cloves garlic, peeled and minced
1 teaspoon cayenne pepper
1 teaspoon Tabasco sauce
½ lb okra, sliced into rounds
¾ lb picked crabmeat, plus 4 claws (if you can get hold of them)
1 x 14-oz can diced tomatoes
sea salt and freshly ground black pepper
juice of 1 lemon
a small bunch of fresh curly parsley

Wine suggestion:
New Zealand red – a young Pinot Noir, served lightly chilled

If you've got shells on your shrimp, peel them and keep the heads and shells aside for your broth. Heat a large saucepan over a medium to high heat and add a lug of olive oil and your sliced sausages. Let them get some nice color. While that's happening, put a large stock pot on a high heat, add another lug of olive oil, and fry any shrimp heads and shells for about 5 minutes. Use a rolling pin to bash them up in the pot and release all their lovely flavors, then pour in your chicken broth, bring to a boil, and leave to simmer for 20 minutes.

Move your cooked sausages to a plate and add the flour to the fat left behind in the pan. Turn the heat down to low and stir. You want the roux to have a semi-loose, doughy consistency, so add a splash of olive oil if there isn't a lot of fat. (You also want the roux to get really nice and dark, so have a bit of patience and keep stirring to stop it sticking. It might take around 10 minutes to get it to the right darkness. Peanut butter color is a good starting point, but you can take it even darker if you prefer by stirring and cooking it for another 20 to 30 minutes.) After about 2 minutes, add a splash more olive oil to the roux along with the holy trinity of onion, bell peppers, and celery. Stir and cook for about 5 minutes, then scrunch up your bay leaves to help bring out their flavors and stir these into the trinity mixture with the thyme leaves. Fry for 5 minutes, then add your garlic, cayenne, Tabasco, and the okra, which will act as a brilliant thickening agent. Give it all a good stir and fry for a couple of minutes.

At this point, add your broth. If you've got shrimp shells in there, pour it through a large strainer. Stir and bring everything up to a boil. Add your crab claws, if using, and canned tomatoes and simmer for 5 to 10 minutes. Stir in your cooked sausages, peeled shrimp, and crabmeat, and leave on a medium heat to tick away for another 5 minutes.

Have a taste and add salt and pepper and a good squeeze of lemon juice if you think it needs it. Keep tasting and seasoning until it's got some kick. Roughly chop the parsley and sprinkle into your gumbo. This is lovely served in bowls over some rice, but you can also put that wonderful big pot right in the middle of the table and let everyone go fishing. What a celebration!

CAJUN BLACKENED FISH STEAKS

Serves 4

4 x ½-lb white fish fillets such as branzino, mahi-mahi, snapper, pacific cod, bream, or pollock (approx. ¾ inch thick), skin on, scaled, and pinboned
1 lemon

For the rub
10 sprigs of fresh thyme, leaves picked
4 sprigs of fresh oregano, leaves picked
2 cloves garlic, peeled
2 teaspoons smoked paprika
1 teaspoon cayenne pepper
1 teaspoon sea salt
1 tablespoon finely ground black pepper
2 tablespoons olive oil
1 lemon

Wine suggestion:
French white – an Alsace Pinot Gris

★　　★　　★　　★　　★　　★

This is my version of a classic Southern dish, but just a word of warning: it is seriously spicy! The way I heard it, this brilliant rub was invented by an African-American chef working at Commander's Palace, a posh New Orleans restaurant. The famous head chef there, Paul Prudhomme, took this recipe, added his own little tweaks, and introduced blackened fish to the rest of the world. Basically it's a bold rub that fragrantly flavors fish and meat and goes dark when it cooks, thanks to the paprika and garlic. Traditionally this dish has been made with the locally caught redfish, but it's also great with any whole or filleted white fish. It goes with so many things, including chicken, pork, lamb, and beef. When I was in Louisiana, I cooked it on a charcoal grill, but I've shown you below how to do it indoors in a pan. Don't be scared by how black the spices go: they'll look burned, but the taste will be amazing.

To make the rub, bash up your fresh herbs and garlic in a pestle and mortar until you've got a nice coarse paste. Mix in the spices, salt, pepper, and olive oil, then squeeze in the juice of half the lemon, making sure not to let any pips get in there, and stir well.

Lightly score the skin of your fish in lines about ¾ inch apart. Using your fingers, smear the rub all over both sides of the fish and into the cuts you've made. Put a nonstick frying or grill pan over a medium-high heat and let it get nice and hot. Put your fish in the pan, skin-side down, and let it cook for 3 to 4 minutes. It will get quite smoky, so you might want to open a window! Turn the heat down to low, then, very carefully, flip your fish over and cook for another 3 to 4 minutes on the second side.

Cut your remaining lemon half and your second lemon into wedges for squeezing over. Serve them with your fish, a nice salad, and boiled or steamed baby potatoes dressed in good olive oil or butter. Don't forget a nice cold glass of wine!

LOUISIANA SEAFOOD BOIL

If you had twenty buddies coming around to your place for a party, you could make this and really blow them away. The real deal involves a massive cast-iron pot on an outdoor gas burner and is cooked in the yard, but it can easily be adapted and cooked in your kitchen.

Crawfish are so easy to get hold of in Louisiana that I just couldn't resist popping some in. Adding razor clams or mussels instead of some of the shrimp would also be exciting. The traditional accompaniments are saltine crackers and seafood sauce or mayo, but I think a good old Marie Rose sauce and some lemon halves for squeezing over work brilliantly here.

Serves 6   ★   ★   ★   ★   ★   ★

2 medium onions, peeled
2 celery stalks, halved
1 lemon, quartered
a small bunch of fresh flat-leaf parsley
6 garlic cloves, unpeeled
3 fresh bay leaves
a thumb-sized piece of ginger root, unpeeled, thickly sliced
2 tablespoons kosher salt
2 teaspoons black peppercorns
2 teaspoons cayenne pepper
1 tablespoon coriander seeds
1 tablespoon black mustard seeds
1 dried chile, crumbled
2 teaspoons fennel seeds
5 whole allspice berries
2 whole cloves
1¾ lb small red-skinned potatoes
4 ears corn, husked and each cut into 3 pieces
2 medium crabs
18 extra-large shell-on raw shrimp

For the Marie Rose sauce
scant 1 cup mayonnaise
3 heaping tablespoons ketchup
1 splash of Worcestershire sauce, such as Lea & Perrins
1 splash of good brandy
juice of 1 lemon
sea salt and freshly ground black pepper

Wine suggestion:
French white – a Loire Sauvignon Blanc from Sancerre or a Pouilly Fumé

Put 8 quarts of water into your biggest saucepan and add your onions, celery, lemon, parsley, garlic, bay leaves, ginger, and all of your spices. Bring a water to a boil, then lower the heat and simmer for about 5 minutes.

While that's happening, mix all your Marie Rose ingredients in a bowl, season to taste with salt and pepper, and put to one side.

Try to use potatoes that are roughly the same size – if you've got any that are much bigger, chop them in half. Add them to the pan and bring back to a boil. Add the corn. After 10 minutes add the crabs and cook for 5 minutes, adding your shrimp for a final 5 minutes. Turn off the heat and allow everything to cool in the pan for a few minutes.

Use tongs or a perforated spoon to get the beautiful fragrant veggies and seafood out of the broth, then pour the cooking liquid away. Serve it all on a nice big platter or on a few sheets of newspaper as they do in Louisiana, with your Marie Rose sauce on the side. Don't forget crab picks and crackers for the claws so you can get to all that lovely meat. Great with some local beer or chilled white wine.

MUFFULETTA

Serves 8–10

When I was in New Orleans everyone made such a fuss over these big round sandwiches, and I have to admit that at first I didn't get it. Then, one day, I picked a few up from the legendary Central Grocery on Decatur Street in the French Quarter to share with friends. They were absolutely huge and I didn't feel up to eating a whole one. A few hours later we were hungry again and attacked the leftovers, and I have to say they were still ridiculously soft and a total pleasure to eat. I later learned that it was a working person's sandwich and just one would have seen someone through a whole day. They'd have a bit for lunch, some later, and even go home and bake the last bit in the oven for dinner until the cheese was melted and it was warm and delicious. What a clever sandwich.

Start by picking up a large good-quality **focaccia or loaf of Italian bread** from your local bakery – if you can get a loaf that's around 8 x 12 inches and nice and deep, you'll be laughing.

Muffulettas are made with olive salad – a jarred mixture of olives, peppers, dried herbs, cauliflower, and carrots. If you can find a jar of that, great. If not, just head to your local deli and get a nice selection of **olives** and whatever **pickled vegetables** you fancy – a couple of good handfuls should do it – a few slices of **prosciutto**,

smoked ham, salami, and provolone cheese, and a ball of gorgeous buffalo mozzarella. You'll also need a couple of lovely ripe tomatoes.

To make your muffuletta, slice your focaccia in half and open it out on your board. If your olives and veggies came packed in oil, pour some of it over the bread and spread it out. If not, just drizzle over some good-quality extra virgin olive oil, then scatter over a good layer of olives and veggies.

Cover with a nice layer of prosciutto, then slice up your tomatoes and layer these on top. Sprinkle over a little sea salt and a nice bit of freshly ground black pepper. Slice up the buffalo mozzarella and layer this over the tomatoes. Top with slices of smoked ham, provolone cheese, and finally a few slices of salami.

Put the top of the focaccia back on and really squeeze down to push all the ingredients together. Cut it up as you like – I reckon 8 pieces is about right – and let your mates tuck in!

HUNTING 'GATORS

When I reached Cajun country, I was invited to go alligator hunting with some of the locals I met – namely, Sydnie Mae, her boys, and her eleven-year-old granddaughter, Whitney. It wasn't gung-ho, gun crazy, or bonkers, but it also wasn't the kind of hunting I'm used to. In Britain, hunting is all about etiquette and dressing the part. But out on the bayou in the midday sun, it's a totally different story. You can't wear wellies or tweeds because it's too damn hot! Instead, you need your shades, your Bud Lights in a cooler, and most importantly, a loaded pistol, to guard against the local wildlife!

Obviously I was slightly nervous about going out to hunt alligator, but I was in good hands as it's a highly regulated hunt. Sydnie Mae has a license to kill only seven adult alligators during the season. It's a testament to her and others like her, who stick to the strict guidelines, that the alligator population, which was near extinction about 100 years ago, now increases year on year to the point where it needs to be controlled.

Alligator is an everyday ingredient in Louisiana, as common as pork is in the UK. I kid you not – go into any regular restaurant or bar and, alongside the other local delicacies of turtles, frogs' legs, and catfish, you'll see gator on the menu. And you know what? It's bloody delicious! I think it's just the idea of eating these animals that freaks us out. But it's local and it's fair game for dinner in Louisiana. You might be surprised to find that the meat is white – a lot like chicken or pork, but with an underlying taste that sets it apart, and a slightly different texture.

On the same day that I caught an alligator, I managed to kill it, skin it, gut it, clean it, cook it, *and* eat it – talk about living off the land! I decided on a couple of recipes that I wanted to try out using the alligator meat, so as the day ended I made up a little fire, sat by the bayou under a tree in the afternoon sun, and cooked. Watched by a herd of curious cattle and surrounded by Sydnie Mae's family and friends, it was the perfect way to end the day. Both recipes can be made with chicken and pork with great success, which is a good thing, as I doubt you'll find much alligator

I absolutely love the big bold flavors in this dish. This recipe obviously uses alligator, which is as common in Louisiana as pork chops are in Britain, but don't let that put you off because you'll get equally amazing results using chicken breast, pork loin, or even shrimp. The marinade has real attitude and the fresh, zingy salsa goes so well with it. If you've got time, it's nice to leave your meat marinating overnight, but it will still be delicious if you only marinate for 30 minutes. If you can't get hold of green tomatoes for your salsa, use a couple of extra red ones instead. Just be sure to seed them first or the salsa will be too wet.

My Cajun mate, Dave Allemond, who runs the McGee's Landing restaurant in Henderson, adds Creole mustard to his marinade because he says it "makes the flavors sing." Creole mustard is similar to whole-grain French mustard and adds a really nice heat. After trying Dave's wonderful food, I'm not going to argue with him.

★　　★　　★　　★　　★　　★

Get started by making your marinade. Whack the cayenne, paprika, and a pinch each of salt and pepper into a pestle and mortar with the fresh herbs and grind them together. Add your garlic, olive oil, and mustard and grind again – the oil will help all the flavors come out. When you've got a thick sticky paste, transfer it to a large bowl and toss your pieces of meat in it until they are completely coated. Cover with plastic wrap, then pop the bowl into the refrigerator and leave for at least 20 to 30 minutes or, if you really want those flavors to do their work, for a few hours or even overnight.

Preheat your oven to 400°F and pop your aluminium foil–wrapped sweet potatoes in to roast for about 1 hour. When they're nearly ready, make your salsa. It's lovely and fresh, with the right amount of heat, crunch, herbiness, acid, and salt to bring it all to life. Put all your salsa ingredients into a bowl, with a good pinch of sea salt to bring out the flavor of the tomatoes. Give it all a good mix.

When the sweet potatoes are ready, take them out of the oven but leave them in the foil so they stay warm. Put a large frying pan or wok on a high heat and get it screaming hot. Quickly but carefully add your pieces of marinated meat and let them cook for a few minutes on each side so they get some nice color.

Unwrap your sweet potatoes and put them on plates. Score them down the middle, then gently squeeze them so they pucker up. Serve your lovely cooked meat on top, and cover with a few spoonfuls of fresh salsa. And that's it – beautiful meat, soft sweet potatoes, and fresh lively salsa!

CAJUN ALLIGATOR WITH SWEET POTATO & SALSA

Serves 4

4 sweet potatoes (approx. ½ lb each), wrapped in aluminium foil
1¾ lbs alligator tail, chicken breasts, or pork loin, cut into ½-inch-thick slices

For the Cajun marinade
1 teaspoon cayenne pepper
1 teaspoon paprika
sea salt and freshly ground black pepper
a small bunch of fresh oregano, leaves picked
a small bunch of fresh thyme, leaves picked
1 fresh bay leaf, spine removed, leaf torn into pieces
2 cloves of garlic, peeled and roughly chopped
3 tablespoons olive oil
1 teaspoon whole-grain mustard

For the salsa
3 scallions, trimmed and minced
½ fresh red chile, or to taste, seeded and minced
2 green tomatoes, diced
1 red tomato, seeded and diced
a small bunch of fresh curly parsley, finely chopped
2 tablespoons cider vinegar
⅓ cup extra virgin olive oil

Wine suggestion:
Californian red – Pinot Noir

POPCORN 'GATOR & AIOLI

Serves 4–6

1–1½ lbs alligator tail
(or substitute meat or fish, see
introduction), cut into ¾-inch cubes
sea salt and freshly ground
black pepper
1 heaping teaspoon
cayenne pepper
2 cups all-purpose flour
⅔ cup buttermilk
1 quart corn oil or canola oil
1 lemon, cut into wedges, for serving

For the aioli
2–3 fresh red chiles
1 large red bell pepper
heaping ½ cup
good-quality mayonnaise
juice of 1 lemon

Wine suggestion:
French rosé – a dry
southern Grenache

The buttermilk used in this recipe is a sour culture with a nice thickness and acidity to it. Usually used for baking cakes and breads, here it helps achieve a double whammy of a wonderfully crunchy outside and nice tender inside.

In Louisiana, alligator is readily available, but elsewhere, it's not! Instead, try pork loin, chicken breast, swordfish, squid, or even some nice peeled shrimp. As always, please be careful when you're deep-frying, and remember, this food is a real treat so have it with something light to balance the indulgence. You may have leftover aioli, so simply pop it into the refrigerator and use it later in the week.

★ ★ ★ ★ ★ ★

Prick the chiles all over with a small sharp knife and put them and the bell pepper directly over the flame of your stove top, in a hot dry grill pan, or under a hot broiler. You need to blacken them all over, and the bell pepper will take slightly longer than the chiles. When they are blistered and black all over, and look almost ruined, pop them into a sandwich bag or a bowl covered with plastic wrap. This will help steam them so they can be easily peeled. After about 10 minutes peel away the skins, then seed everything and chop until nice and fine. Stir in your mayo, a sprinkle of sea salt, and the lemon juice to give it a bit of an edge, and put it to one side.

Toss the meat in a bowl with a nice pinch of salt, pepper, and cayenne. Get yourself 2 large bowls and pour your flour into one and your buttermilk into the other. Toss your seasoned meat in the flour until it's nicely coated, then shake off the excess and dip it into the buttermilk then back into the flour. These two layers of flour will give you the most lovely popcorn effect and an incredible crispy surface.

Pour your oil into a large sturdy saucepan and put it over a high heat until it reaches 350°F. If you don't have a thermometer, pop a little piece of potato in as your gauge. When it turns golden and rises to the top, you'll know the oil is hot enough. If you cook this in batches, the oil will stay at the right temperature. Carefully lower batches of meat into your hot pan of oil or deep fryer, and move the pieces around so they fry evenly for 3 to 4 minutes. Just be sure to keep an eye on the pan. When the pieces are golden and puffed up like popcorn, they're done. Use a perforated spoon to transfer them to paper towels to drain, then season with sea salt.

Pile the popcorn 'gator on a plate next to a bowl of your aioli for dipping. Sprinkle with cayenne and serve straightaway, with some lemon wedges for squeezing over and some cans of ice-cold beer. Happy days!

WHIZZING AROUND ON A BIT OF TIN ABOVE A LOAD OF 'GATORS IS A LITTLE BIT DIFFERENT FROM DRIVING ROUND ESSEX...

McGEES ATCHAF

GOLD
HOTTER BY THE DROP®
PEPPER SAUCE
2 FL. OZ.   59 mL

Michelob ULTRA

"LOUISIANA" THE PERFECT HOT SAUCE
ONE DROP DOES IT®

In the kitchen with the naked chef

Jamie Oliver lends a helping hand in Henderson

Krista Richmond

Mc Gee's Landing restaurant reopens after the second hurricane destroys it in two years. What a great night!

BREAD PUDDING & CHOCOLATE-BEER SAUCE

If you want something insanely delicious, this is where it's at! In Britain we love tucking into bread pudding in the depths of winter, but the people of Louisiana love to eat it in the middle of a hot summer. That's why I thought it would be the perfect dessert to serve at the relaunch of the McGee's Landing restaurant. What's also great about this pudding is that it's a clever way of using up all sorts of leftover bread, including brioche, croissants, even panettone.

You might think beer is an odd choice for the sauce, but beer has malt in it and malty flavors go really well with chocolate. Sometimes I'll use other wonderful things like Chianti, sweet wine, brandy, and even vodka in my chocolate sauce. This is a real show-stopper, and although death-by-chocolate might sound like a brilliant way to go, remember it's a treat.

★　　★　　★　　★　　★　　★

Serves 8–10

For your pudding
5 large eggs, preferably free-range or organic
5 tablespoons unsweetened cocoa powder
5 tablespoons sugar, plus extra for sprinkling
1 cup heavy cream
3 cups reduced-fat milk
1 x 28-oz loaf of white bread, ends removed, sliced into ¼-inch-thick slices
1 x 4-oz bar good-quality bittersweet chocolate (70% cocoa solids)
a small handful of pecan nuts, roughly chopped
optional: a container of strawberries, to serve
optional: vanilla ice cream, to serve

For your sauce
½ cup brown ale
½ cup heavy cream
2 tablespoons sugar
1 x 4-oz bar good-quality bittersweet chocolate (70% cocoa solids)
sea salt

Wine suggestion:
Californian sweet white – an Orange Muscat

Preheat your oven to 350°F. Crack your eggs into a large mixing bowl with the cocoa powder and sugar and whisk until smooth and silky. Gradually whisk in the cream and milk until combined. Cut your slices of bread into rough triangles and add them to the mixing bowl. Push them down gently and leave them for 30 seconds, or until they've soaked up that lovely chocolate custard. It's best to do this a few slices at a time rather than all at once.

You'll need an ovenproof dish or pan about 9 x 13 inches and 2½ inches deep to cook your pudding. Layer your soaked bread triangles in the dish, then pour over any remaining custard so it fills the dish.

Leaving the chocolate in its wrapper, smash it against the worktop to break it into chunks (this works well if the chocolate is cold). Unwrap and poke these chunks between your slices of bread. They'll melt into wonderful warm pools and be nice little surprises as you're eating. Instead of chocolate, you can also try dried or candied fruits, mixed nuts, banana slices, or small pieces of caramels – lovely!

Scatter your chopped pecans over the top of the pudding, then sprinkle over some sugar evenly from a height. Pop the pudding into the oven for 25 to 30 minutes, or until it's golden and the custard is delicately setting, but still wobbly.

While that's happening, get a medium saucepan over a medium-high heat and add your beer, cream, and sugar. Keep stirring and as soon as it comes to a boil, take it off the heat. Smash up your chocolate as you did before and stir the whole lot into the hot cream mixture with a small pinch of salt. Serve your pudding with your chocolate-beer sauce drizzled over the top. Lovely with a few fresh strawberries and a scoop of vanilla ice cream.

As an English kid, I could never get my head around the idea of sweet potato or pumpkin pie. I thought, "What's all that about? They're vegetables, not desserts!" But now that I'm older and wiser, I completely get it, and I can promise you that this is one delicious dessert.

I've fixed the original recipe up a bit because in Louisiana their sweet potatoes are boiled first, which I think takes away from their wonderful flavor. Roasting them whole, as I've done here, is easy and gives them a much better, nuttier taste. I've also lowered the sugar content, as, like many recipes from the region, it was too insanely sweet for my taste.

Preheat your oven to 400°F. Make your pastry (see page 122), and while it's in the refrigerator for 30 minutes, prick your sweet potatoes with a fork, lay them on a sheet pan, and pop them into the oven – they'll need about 50 minutes to an hour, until they're soft and cooked through. When they're ready, take them out of the oven and turn the temperature down to 350°F.

After the pastry has had 30 minutes in the refrigerator, continue through the method on page 122 until baked blind.

While the pie crust is in the oven, peel the skins from the roasted sweet potatoes and discard. Put the flesh into a large bowl and mash it up. Melt your butter in a saucepan on a low heat and add it to the sweet potato with the sugar, flour, nutmeg, a large pinch of cinnamon, and the vanilla extract. Whisk 2 eggs in a separate bowl, pour them into the mixture, then mash everything together until completely combined.

Spoon your sweet potato mixture into the cooled pie crust, and use a fork or spoon to spread it out evenly. Dust a clean surface and a rolling pin with flour and roll out your leftover pastry (plus any bits that you trimmed off the sides). Cut it into long strips, a bit longer than the width of your pie. Drape these strips over the top, crisscrossing them as you go so you get a nice lattice design on the top. Tidy up the sides, then beat your remaining egg and brush it over the pastry. Put the pie into the oven and bake for 45 to 50 minutes, until gorgeous and golden.

Make your clementine cream just before serving by whipping the cream, clementine zest and juice, and sugar together until you've got soft peaks. Take your pie out of the oven and let it cool for about 25 minutes before serving with the clementine cream. Lovely with a few slices of clementine on the side.

PS: If you're looking for something different to make at Christmas, try making individual ones instead of your regular mince pies.

SWEET POTATO PIE

Serves 10–12

1 x sweet pastry recipe
(see page 122)
2¼ lbs large sweet potatoes
3 tablespoons unsalted butter, melted
½ cup superfine sugar
¼ cup all-purpose flour
¼ teaspoon ground nutmeg
ground cinnamon
2 teaspoons vanilla extract
3 large eggs, preferably
free-range or organic

For the clementine cream
1 cup heavy cream (or natural yogurt
for a slightly "skinnier" version)
zest and juice of 3 clementines
2 tablespoons superfine sugar
optional: 4 clementines, peeled
and sliced into rounds, to serve

Wine suggestion:
Italian sweet white –
a Moscato d'Asti

Thanks to the existence of the mighty Mississippi River, there are loads of beautiful bayous right across the state of Louisiana (these are basically streams or creeks, but they're not like any streams or creeks I've seen at home in Britain). Louisiana bayous have a sort of wild, swampy charm about them that I love. Wild pecan trees grow along the banks, so there's no shortage of this delicious nut.

Another ingredient Louisiana has in abundance is molasses, thanks to the fields and fields of sugarcane. I've used both these ingredients to make this beautiful, and quintessentially Southern, dessert.

★　　★　　★　　★　　★　　★

Start by making the pastry (see page 122), adding the optional vanilla seeds and orange zest from the list of ingredients.

Preheat your oven to 350°F. Take half your pecans and put them inside a clean dish towel or in a sandwich bag. Use a rolling pin to bash them up finely.

After the pastry has had 30 minutes in the refrigerator, continue through the method on page 122 until baked blind.

To make the filling, use a whisk to mix the eggs, sugar, and cinnamon in a bowl. Add your finely bashed pecans and mix again with a spoon until completely blended and smooth. Add the molasses, melted butter, and bourbon, mix well, then fold in your reserved pecans. Pour this mixture into the tart crust.

Put the tart into the oven and bake for 25 to 30 minutes, until the filling starts setting at the sides. Remove and leave to cool in its pan for an hour (if you can wait that long), to really help it set, before serving. I think a slice of slightly warm tart with a scoop of vanilla ice cream is absolute heaven.

BOURBON PECAN TART

Serves 10–12

1 x quantity sweet pastry
(see page 122)
3¾ cups pecan halves
3 large eggs, preferably
free-range or organic
¾ cup superfine sugar
1 teaspoon ground cinnamon
scant ½ cup molasses
or black treacle
3 tablespoons unsalted
butter, melted
3 tablespoons bourbon whiskey
vanilla ice cream, to serve

Wine suggestion:
Spanish sweet sherry –
Pedro Ximénez

SWEET PASTRY

Makes generous 1 lb

2 cups plus 2 tablespoons
all-purpose flour, plus
extra for dusting
½ cup confectiohers' sugar
9 tablespoons good-
quality unsalted cold butter,
cut into small cubes
optional: 1 orange
optional: 1 vanilla bean, halved
and seeds scraped out
1 large egg, preferably
free-range or organic, beaten
a splash of milk

Everyone needs a good, basic pastry recipe, and this is one you can rely on. It's easily adaptable if you want to add extra flavors like orange zest or vanilla – or even a pinch of nutmeg or cinnamon – and is really simple to throw togather.

If you have any pastry left over, simply wrap it in plastic wrap and freeze it to use another time.

★　　★　　★　　★　　★　　★

You can make your pastry like this by hand, or pulse it in a food processor. From a height, sift your flour and confectioners' sugar into a large mixing bowl. Using your fingertips, gently work the cubes of butter into the flour and sugar until the mixture resembles bread crumbs. If using orange or vanilla for extra flavor, either finely grate in the zest of your orange or add the seeds from the vanilla pod and mix again.

Add the egg and milk to the mixture and gently work it together using your hands until you have a ball of dough. Remember not to work the pastry too much at this stage or it will become elastic and chewy, not crumbly and short.

Sprinkle a little flour over the dough and on a clean worktop, and pat the ball into a flat round about 1inch thick. Sprinkle over a little more flour, then wrap the dough in plastic wrap and pop it into the refrigerator to rest for at least 30 minutes. Get yourself a 9½-inch nonstick loose-bottomed tart or quiche pan (approx. 1¼ inch deep) and, using a splash of vegetable oil on a paper tower, lightly oil the inside.

Dust a clean surface and a rolling pin with flour, then carefully roll out your pastry, turning it every so often, until it's just under ¼ inch thick. Carefully roll your pastry around the rolling pin, then unroll it carefully over your oiled pan. Ease the pastry into the pan, making sure you push it into all the sides. Trim off any excess by running a knife along the top of the pie crust, then prick the base of the pie crust all over with a fork and pop it into the freezer for 30 minutes. Preheat your oven to 350°F.

Get yourself a large square piece of parchment paper, scrunch it up, then unwrap it and use it to line your pie crust, pushing it right into the sides. Fill the pie crust right up to the top with rice, and bake blind for 10 minutes in your preheated oven. Take the pie crust out, carefully remove the rice and parchment paper (you can save the rice to use for blind baking another time), then return the crust to the oven to cook for a further 10 minutes, until it's firm and almost cookie-like. Let cool.

To help me get my head around American food, I wanted to go straight back to the most original kind of American cooking: the kind done before America was even called America. Since the people with the longest history in the U.S. are, without question, Native Americans, and since a large percentage of them live in Arizona, that state was at the top of my list of places to go. It might seem like an odd state to include in this cookbook – it certainly isn't overly "foodie" – but I'm so glad I did. As with a lot of places in the world, when you look for good food, you'll find it . . .

Many of the Native American tribes in the U.S. live on "reservations": land reserved by the U.S. government for Native Americans to live on. The largest of these in America is the Navajo Reservation, which sprawls across 17 million acres of land in Northern Arizona, New Mexico, and Utah. The Navajo number about 165,000 people, which is like the population of a medium-sized city or town having a whole state to live in!

It takes seven or eight hours to drive from one end of the reservation to the other, passing little more than a handful of houses and very few gas stations (which can be a bit nerve-racking!). The people I met in Navajo country were absolutely second to none, but one of the biggest characters of all was the land itself. The natural beauty of the place was like nothing I've ever seen: extreme, surprising, dramatic, incredibly rugged, and completely unspoiled by any type of commerce, tourism, or business. The Navajo call this part of America the wilderness – it's their backyard, somewhere they love, respect, and take care of. One of the parts I loved was called the Painted Desert, and rightly so. At sunset, especially, you can see for miles and miles in every direction, and watch the colors of the rocks change right in front of your eyes.

There is something wonderfully prehistoric about the scenery of Arizona – if a dinosaur had appeared on the horizon it would have made perfect sense to me, because in many ways this trip was like walking through a door and into another time. It gave me a chance to get to know some lovely families and share their traditions, rituals, and spiritualism; ways of living that evolved long before the white man moved in. In this chapter I'm going to take you back to a more ancient form of cooking – with hearty, comforting, rustic, and totally delicious dishes. It was an honor to learn about the food culture of the Navajo, and I feel that the recipes in this chapter help to put the best of American food into perspective.

Today, Arizona is a real mixture of influences. You've got the meat, corn, squash, and beans that the Native Americans have thrived on for hundreds of years, thrown in with ingredients like tomatoes and chiles, which the Spanish brought with them when they settled there in the mid 1500s. Those ingredients really fired up the Native dishes and made them more colorful and dynamic. The recipes in this chapter range from old-school Native American to Spanish- and Mexican-inspired dishes, as well as a few that I made up, based on what I bought, what I saw, and how I felt at the time.

This is definitely a part of America I'll be visiting again one day, and somewhere well worth traveling through if you get the chance.

You lot know I'm a big salad fan, so I made up a salad based on the ingredients available in Arizona. A lot of the people who tried it, aside from thinking it was damn good, were surprised by the incredible texture and flavors you get when you barbecue, roast, or grill avocado. It's hot, zingy, and will definitely wake up your taste buds. The more interesting the salad leaves you use, the better the salad will be, so get creative.

P.S. I've called it "mad dog" because the dog at the sheep farm I was visiting came and stole some right off the plate straight after I made it . . . cheeky thing!

MAD DOG SALAD

Preheat your oven to full whack. Halve, pit, and peel your avocados and lay them on a sheet pan. Drizzle over some olive oil and season generously with salt, pepper, and a really good pinch of cumin seeds. Toss until nicely coated, then roast in the hot oven for about 15 minutes so they get a bit of color. While this is happening, get another sheet pan, lay out your tortilla chips, and sprinkle over your Cheddar, pine nuts, and pumpkin seeds. You're going to pop this pan into the oven about 4 minutes before the avocado is ready to come out, so the cheese has time to melt and the nuts and seeds toast a little.

Mix your cress or alfalfa and salad leaves together. Drizzle over the lemon juice and three times as much extra virgin olive oil and sprinkle over a good pinch of salt and pepper. Quickly toss together so everything is perfectly dressed. Take your avocados and pan of tortillas out of the oven.

Put your cheesy tortilla chips, nuts, and seeds on a platter or divide between plates, slice or tear over the avocado, then scatter your lovely dressed salad over the top. Finish by sprinkling over as much fresh chile as you dare. Gorgeous!

Serves 4

3 ripe avocados
olive oil
sea salt and freshly
ground black pepper
cumin seeds
2 large handfuls of
regular tortilla chips
a large handful of freshly
grated Cheddar cheese
a handful of pine nuts
a handful of pumpkin seeds
a large handful of cress or alfalfa
4 good handfuls of mixed
interesting salad leaves,
washed and spun dry
juice of 1 lemon
extra virgin olive oil
2 Scotch bonnets or other
interesting chiles, seeded
and thinly sliced

Wine suggestion:
Spanish rosé – from
the Garnacha grape

MEXICAN BREAKFAST

The Mexican name for this dish is *huevos rancheros* – eggs with chiles, tomatoes, and bell peppers in burritos. It's absolutely great if you've got a few friends around, and even better if you've got a hangover you're trying to shake off. If you wanted to take this dish one step further, for a late brunch you could serve it with black beans, some steamed rice, and a bottle of Tabasco or chili sauce beside it. Give it a go.

Serves 6

★　　★　　★　　★　　★　　★

olive oil
1 onion, peeled and thinly sliced
2 cloves garlic, peeled and thinly sliced
2 red bell peppers, seeded and thinly sliced
2 fresh red or orange chiles, seeded and thinly sliced
1 large dried chile
3 fresh bay leaves
sea salt and freshly ground black pepper
1 x 14-oz can diced tomatoes
2 large tomatoes, sliced
6 large eggs, preferably free-range or organic
6 tortillas
6 oz block Cheddar cheese, to serve

Get a large frying pan (make sure you've got a lid to go with it) on a high heat and add several good lugs of olive oil. Add the onion, garlic, peppers, fresh and dried chiles, bay leaves, and a good pinch of salt and pepper. Stir and cook for 15 minutes to soften and caramelize the vegetables. Pour in your canned tomatoes and use a spoon or potato masher to break them up a bit. Bring to a boil, then turn down to a medium heat and cook for a further 5 minutes so the sauce starts to reduce down.

When you've got a nice thick tomato stew consistency, have a taste and add a pinch more salt and pepper if you think it needs it. Lay your sliced tomatoes over the top of the mixture, then use a spoon to make small wells in the tomato stew, and crack in your eggs so that they poach in the thick, delicious juices. Try to crack them in as quickly as you can so they all get to cook for roughly the same amount of time. Season from a height, put the lid on, and let the eggs cook for 3 to 4 minutes. Warm your tortillas while this is happening. You can pop them into the oven at 350°F for a few minutes, microwave them for a few seconds, or even lay them over the lid of the pan so they heat up as the eggs cook.

Take the lid off and check your eggs by giving them a poke with your finger. When they're done to your liking, turn the heat off and take the pan to the table with your warmed tortillas, your Cheddar, and a grater so your friends can get involved and make their own. Personally, I like to grate a bit of cheese right onto a warm tortilla, spoon an egg and some of the wonderful tomato stew on top, wrap it up, and eat it right away. What a beautiful way to wake up!

CHILE CHEESE CORN BREAD

This is one of the most delicious corn breads I've ever had. You get incredible flavor from the onions and corn, while the cornmeal gives it a rustic, spongy texture that's so brilliant. Two of my favorites, chiles and cheese, do their thing in this bread and really take the flavor to a whole other level.

You can serve this corn bread alongside soups or stews, but frankly, I think a good slice of this, with a bit of crunchy salad, makes a brilliant lunch. You could also reheat it in a dry pan the next day for breakfast and eat it with poached eggs and some smoky bacon . . . totally delicious.

Serves 10

★ ★ ★ ★ ★ ★

½ stick (¼ cup) butter
2 onions, peeled and thinly sliced
2 ears corn
4 large eggs, preferably free-range or organic, beaten
2⅔ cups coarse cornmeal or polenta
1 cup whole milk
1 teaspoon baking powder
⅓ cup all-purpose flour
sea salt and freshly ground black pepper
Scant 1½ cups freshly grated sharp Cheddar cheese
3 fresh green chiles, 2 of them seeded and minced, the other thinly sliced
olive oil

Preheat your oven to 400°F. Put your butter into a frying pan on a medium heat and add your sliced onions. Fry gently for 15 to 20 minutes, until they've caramelized and are golden and sticky. While that's happening, get your corn ready. Hold the cobs upright on the board and carefully run a small knife from the top of the corn to the bottom, cutting all the kernels off. Add these to the pan with the onions and cook for a further 5 minutes, then remove from the heat and set aside to cool for a few minutes.

In a bowl, mix your eggs, cornmeal, milk, baking powder, flour, a good pinch of salt and pepper, and most of your grated cheese. Beat until well mixed, then stir in your cooled onion and corn mixture and your 2 minced chiles. Grease a 9-inch skillet or cake pan with some olive oil, line the base with parchment paper, and pour in your mixture.

Sprinkle the chile slices on top, then pop the corn bread into the oven to bake for 35 minutes. About 10 minutes before it's ready, pull it out, sprinkle over your remaining Cheddar, and return it to the oven. Once ready, let it cool for 15 minutes, then turn it out on to a wire rack or serving plate, cheesy side up. Serve this straight away because it's unbelievably good when it's warm.

One night during my trip I stayed in a hunting shack in the middle of the Painted Desert. We drove for an hour or more through the middle of nowhere to get there, and there was nothing but land as far as the eye could see. That night was easily the coldest I've ever experienced! So in the morning I was happy to go and warm up by the fire watching this Navajo breakfast being made. It's a delicious one-pot hearty breakfast of fried bacon with potatoes and onion, mixed with egg at the last minute until it sets. Served with warm flatbreads, a pinch of cayenne pepper, and some hot coffee, it really set me up for the day.

SCRUMPTIOUS NAVAJO BREKKIE

★　　★　　★　　★　　★　　★

Serves 4

Thinly slice your potatoes. If you've got a box grater with a slicer attachment, or a mandolin, use that – just be careful not to slice your fingers! Heat a large nonstick frying pan (one that's got a lid) on a medium heat. Add the chopped bacon and sliced onions to the pan with a small lug of olive oil, fry for a few minutes until lightly golden, then add your potatoes. Keep frying for about 10 to 15 minutes on a medium heat, separating the potato slices with a spoon as you stir, until the potatoes are soft and tasty. Season to taste with a good sprinkle of salt and pepper.

Beat the eggs in a bowl with a pinch of salt and pepper. Turn the heat under your pan down to low, give it a final stir, then add your eggs and slowly stir and scramble them in. Pop the lid on – if it's a nice thick pan that holds its heat well, you can take it off the heat now and just let the hot pan cook the eggs so they are set but still have a bit of a wobble in the middle – if not, keep it on the heat for another minute or two. Serve right away with some warm flatbreads (see page 139) or toast and a sprinkle of cayenne pepper. You can even melt a bit of cheese over the top if you like.

1¾ lbs red-skinned potatoes, scrubbed
6 slices of smoked bacon, the best quality you can afford, roughly chopped
1 medium onion, peeled and thinly sliced
olive oil
sea salt and freshly ground black pepper
6 large eggs, preferably free-range or organic
4 flatbreads or pieces of toast, to serve
cayenne pepper, to serve
optional: a handful of freshly grated Cheddar cheese

VENISON & JUNIPER STEW

Serves 6–8

¼ cup all-purpose flour
sea salt and freshly ground black pepper
1¾ lbs stewing venison or beef,
cut into ¾-inch chunks
olive oil
2 onions, peeled and roughly chopped
3 carrots, peeled and roughly chopped
2 celery stalks, trimmed
and roughly chopped
1 tablespoon juniper berries,
crushed in a pestle and mortar
2 sprigs of rosemary, leaves
picked and chopped
a pat of butter
6 sprigs of fresh Italian parsley
2 beef bouillon cubes, preferably organic
1½ lbs baby potatoes, scrubbed
clean, larger ones halved
1 clove garlic, peeled and minced

Wine suggestion:
Californian red – a Merlot from the
Napa Valley or Sonoma County

The Navajo love their lamb and mutton, but back in the day – at the right times of the year – they'd also get out there and hunt things like elk, which they'd stew with wild juniper berries. What's amazing for me is that thousands of miles away in Britain we were hunting deer for venison and stewing that with juniper too. I guess some combos are just brilliant, no matter where you live. Don't worry if you can't get venison, because stewing beef will also be delicious. Really nice served with some rice, beans, a baked potato, or flatbreads (see page 139), or, if you're a bit more traditional, some nice steamed greens. A humble but delicious stew.

★　　★　　★　　★　　★　　★

Dust a cutting board with 2 tablespoons of flour and a good pinch of salt and pepper, and toss your chunks of meat through this mixture until well coated. Heat a large saucepan or Dutch oven on a high heat, add a few lugs of olive oil, and fry your meat for 3 minutes to brown it. Add your chopped onions, carrots, celery, crushed juniper berries, rosemary, and the pat of butter. Add a few tablespoons of water, give everything a good stir, then pop the lid on the pan and let everything steam for 4 to 5 minutes so the flavors really mingle together.

Take the lid off so your meat and veggies start to fry, and stir every so often for 5 to 10 minutes. Chop your parsley stalks finely, and once the onions start to caramelize, add them to the pan with your remaining 2 tablespoons of flour and your crumbled bouillon cubes. Stir, and pour in enough water to cover the mixture by a couple of inches. Put the parsley leaves aside for later.

Bring to a boil, then turn the heat down to medium low so that the stew is just simmering. Add your potatoes and slow cook for at least 2 hours with the lid slightly askew, or until the meat falls apart easily. Keep an eye on it as it cooks, and add splashes of water if you think it looks too dry.

Put your minced garlic in the middle of a cutting board. Add most of your parsley leaves with a teaspoon of sea salt and ½ a teaspoon of black pepper. Chop everything together so you get a kinda chunky paste. Add this to the stew and stir through. Chop the last of your parsley leaves and sprinkle over the stew before serving.

These flatbreads are a sort of cross between Mexican tortillas and Indian naan breads. They're used for breakfast, lunch, or dinner and carry, complement, or mop up whatever is being served with them. Apparently, in the old days, if a Navajo woman couldn't whip up a batch of fluffy flatbreads, her chances of marrying a decent guy were pretty low. No pressure! These are brilliantly simple to make.

★　　★　　★　　★　　★　　★

Mix your flour, salt, baking powder, and herbs or spices (if using) in a large bowl, using a fork. Make a well in the center, then pour in the olive oil and about ⅔ cup of warm water. Use the fork to gradually bring in the flour from the edge of the bowl, and add another splash of water if you think it's too dry. Once it starts to combine, wet your hands and use them to really bring it all together until you have a nice ball of dough.

Dust your hands and a clean worktop with flour and knead the dough with your hands until it is smooth and elastic. This will take 5 to 10 minutes. Pop the dough back into the bowl, dust it with a bit more flour, then cover and leave to relax.

Divide your dough into 10 equal-sized balls, then lightly oil your hands and squeeze each ball between your palms to flatten it slightly. Dust with a little flour as you go, and pat and slap the dough from the palm of one hand to the top of the other. Turn and twist the dough about in a circular movement as you go and keep slapping from hand to hand – each flatbread should be about ½ inch thick. You'll probably mess up a few, but practice makes perfect.

Normally the flatbreads are cooked as you're making them. You can do this on a grill or in a nonstick frying pan on a medium heat. Cook them for a few minutes on each side and check the underside – you want them to puff up with a nice bit of golden color. Keep them warm in a basket covered with a dish towel until you're ready to serve them.

Serve them while they're lovely and warm, or you can reheat them with anything from burgers, to stews and soups, to salads.

NAVAJO FLATBREADS

Makes about 10 flatbreads

Scant 5 cups white bread flour,
plus extra for dusting
1 teaspoon salt
2 heaped tablespoons baking powder
optional: 1 teaspoon dried herbs or spices,
such as thyme, parsley, sumac (see
page 66), or crushed fennel seeds
⅓ cup olive oil

TEMPERATURES IN THE ARIZONA DESERT CAN DROP TO -24°F IN THE WINTER AND SOAR TO 106°F IN THE SUMMER. SHEEP FARMING HERE IS NOT AN EASY JOB.

When you're in the middle of Navajo country, with dry rocky land as far as the eye can see, you can't imagine that you'd be able to enjoy a watermelon salad like this. But amazingly, I learned that watermelon has been a part of the Navajo diet for a really long time. Back in the day they'd bury them underground to preserve them, then dig them up when they needed them, and they'd still be juicy and delicious. This is a method of preserving food that has been used in Britain for ages too. We call it "clamping," and it's most commonly used for root vegetables. Bizarrely, it works better than a refrigerator, and this just proves that the Navajo were great gardeners as well as hunters. Feel free to add watercress, arugula, or other nice leaves to this salad.

WATER-MELON SALAD

 ★ ★ ★ ★ ★

Put a frying pan on a medium heat and add your pumpkin and sunflower seeds with a little drizzle of olive oil, a good pinch of salt and pepper, and a pinch of chile powder. Toss and fry for a few minutes. Don't stand directly over the pan, though, as the seeds can sometimes pop up quite high. Once the seeds are lightly colored and nicely toasted, take the pan off the heat and put to one side.

Remove the skin and as many seeds as possible from your watermelon half, then chop the flesh up into wonky chunks. Cut your cheese into similar chunks. Put the watermelon into a bowl with most of your mint leaves and all your sliced scallions. Squeeze over the juice of your limes to make it sing, drizzle over a good lug of extra virgin olive oil, add a good pinch of salt and pepper, and toss everything together. Arrange your dressed watermelon mixture on a platter or board, or divide between plates, add the chunks of cheese, and scatter over your toasted seeds. Finish with a sprinkle of sliced fresh chiles if using (as much as you dare), and your remaining mint leaves.

Serves 4

a large handful of pumpkin seeds
a large handful of sunflower seeds
olive oil
sea salt and freshly ground black pepper
chile powder
½ small watermelon
6 oz. sheep's cheese or
hard goat's cheese
a small bunch of fresh
mint, leaves picked
3 scallions, trimmed and thinly sliced
2 limes
extra virgin olive oil
optional: 1 Scotch bonnet or other
interesting chile, seeded and thinly sliced

Wine suggestion:
Tuscan white – a Vermentino

This is a fantastic Mexican-inspired soup – the kind of soup where you've got to go with it and let the flavors just blow you away! It uses tortilla chips the way you would use croutons in a French onion soup and the results are delicious and tasty. I'd never tried this before visiting Arizona. Having the freshness of chiles and the chunks of beautiful ripe avocado floating on the top is really nice, because avocado is lovely in hot dishes too. I think it's nicest when people help themselves to the garnishes, but you could also chuck everything right in the pan just before serving. By the time you've got drinks on the table, the tortilla chips will have softened slightly in the soup and will be delicious.

RUSTIC TORTILLA SOUP

Serves 4

Get a large saucepan on a low-to-medium heat and pour in a good lug of olive oil. Add the onion, garlic, carrots, and bell peppers and fry gently for 10 to 15 minutes until softened, stirring every so often so they don't catch on the bottom of the pan.

Add the chopped fresh tomatoes and bay leaves, crumble in the bouillon cubes, and add the canned tomatoes. Pour in about 2 tomato cans' worth of water, then bring to a boil and turn down to a simmer for about 20 minutes, stirring occasionally.

Preheat your oven to 350°F. While the soup blips away, peel and pit your avocado and dice into ½-inch cubes. Put these on a plate, grate over your lime zest, and squeeze in the juice to keep the avocado from browning. Put in the center of the table next to a plate with your slices of green chile.

Lay your tortilla chips on a sheet pan, drizzle with a good lug of olive oil, and sprinkle over the dried sage. Heat in the oven for a few minutes until warmed through. Meanwhile, check on your soup. If you like it looser, you can add a bit of water to it at this point; if you like your soups thicker, you can let it cook for a bit longer. I quite like to mash the soup up a little to get a bit of pulpiness going, but if you like it chunky, leave it as is. Have a taste, season with salt and pepper, then give it a stir and taste it again.

Once you're happy with the flavors, divide the soup between bowls and take them to the table, with the warm tortilla chips.

For the soup
olive oil
1 onion, peeled and roughly chopped
2 cloves garlic, peeled and crushed
2 large carrots, peeled and roughly chopped
2 green bell peppers, seeded and roughly chopped
2 yellow bell peppers, seeded and roughly chopped
2 large tomatoes, roughly chopped
2 fresh bay leaves
2 chicken bouillon cubes, preferably organic
1 x 14-oz can diced tomatoes
sea salt and freshly ground black pepper

For the garnishes
1 ripe avocado
1 lime
1 fresh green chile, thinly sliced
2 large handfuls of tortilla chips
1 heaped teaspoon dried sage

Wine suggestion:
Spanish white – a Rueda Verdejo

SHEEP IS LIFE

The wonderfully rugged and sturdy churro sheep, with their long straight horns and thick woolly coats, have been farmed by the Navajo for centuries. They are one of the oldest breeds of sheep in the world and have played an absolutely crucial role in Navajo society, so much so that the Navajo word for sheep is the same as their word for mother. They also have a saying, "Sheep is life," and when you see the way the Navajo respect their sheep, care for them while they're alive, then use every last bit of them for food, clothing, and other household materials, you can completely understand where that must have come from.

A lot of my time in Arizona was spent at my good mate Roy's. He's a Navajo farmer who also acts as the mayor of the reservation and is really involved in the community. Slaughter is an unavoidable part of farming, and it's not something anyone could ever enjoy watching. I've seen my fair share over the past few years, and I would say that most modern-day slaughter is pretty clinical and mechanical. What I saw at Roy's farm on this day was totally different: a traditional, simple process that was respectful and peaceful for the animal. After the lamb for our meal had been chosen, its legs were tied together with woven wool so it could be taken out of the pen. It was blessed and a prayer was said over it before one of the women – traditionally the ones in charge of butchery – slit its throat and drained the blood. The whole thing was really very efficient and the lamb didn't seem distressed in the slightest – the ideal scenario for both sides.

People these days prefer to buy their meat in a package and be as far removed from the whole process of life and death as possible. That's completely understandable, but I also think there's something really special about seeing a community that understands this cycle so intimately and places such huge value on the life of an animal.

Roy gave me two beautiful legs of lamb to cook, and I felt absolutely honoured to be able to take those cherished bits of meat and turn them into something delicious we could share

EPIC CHURRO LAMB

Serves 10

I first cooked this dish on the Navajo reservation using churro lamb that had just been slaughtered. Roy (the sheep farmer who'd generously provided the lamb) and I made this together, and it turned out beautifully. I've since tweaked the recipe a bit to my taste by adding a few other ingredients. But, as far as I'm concerned, the heart and soul of the dish still respects the wonderful churro lamb.

I served this to the elderly Navajo ladies who'd helped us butcher the lamb. They certainly looked like they'd cooked a few great meals in their time, and although they couldn't speak a word of English, I think they approved!

★　　★　　★　　★　　★　　★

1 large leg of lamb on the bone (4½ to 6½ lbs)
10 flatbreads or tortillas, to serve (or see recipe on page 139)

For the marinade
10 juniper berries
a small bunch of scallions (about 10), trimmed and minced
4 cloves garlic, peeled and minced
a bunch of fresh mint, leaves picked
sea salt and freshly ground black pepper
olive oil

For the salsa
3–4 fresh red chiles
3 green bell peppers
a small bunch of fresh mint, leaves picked
2 scallions, trimmed
2 ripe plum tomatoes
sea salt and freshly ground black pepper
extra virgin olive oil
a slug of white wine vinegar
1 heaped tablespoon sumac (see page 66)

Wine suggestion:
French red – from Cahors

Make your marinade in a pestle and mortar or a food processor. Bash or blitz the juniper berries with the chopped scallions, garlic, mint leaves, a good pinch of salt and pepper, and a few lugs of olive oil to make a paste. Lay the lamb on a board and stab around the leg with a small knife. Stick your finger right into these holes to make them slightly bigger, then rub the marinade all over the lamb and make a point of getting it into all of the holes. Wrap the lamb in plastic wrap or pop it into a covered roasting pan to marinate in the refrigerator for at least 2 hours or overnight if possible.

Take your lamb out of the refrigerator and let it come up to room temperature. Preheat your oven to full whack. Put the lamb in a roasting pan, season it all over with a generous amount of salt, then put it into the hot oven. Turn the temperature down immediately to 400°F and roast for about 1 hour for a 4½ lb leg, about 1½ hours for a 6½ lb one. When the meat comes away from the bone and is beautiful, take it out of the oven, cover it with aluminium foil, and let it rest for 15 to 20 minutes while you make your salsa.

Prick your chiles all over and put them and the bell peppers over a flame on your stove top or into a hot dry grill pan, turning them until black and blistered all over. Pop them into a bowl, cover with plastic wrap, and allow them to steam for about 10 minutes. Peel away the skins (you can wear rubber gloves to do this if you want), then chop the flesh on a board with your mint leaves, scallions, tomatoes, and a pinch of salt. When it's as fine as you like it, scrape it into a bowl, loosen with a swig of extra virgin olive oil, and add your vinegar and sumac. Have a taste and season to your liking.

I like to serve this with some lovely white beans. Put a couple of cans of beans into a saucepan with a slug of white wine vinegar and a little dried thyme and season to taste with salt and pepper. Carve your lamb, and serve it with some of that wonderful salsa, a good spoonful of beans, and a few warm flatbreads. What a feast.

The Navajo refer to beans, corn, and squash as the "three sisters." These staple ingredients of their diet grow very harmoniously together. Beans climb up the corn and the squash grows beneath it, allowing lots of food to be grown in one space – something I started to do in my garden a few years ago. It was great to see it happening firsthand. Traditionally they'd eat the three vegetables fresh in the summer months, then dry and store them away for the winter. The key ingredients in this hearty stew have been around for thousands of years. Faithful to the simple cooking style of the Navajo, they prove that sometimes the simplest meals can be the most nourishing and delicious.

THREE-SISTERS LAMB STEW

★   ★   ★   ★   ★   ★

Serves 6–8

Preheat your oven to 350°F. Trim most of the fat from your meat (but leave a little for flavor), then cut the meat into ¾-inch chunks and season all over with a good pinch of salt and pepper. Put a large pan on a high heat and add a few lugs of olive oil, then your meat, onions, carrots, celery, and cumin seeds. Move everything around and fry for 10 to 15 minutes, until the vegetables have softened and colored lightly. Stir in your canned tomatoes and crumble in your bouillon cubes, then add 2 cans' worth of water. Bring to a boil, then turn the heat down to medium, put a lid on, and leave to simmer gently for around 2½ hours. Keep an eye on it as it cooks, and add splashes of water if you think it looks too dry.

While this is cooking, roughly slice your squash into 1-inch wedges and put into a sheet pan. Toss in a little olive oil, salt and pepper, crumble over your dried chile, and put into the oven to roast for 45 to 50 minutes, until golden, intense, and delicious.

After about 2 to 2½ hours, the meat in your stew should be tender, so test it by taking out a piece: if it pulls apart easily, it's done; if not, cook a bit longer. When you're happy, add the roasted squash to the stew with the corn and simmer for a further 10 minutes. Add a glass of water if you feel it needs a bit more liquid, or, if you think it's a little loose, remove the lid and let it thicken for a few more minutes. Remove from the heat, have a taste, and season very carefully with salt and pepper. Keep tasting and seasoning until it's perfect, and serve with rice, beans, bread, or potatoes.

1¾ lbs boneless lamb or mutton shoulder
sea salt and freshly ground black pepper
olive oil
2 onions, peeled and roughly chopped
2 large carrots, peeled and roughly chopped
2 celery stalks, trimmed and roughly chopped
½ teaspoon cumin seeds
1 x 14-oz can diced tomatoes
2 chicken, beef, or lamb bouillon cubes, preferably organic
1 butternut or acorn squash, halved lengthways, seeds scraped out, skin left on
1 dried chile
2½ cups frozen corn

Wine suggestion:
Spanish red – a Rioja or Ribera del Duero

NAVAJO

The Navajo way of life didn't seem to me to be so much based around religion as it was a spiritual way of looking at things. The Navajo believe the planet will provide for you if you respect it, and they used to believe the land was everyone's: there were no borders or lines to cross and no one could lay claim over land because it wasn't anyone's to take. And OK, for the first few hours you might think it's some crazy hippie stuff you're hearing, but once you get to know the people and translate what they're saying into your own life, you start seeing things differently.

You realize that what they've been doing, and what they are trying to hold on to in a modern America, are things that countries like Britain are only just starting to get excited about: growing food locally, sitting down as a family, being in touch with the food you eat, taking what you need rather than taking everything. When I wrote *Jamie at Home* a few years ago, I was trying to explain that, although I was just a thirty-year-old lad, when you plant something and it grows, that somehow turns you into a bit of a softie. In many ways, I felt right at home with their views.

But it would be wrong and untrue of me to sit here and pretend it's all fun and games for them at the moment, because it's definitely not. America's Native population, in general, is in a really tough place. I don't think anyone could deny that. It's no secret that the bad treatment of the Native Americans started centuries ago, when America was being settled by Europeans, and the English, as well as other nationalities, were all part of disrespecting the locals – so don't go thinking I'm slagging off modern America when I talk about the hard times they're going through. The statistics speak for themselves: the average wage in America is $30,000 a year, yet the average wage among the Navajo is $6,000 – a quarter of the national average! Unemployment in some parts of the reservation is 75 percent. Type 2 diabetes affects 50 percent of the adult Navajo population, and life expectancy is not what it should be. The majority of the reservation have replaced their ancestors' diet with cheap, easy, fast food, and the state of things ain't good.

Historically, the Navajo were self-sufficient: hunting and living off the land, eating well, rarely fighting, and living well into their nineties and even their hundreds. The white man put an end to that by culling their animals, stripping them of their land, replacing their Native names with anglicized ones, and moving them onto reservations. To this day they're caught between U.S. federal law and their own tribal laws. What's interesting is that throughout America issues like family, community, and sustainability are becoming more and more important, and all of those things were central to the Navajo's original way of life. If America is coming full circle, maybe the Navajo can gain back some of what they've lost over the years, because without a doubt I think they represent a broken and precious part of America.

My time in this beautiful part of the country was inspiring, but short—and I left with lots of questions. The issues around the problems Native Americans are facing are complicated, far too complicated for me to fully understand in so little time. On my travels through the U.S. I met loads and loads of immigrants, and throughout its history America has been built on immigration, those who've come looking for the American dream and are, in lots of cases, escaping war, poverty, and other terrible situations. I really do believe in the American dream myself. I believe that anything can happen there, so when I see the people who've been there the longest struggling like the Navajo are while so many around them are succeeding, I wonder why.

The way I look at it is that when people make the choice to move to America, in some way they've already become American and have bought into everything that means. The difference for the Native Americans is that they had a system – and a lifestyle – that worked, and worked well. They didn't want to change; they had the American way put on them. For their culture and traditions to survive now, I think they'll need an entrepreneurial spirit, investment in the community, and, most importantly, their young people to do what we hope all young people will do: take the best of the past and use that to make the best of the future. I truly hope that happens for them.

Jackrabbits, or hares as we Brits call them, are (like rabbits) an absolute joy to eat. Because they're such active animals their meat really benefits from slow stewing like this. Ask your butcher to joint one for you, and give you the liver and kidneys as well. Navajo legend has it that people who make round dumplings get stoned to death by hail! I certainly don't want any of their spirits angry with me, so I've made my dumplings Navajo-style: finger-shaped. Since first making them, I've adjusted the recipe to my taste to make them slightly lighter and fluffier. They are sort of a Navajo halfway house now, but I think that the integrity of the old-school dumpling is still there.

RABBIT STEW & DUMPLINGS

★ ★ ★ ★ ★ ★ Serves 4–6

Mix the 2 tablespoons of all-purpose flour in a bowl with a pinch of salt and pepper and the meat. Toss everything together until well coated. Put 4 good lugs of olive oil into your largest Dutch oven or similar pan over a high heat. Let the oil heat up, then add your coated rabbit and let it brown on all sides. Once it's browned, add all your chopped vegetables and cook for about 10 minutes so the veggies soften and color slightly. Add the 2 teaspoons of all-purpose flour along with the reserved liver and kidneys and give everything a good stir. Crumble in your bouillon cubes and add 1¼ quarts of water. Season, bring to a boil, then turn the heat down to a low simmer and cook with the lid on for around 1½ hours or until the meat pulls easily from the bone. As it's cooking, keep an eye on it and add a splash of water if it looks dry at any stage. When it's ready, add enough water to loosen the stew if it needs it – the dumplings will need some extra liquid to suck up as they cook. Either leave the rabbit pieces whole, or you can remove them from the stew and shred the meat from the bones.

Mix your self-rising flour and cornmeal in a bowl. Grate in your chilled butter and add a good pinch of salt, pepper, and the herbs. Use your fingertips to rub the butter into the mixture so you end up with a nice bread-crumb texture, then add 3 to 4 tablespoons of cold water to combine everything. Lightly flour a clean worktop and knead for a minute or two so you get a nice smooth dough. Divide this into 12 balls and use your hands to roll them out into long, finger-sized dumplings.

Lay the dumplings on top of the stew and give the pan a good shake so they get covered in some of the juices. Put on a medium heat with the lid on and leave to blip away for 30 minutes. Once the dumplings are puffy and cooked through, tear up your reserved celery leaves and scatter them over. Take the whole thing right to the table with a little pot of cayenne pepper for sprinkling over. Serve with some lovely fresh greens.

2 heaping tablespoons all-purpose flour, plus 2 teaspoons
sea salt and freshly ground black pepper
1 jointed whole rabbit (approx. 3½ lbs), liver and kidneys reserved
olive oil
2 onions, peeled and thinly sliced
4 large carrots, peeled and sliced at an angle
2 celery stalks, trimmed and roughly chopped, small inner leaves reserved
2 chicken bouillon cubes, preferably organic
cayenne pepper, to serve

For the dumplings
1⅓ cups self-rising flour
1¼ cups fine cornmeal
10 tablespoons chilled butter, cut into cubes
a pinch of sea salt and freshly ground black pepper
1 teaspoon dried sage
3 sprigs of fresh rosemary, leaves picked and finely chopped

Wine suggestion:
French red – Châteauneuf-du-Pape

THE NATIVE AMERICANS I MET, INCLUDING JAMES, WERE DESPERATE FOR CHANGE AND PINNING THEIR HOPES FOR THE FUTURE ON BARACK OBAMA

CHICKEN MOLE

Mole (pronounced mo-lay) sauce is an absolutely delicious Mexican sauce. With New Mexico just next door, I couldn't resist. Don't be put off by the idea of using chocolate in a dish like this: it's added to bring all the flavors together and give it a rich thickness. It's great with chicken, whether roasted or boiled, and also great with pork, beef, lamb, or served beside roasted fish. A good mole should be sweet, spicy, silky smooth, and a pleasure to dip any bit of lucky old meat into. It should also have a tiny edge of acidity to help it cut through the richness of the meat. Give it a go.

Serves 6–8

★　　★　　★　　★　　★　　★

For the chicken boil
4–5 lbs chicken, preferably free-range or organic
1 teaspoon sea salt
2 onions, peeled and quartered
2 celery stalks, roughly chopped
6 fresh bay leaves
2 cinnamon sticks
10 black peppercorns
4 cloves garlic, peeled

For the chocolate mole
5 large dried red chiles
olive oil
2 onions, peeled and roughly chopped
2 cloves garlic, peeled and thinly sliced
1 teaspoon cumin seeds
1 teaspoon ground cinnamon
2 heaped teaspoons sesame seeds
1 x 14-oz can diced tomatoes
2 heaped teaspoons unsweetened cocoa powder
sea salt and freshly ground black pepper
1 x 4-oz bar good-quality bittersweet chocolate (70% cocoa solids), broken into chunks
red wine vinegar

Put your chicken into a large saucepan with all the other boil ingredients and cover with cold water to come an inch or so above it. Bring to a boil, then turn down to a low simmer, cover with a lid, and cook for 1 to 1½ hours, or until the meat just pulls and shreds apart beautifully. Skim away any foam that rises to the top from time to time. Check after 30 minutes and top up with a little hot water if it looks as though it's cooked down a lot.

While your chicken is cooking, get your mole sauce together. Put your dried chiles into a bowl and cover them with 3½ cups of boiling water. Let them soak in this for about 10 to 15 minutes, so they soften and start to release their incredible flavors. Get a large saucepan on a medium heat and add a good lug of olive oil, your onions, sliced garlic, soaked chiles (make sure you save their water), cumin, and ground cinnamon. Slowly cook everything for 15 to 20 minutes, until the vegetables have softened and sweetened. Stir in the sesame seeds and canned tomatoes, then fill the empty can with some of the water you soaked your chiles in and add this too. Bring to a boil, then turn down and simmer for 5 minutes.

Add your cocoa powder and a good pinch of salt and pepper, stir really well, and cook for another 5 minutes. At this point, add the chunks of chocolate and stir them in gently until melted, then pour the sauce into a food processor or liquidizer (you may need to do this in batches). Pop on the lid, cover with a dish towel, and liquidize for a few minutes. Take the lid off and have a taste. This is where you get the seasoning exactly right, so add a slug of red wine vinegar for that hint of acidity and a pinch more salt and pepper if need be. You want the sauce to have a fairly loose consistency, so add another splash of chile water if it looks too thick. When it's lovely and smooth, pour it into a bowl, cover it with aluminum foil, and put it into a large saucepan with a couple of inches of simmering water to keep it warm until your chicken is ready.

Using tongs, move the chicken from the pan to a large cutting board and get rid of the bones. Take 2 forks and shred the meat into bits and pieces. Pile it on a platter with a pair of tongs and pour over some of that gorgeous mole sauce, then take it to the table with some simple boiled rice, a few warm flatbreads, a fresh green salad, and the rest of your fantastic chocolate mole in a jug.

This green chili is so delicious, simple to make, and a total pleasure to eat. In England, we're sort of brainwashed into thinking of chili as just being chili con carne, but this is completely different and I absolutely love it. I think it's cleaner, braver, and fresher than your average chili. You can make your own flatbreads (see page 139) or use tortillas, or you can even serve with chapatis or naans instead.

★　　★　　★　　★　　★　　★

Put a large saucepan on a high heat and add a little olive oil. Add the ground pork, dried sage, and a good pinch of salt and pepper. Use a wooden spoon to break the meat up a bit and stir it about, then cook for a few minutes, stirring occasionally. Add your onions, garlic, bell peppers, and chiles, stir everything together, then fry for 15 minutes on a high heat until any liquid from the pork has evaporated and everything is starting to turn golden. When it looks good, stir in your chopped tomatoes and half a glass of water. Remember that it's supposed to be quite dry (in a really wholesome and nice way), not stewy and wet, so don't add too much water.

Turn the heat down to medium and let it tick away for 10 minutes or so while you wash and roughly chop up the lettuce. Pick the leaves from the bunch of mint and roughly chop them. Trim and thinly slice your scallions.

When you're ready to serve your chili, warm your tortillas in the oven at 350°F for a few minutes or in a dry pan for 30 seconds. Taste your dense chili. More than likely it will need another good pinch of salt and pepper. If you want to give it a nice fresh edge, you can squeeze in the juice of a lime. Stir in half of your chopped mint.

Push a warm tortilla or flatbread into each of your little bowls and spoon some delicious green chili on top of each one. Top with your chopped lettuce and a dollop of yogurt. Sprinkle over the rest of your mint and the scallions and serve right away with some cold beers.

GREEN CHILI

Serves 4

olive oil
1¾ lbs ground pork, the best
quality you can afford
1 teaspoon dried sage
sea salt and freshly ground black pepper
2 onions, peeled and roughly chopped
3 cloves garlic, peeled and thinly sliced
2 green bell peppers, seeded
and roughly chopped
6 small green chiles, roughly chopped
4 large, ripe red tomatoes,
chopped into small chunks
1 romaine lettuce, leaves
washed and spun dry
a small bunch of fresh mint
4 scallions
1 package flour tortillas
optional: 1 lime
sour cream or natural yogurt, to serve

THE PAINTED DESERT IS A BEAUTIFUL
BUT BARREN PLACE. WITH SO FEW NATURAL
RESOURCES, YOU'D HAVE TO BE INCREDIBLY
CLEVER AND RESOURCEFUL TO
CARVE OUT A LIFE HERE.

PEACH COBBLER

Even though this recipe is dead easy, the results are so delicious it's worthy of any occasion. The combination of hot juicy peaches in their own gorgeous syrup with soft-yet-crisp little scone-like dumplings is just amazing. You can assemble this, bake it ahead of time, then bring it back to life when you're ready to serve it by adding a splash of water and warming it up in the oven. Best served hot, with a few spoonfuls of vanilla ice cream melting over the top.

Serves 6

★　　　★　　　★　　　★　　　★　　　★

8 ripe peaches, halved, pitted and cut into wedges
1 vanilla bean, halved lengthways and seeds scraped out
zest of 1 lime
scant ¼ cup light brown sugar
zest and juice of 1 orange
1 inch ginger root, peeled and finely grated

For the cobbler topping
¼ cup pine nuts
scant 1 cup self-rising flour
¼ cup superfine sugar
salt
7 tablespoons unsalted butter, chilled
optional: confectioners' sugar, to serve
good-quality vanilla ice cream, to serve

Wine suggestion:
French sweet white – a Muscat de Beaumes-de-Venise

Preheat your oven to full whack. In an earthenware cooking dish (approx. 10 inches in diameter), toss your peaches gently with the vanilla seeds, lime zest, brown sugar, orange zest and juice, and grated ginger. Put the dish into the oven and immediately turn the temperature down to 375°F. Cook for about 10 to 15 minutes, until the peaches have softened slightly – the time it takes will depend on their ripeness.

Meanwhile, mix your cobbler topping. If you're using a food processor, whiz up your pine nuts, then tip in your flour, sugar, and salt. Cut your butter up into cubes, add to the processor, and pulse until the mixture resembles fine bread crumbs. Tip this mixture into a bowl. If working by hand, pop your pine nuts into a sandwich bag and bash them up with a rolling pin. Tip them into a bowl with the flour, sugar, and a pinch of salt, then use a box grater to grate in your chilled butter. Using your fingertips, gently rub the butter into the mix until it starts to resemble fine bread crumbs. At this point add 2 tablespoons of water to bring everything together, and when you have a firm dough put it to one side.

Remove your dish of peaches from the oven and pour in half a glass of water. Gently mix in and scrape around the edges to make sure nothing is catching, then use a tablespoon to dollop 6 big spoonfuls of dough on top of the peaches. Return the dish to the oven for around 20 minutes. When it's bubbling, golden on top, and nearly perfect, get your ice cream out of the freezer.

Make sure your gang are at the table and ready to eat. Dust your cobbler with confectioners' sugar, if using, then spoon a few scoops of ice cream on top and give it a minute to let the ice cream marble into the beautiful peach syrup. Take it to the table and don't expect much to come back!

You'll find a huge variety of cookies in America, from the much-loved chocolate chip, to oatmeal and raisin, to peanut butter. In an area like Arizona, where there are loads of pine nuts, it's no surprise to find them in all sorts of things, from breads and stuffings to pastes, but they're especially good in these delicious cookies. When they're mixed with almonds, like they are here, you get an Arizona twist on the classic American peanut butter cookie, and a damn tasty one at that! If you're wondering what that vibrant pink drink in the picture is, it's strawberry orchata (see page 178). Kids and adults love it just as much as these cookies, so it's well worth making.

★　　　★　　　★　　　★　　　★　　　★

Preheat your oven to 350°F. Spread the almonds and pine nuts on a cookie sheet and put them into the hot oven for 5 minutes. Once they're beginning to color slightly, take them out and save a couple of handfuls for later. Blitz the rest up in a food processor until you get coarse crumbs. Add your sugars, butter, egg, golden syrup, vanilla extract, flour, and baking soda, and pulse for a few minutes until nice and smooth.

Spoon this mixture into a large bowl and add the oatmeal. Roughly chop the reserved nuts and fold these into the mixture really well, using a wooden spoon.

Line 2 large cookie sheets with parchment paper. Use a tablespoon to spoon dollops of the cookie mixture onto your sheets, leaving enough space between them for the cookies to spread without touching. Resist the urge to flatten them down if they are sitting quite high on the sheet.

Bake the cookies in the hot oven for 10 minutes, until golden around the edges. If they're still a bit gooey in the middle when you take them out, that's all right, because they'll harden up a bit as they cool. Leave them on the sheet for about 10 minutes, then carefully transfer them to a wire rack to cool for 5 minutes or so – I like to eat mine warm. Pop the rest in a cookie jar and they'll keep for a few days.

ALMOND & PINE NUT COOKIES

Makes about 24 cookies

1¼ cups whole raw almonds
a large handful of pine nuts
heaping ½ cup superfine sugar
½ cup (packed) light brown sugar
7 tablespoons unsalted butter
1 large egg, preferably free-range or organic
2 tablespoons golden syrup, such as Lyle's, or honey
1 tablespoon good-quality vanilla extract
1⅓ cups all-purpose flour
1 teaspoon baking soda
heaping ⅓ cup quick-cook oatmeal (not instant)

At a fantastic out-of-the-way Mexican restaurant called El Metate in Gallup, New Mexico, the very sweet owner, Rebecca, taught me how to make proper Mexican tamales. To see her teaching me how to make these, go to www.jamieoliver.com/how-to. Tamales can be sweet, like these, or savory. They are basically filled Mexican dumplings – I think they're brilliant. The corn husks they're wrapped in are used throughout Mexico. If you buy corn in season, it often comes in husks, but the dried husks I'm using here work a treat. You can pick them up online or at Whole Foods Market stores. Otherwise, things like parchment or wax paper will also do the trick.

★   ★   ★   ★   ★   ★

Soak your corn husks in a bowl of warm water or, if you're using parchment paper, cut yourself 16 pieces about half the size of a page in this book. In a separate bowl, mix the cornmeal, flour, salt, baking powder, sugar, coconut, and chopped pineapple. Add the lime zest and juice and pour in just over ⅔ cup water to bring everything together. Mix well, until you've got a thick spoonable paste.

Put a large saucepan of water on to boil – the pan needs to be big enough to fit a colander on top. Take a soaked corn husk or piece of parchment paper and spoon a heaping tablespoon of your pineapple mixture into the middle of the husk or paper; if the husks are thin you might have to layer two on top of each other. Fold the sides in to cover the filling, then twist the ends and use string to tie them so they look like British Christmas crackers.

Lay your prepared tamales in a large colander or steamer, making sure they're all in one layer and not overlapping. Cover the top of the colander with aluminum foil and seal it nice and tightly. If you don't have a colander large enough, you can always steam the tamales in 2 batches. Pop the colander on top of your pan of boiling water and steam for about 20 to 25 minutes. About 5 minutes before they're due to be ready, start making your chocolate sauce.

Gently bring the cream to a boil in a saucepan on a medium heat. As soon as it starts to boil, take the pan off the heat and stir in your chocolate pieces until they're perfectly melted and combined. Add the cubes of butter and a pinch of salt and stir well until the butter is melted.

Open one of the tamales to check that it's perfectly cooked – it should be solid and the wrapping should peel away from it easily. Take them off the heat and let them cool down slightly so they're cool enough to handle but still warm and delicious. Lay them on a platter next to a jug of your warm chocolate sauce and let everyone get involved and unwrap their own.

SWEET TAMALES 'N' CHOCOLATE

Makes about 16 tamales

32 dried corn husks or 16 rectangles of parchment or wax paper, each ranging 6 x 8 inches

For the tamales
1⅔ cups fine cornmeal
1 heaping tablespoon all-purpose flour
pinch of sea salt
½ teaspoon baking powder
¼ cup sugar
heaping ½ cup unsweetened shredded coconut
½ pineapple (approx 6 oz), peeled, core removed, halved, and really finely diced
zest and juice of 1 lime

For the chocolate sauce
scant 1 cup heavy cream
1 x 4-oz bar good-quality bittersweet chocolate (70% cocoa solids), broken into small pieces
2 tablespoons unsalted butter, cubed
a pinch of sea salt

HOT! CHOCCY & CHURROS

Makes 6 little cups of mind-blowing hot chocolate and about 20 churros

For the churros
1 cup water
5 tablespoons unsalted butter, cubed
scant 1¾ cups all-purpose flour
½ teaspoon baking powder
sea salt
1 large egg, preferably free-range or organic, beaten
1 quart vegetable oil
¼ cup sugar, to serve
1 teaspoon ground cinnamon, to serve

For the chilli hot chocolate
1 quart whole milk
½ teaspoon cinnamon
1 fresh green chile, halved lengthways and seeded
2 heaped tablespoons light brown sugar
2 heaped tablespoons cornstarch
½ x 4-oz bars good-quality bittersweet chocolate (70% cocoa solids), broken into chunks

This is a real treat for anyone who loves chocolate and doughnuts, and it's by far the best hot chocolate I've ever had in my life. Don't be put off by the green chiles in it, because it's brilliant. Churros are small doughnuts, perfect for dunking in the hot chocolate. Usually, they are rolled out into the tursted shape of the horns of churro sheep. I've made mine a little differently but they're just as sweet.

★　　★　　★　　★　　★　　★

Bring the water and butter to a boil in a saucepan on a high heat, then take the pan off the heat and stir in your flour, baking powder, and a pinch of salt until you get a nice smooth batter. Let this cool for a few minutes, then add your egg and beat until well combined.

Pour your vegetable oil into a large sturdy saucepan and put it on a high heat. You want it to reach about 350°F. If you don't have a thermometer, use a little piece of batter as your guide. When it rises to the top and turns crisp and golden, you'll know the oil is hot enough. Please make sure you pay attention.

Put a separate saucepan on a medium heat and add your milk, cinnamon, and chile. Bring to a boil, then turn down to a low simmer for 8 minutes to let the flavors infuse. Mix the sugar and cornstarch together in a small bowl with a few tablespoons of cold water until you have a smooth paste. Pour this into the hot milk and give it a good whisk so it thickens the mixture.

Turn the temperature down a bit and drop in your pieces of chocolate. Whisk until completely melted. Turn the heat right down to low to keep it warm while you fry your churros or serve it straight away . . . up to you!

Take heaping teaspoonfuls of the batter and carefully slide them into the hot oil to fry for 2 to 3 minutes. Do about 10 little churros at a time. Keep watching them and turning them over until they're golden and puffed up all over, then use a perforated spoon to move them to a plate lined with paper towels to drain.

Sprinkle with sugar and cinnamon from a height, then toss around so they pick up the flavors and serve straightaway with steaming mugs of your hot choccy.

CINNAMON ORCHATA

Orchata is another example of the exciting Mexican and Spanish influences that make food in this part of America so wonderful. It's such an exciting way of using rice, and is so delicious. You can also make a strawberry orchata by following the method below, leaving out the cinnamon and blitzing the rice, water, and sugar with 14 oz of hulled strawberries. Serve with delicious cookies like I've done on page 171 and it's very happy days!

Makes 4 large glasses

★   ★   ★   ★   ★   ★

¾ cup long-grain rice
1 quart whole milk
1 teaspoon ground cinnamon
¼ cup light brown sugar
1 or 2 cinnamon sticks

Boil the rice following the package instructions, then drain and run under cold water so it cools down quickly. Pop it into a liquidizer with the milk, ground cinnamon, and sugar. Whiz until smooth, then taste and add a bit more sugar, until it's sweet enough for you. You may need to do this in 2 batches if your liquidizer isn't big enough.

Once it's lovely and silky, strain it into a jug with a load of ice and discard any rice left behind. Snap your cinnamon sticks in half and pop these in. Sprinkle over a little more ground cinnamon and serve.

Get yourself a large sturdy saucepan with a lid and put it on a medium heat with a couple of lugs of **peanut oil**. Add a cup of **popcorn kernels**, put the lid on, and shake the pan every few seconds. When the first kernels start popping, keep the pan moving and add a large pat of **butter** and about 1 teaspoon of a funky **chili powder** (smoked chipotle chili powder is incredible). If you can find some interesting **dried chiles** remove their stalks, bash the chiles to a fine powder in a pestle and mortar, and use that instead of the chili powder. Keep shaking the pan until it's all popped, then tip the popcorn onto a big tray and season to your liking with **sea salt** and 1 teaspoon of **chili powder**, to taste. A brilliant thing to serve for nibbles.

CHIPOTLE CHILE POPCORN

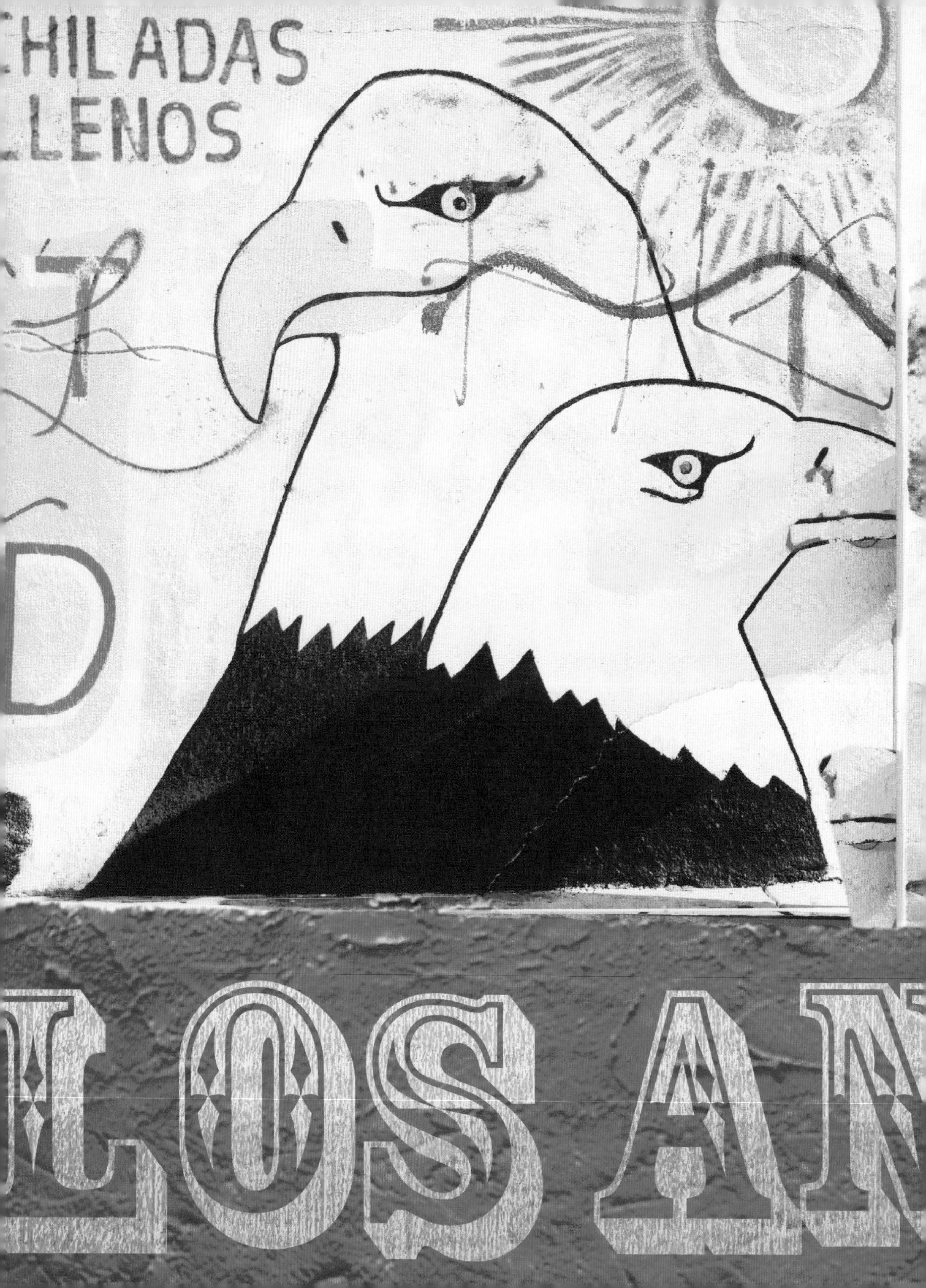

CHILADAS
LENOS
LOS AN

There's no city on earth like Los Angeles. From Beverly Hills in the west to Boyle Heights (where I stayed) in the east, this is definitely a city of contrasts. There is incredible personal wealth in the "city of angels," and in California in general: if just this one single American state were a country, it would be the tenth richest in the world! But there are also neighborhoods where people live in almost Third World–level poverty. As in New York, immigrants surge into LA in search of the American dream, and, as in New York, it is often a case of survival of the fittest.

Since Hispanics make up the majority of LA's population, I wanted to learn as much as I could about this side of Californian food culture. I'm really glad I did, because I found Mexican food so exciting: tasty, in your face, and, more often than not, damn nutritious. My first night was spent with some really wonderful Mexican-American families. They shared their food and their stories with me. Being surrounded by family and good food is the cornerstone of life as a Mexican-American. It was also Oscar night when I arrived in LA, and what a learning experience it was for me to be staying somewhere where I was able to see that iconic Hollywood sign, but be surrounded by people whose day-to-day reality was worlds away from the LA we all imagine.

Sadly, however, East LA is also an area where gang violence and gun crime are huge problems; pretty much everyone I met had been affected by gangs in some way, and the stories they told me ranged from uplifting to downright disturbing. An incredible organization, Homeboy Industries, is tackling the gang problems in a really positive and effective way, which I'll be telling you about later.

Outside LA, the state of California is blessed with exhilarating cities, like San Francisco, and areas of natural beauty, like the Napa Valley, which is dedicated to wine production. Some world-class organic farmers and artisinal food producers work in this area, which allows for the most diverse garden of ingredients: every sort of orchard fruit and fresh vegetable imaginable, incredible cheeses, cured and smoked meats, and plenty of amazing wines to wash them down with. Talk about the good life!

When I think of the food culture in California, I can't help but think of the wonderful chef and food activist Alice Waters, who's been creating delicious, simple food at her restaurant Chez Panisse for a few decades now. In much the same way as Rose Gray and Ruth Rogers, my former employers at London's River Café, Alice blazed a real trail in American food. Her menus focused on great-quality, simple, seasonal ingredients. It might not sound radical now, but when these girls started pushing their simple, common-sense approach to food and refused to be bullied by Michelin-starred notions of what "fine-dining cuisine" should be, they were being experimental to the core.

What I came to realize during my time in LA is that there is definitely a Californian style of putting a plate together. Whether I was making beautiful Mexican tortillas for breakfast or a gorgeous salad full of fresh stuff from a posh farmers' market, this Californian style of plating happens when the food does all the talking, so it looks a little scruffy but still beautiful; like it's fallen on the plate that way. What's cool about it is that this style fits really well with the way I like to cook: lots of citrus and plenty of fresh herbs. Hopefully in this chapter I've managed to capture the color and energy of this incredible city and state, and honor the passion and heart of LA's vibrant Mexican-American community.

Los Angeles

POSTAGE
1½ ¢
WITHOUT
MESSAGE

BEAUTIFUL BREAKFAST TORTILLAS

This will definitely get you going in the morning, especially if you use fresh chiles and chile sauce like I've done here. If that's not your thing, feel free to adjust this to suit your taste – it will still be delicious. Great with a mug of strong coffee.

In America you see generic hot chile sauces everywhere, and good supermarkets and stores should stock some mind-blowing varieties. Just don't mistake them for the sweet chile versions out there. If you're a chile freak, like me, make your own (see page 240). It's simple, so tasty, and you'll have it on hand, ready to spice up all sorts of lovely dishes.

Serves 2

★　　★　　★　　★　　★　　★

1 ripe avocado, halved, pitted, peeled, and chopped
2 limes
sea salt and freshly ground black pepper
1 medium-sized tomato, halved and diced
1 fresh green chile, seeded and minced
a small bunch of fresh cilantro, leaves picked and chopped
a handful of freshly grated Manchego or Cheddar cheese
4 corn or flour tortillas
6 large eggs, preferably free-range or organic
4 scallions, trimmed and minced
a good pat of butter
chile sauce (as hot as you want!), to serve

Roughly mash your avocado with the juice of 1 of your limes and a good pinch of salt and pepper, and put aside. Arrange the rest of your topping ingredients on a plate: the tomato, chile, cilantro leaves, and grated cheese.

Quickly reheat the tortillas in a hot dry pan for 20 seconds on each side until warmed through. Wrap them in aluminum foil to keep them warm while you get on with your eggs.

Beat the eggs in a bowl with the minced scallions and a good pinch of salt and pepper. Melt the butter in a large frying pan on a medium heat and pour in the eggs. Lightly tip the pan as the eggs cook, and when you see a layer forming on the bottom of the pan, sweep a rubber spatula around so you get little handkerchiefs of cooked egg surrounded by wonderful custardy egg. Keep an eye on it and stir gently for a minute or so, until the eggs are starting to scramble but are still loose.

Get your 2 plates and lay a warm tortilla on each one. Divide the scrambled egg between them, top with the chopped tomato and mashed avocado, and sprinkle over your chile, cilantro, and grated cheese. Lay another tortilla on top, and drizzle over some chile sauce. Cut your remaining lime into wedges for squeezing over and dive in.

In the summer, when zucchini are popping up all over the garden, you should be able to find zucchini flowers in good farmers' markets – it's worth trying them if you can, as they're a bit of a seasonal treat, especially when stuffed like they are here. Zucchini tend to grow like the clappers, so have a go at sowing a few seeds and you'll have a really good supply of flowers and zucchini in no time. Pick as many flowers as you want, but always make sure you leave one male and one female zucchini on each plant (a flower on a stem is a male and a flower on a zucchini is a female) so you don't run out.

★   ★   ★   ★   ★   ★

Mix all the stuffing ingredients together in a bowl. Very carefully pull back the petals of each zucchini flower and remove the stamen from inside each one. Be gentle, as the petals tear easily. Take a couple of teaspoons of the stuffing and fill each zucchini flower right up, bringing the petals back around the filling. Lightly twist the ends together to close each flower, then put them all on a tray and put aside. Whisk the batter ingredients together in a clean bowl.

Pour the vegetable oil into a large sturdy pan and put it on a high heat. You want it to reach about 350°F. If you don't have a thermometer, use a little piece of potato as your gauge. When it rises to the top and turns crisp and golden, you'll know the oil is hot enough. Please make sure you are paying attention to what you're doing and don't have any kids running around, because hot oil is dangerous.

Remove the potato, if you've used it, then carefully dip each zucchini, and its flower, into the chili batter, letting any excess drip off. Use a perforated spoon to lower each one slowly into the hot oil, making sure you don't overcrowd the pan, or the temperature of the oil will drop. Deep-fry each batch for 2 to 3 minutes on each side, turning the zucchini to cook them evenly until they're a beautiful light golden color. Use a perforated spoon to remove them to a plate lined with paper towels to drain. Serve right away while they're crisp and hot, with wedges of your naked lime and a bowl of sea salt for sprinkling over. Don't let them get soggy or you won't get the proper experience.

STUFFED ZUCCHINI FLOWERS

Serves 4 as a starter

12 baby zucchini with flowers
1 quart vegetable oil, for frying

For the stuffing
2½ cups freshly grated Mexican ranchero cheese, or good quality crumbled dry ricotta
4 oz soft goat's cheese (chèvre)
a couple of sprigs of fresh marjoram, leaves picked and finely chopped
a few sprigs of fresh mint, leaves picked and finely chopped
zest and juice of 1 lemon
zest of 1 lime
sea salt and freshly ground black pepper
1 fresh green chile, seeded and finely chopped

For the batter
1¾ cups self-rising flour
1½ cups sparkling water
2 teaspoons chili powder

Wine suggestion:
southern Italian dry white –
from the Fiano grape

LA BREA SALAD

La Brea is a really cool district in West Hollywood with all sorts of quirky shops and restaurants. While I was there I had a delicious beet salad at a place called AOC that inspired me to make my own version, so I headed to a fantastic farmers' market and picked up a brilliant mixture of beets in all sorts of different vibrant colors. You can also make this using other veggies like turnips, baby zucchini, patty pan squash, even baby potatoes. And also try varying the herbs and vinegar.

Serves 4

★ ★ ★ ★ ★ ★

For the salad

1¼ lbs smallish raw baby beets (gold, purple, and candy cane if you can get them), trimmed and scrubbed clean
¾ lb baby carrots, scrubbed clean
a large handful of small radishes, trimmed and washed
scant ¾ cup pumpkin seeds
⅔ cup sour cream, to serve

For the dressing

1 clove garlic, peeled and finely grated
juice of 2 blood oranges, if available, otherwise use normal oranges
2 tablespoons honey
2 tablespoons cider vinegar
1–2 fresh red chiles, seeded and minced
sea salt and freshly ground black pepper
a small bunch of fresh mint, leaves picked, a few reserved for garnish, the rest roughly chopped

Wine suggestion:
Italian white – a Soave Classico

Cook the beets and carrots in separate pans of boiling salted water until tender and a knife goes through them easily. A couple of minutes before the carrots are done, add the radishes to the pan to blanch them.

Meanwhile, make your dressing. Put all the ingredients into a large bowl with a good pinch of salt and pepper and the chopped mint – keeping a few leaves back for garnish. Mix everything together really well, then have a taste and add more salt, pepper or vinegar if needed. Don't worry if the dressing seems quite spicy at this point – once it's on your plate with the veggies and sour cream, it'll be perfect.

When the veggies are ready, drain them in batches in the colander, then move them to a tray to steam dry. Once the beets are cool enough to handle, peel off the skins (you might want to put on some rubber gloves to protect your hands from getting stained). Halve or quarter the beets, tossing the lighter-colored ones into the dressing straightaway along with your radishes and carrots.

Once you've dressed the veggies, you can either serve them as they are or put them all into a large roasting pan and pop them into the oven at 400°F for about 15 minutes. This will intensify the flavor and make the veggies golden and sticky – both ways are delicious, so I'll leave it up to you.

Toast your pumpkin seeds in a dry pan until lightly golden.

Just before serving, toss your darker beets in with the other veggies. Taste and season one last time, then smear the sour cream over a serving platter and pile all your delicious veggies on top. Sprinkle with the seeds and reserved mint leaves and enjoy.

RIGO'S STORY

A few of my days in LA were spent with a chef called Rigo, a lovely young man. Brought up in a Mexican family that was bound up in the gang culture, he had lost his father, stepfather, and uncle to drug crime. But, bravely, he decided to turn his back on this life and train as a chef. He's now doing a great job, working in the Four Seasons Hotel in LA cranking out 300 top-class breakfasts there every day, and has a child and a settled family life. Just goes to show that if you've got the guts and the determination to start afresh, it can be done.

On the morning I went fishing off Redondo Beach Pier with my new friend Rigo, we didn't have any luck, so we decided to grill the mackerel caught by the fishermen next to us. They thought we were crazy because they only use mackerel for bait – but they changed their tune once I'd persuaded them to eat these delicious wraps.

Of course, you could also use sardines, trout, slices of salmon, or even strips of lovely chicken with great effect in this recipe, but I think fresh mackerel is something really special. These are great portable wraps, especially when you're sitting at the end of a windy pier.

REDONDO MACKEREL WRAPS

Serves 2 as a main or 4 as a snack

Light your grill or get your grill pan screaming hot.

To make the salad, shave the zucchini into long ribbons with a speed peeler (if it's a big one, you'll want to avoid the fluffy seedy center) and put them into a large bowl. Do the same with the asparagus spears – you will need to lay them on a board to do this, as it is a bit fiddly to hold them and shave! Add the asparagus to the bowl with the scallions, radishes, and most of the chile. Squeeze over the lime juice, add a good lug of extra virgin olive oil, and season well with salt and pepper. Gently toss everything together using your hands – this will give you a beautiful salad base. Put to one side.

Scoop your avocado flesh into a bowl and mash it up with a fork along with the juice from 1 of your limes and a good pinch of salt and pepper. Put this to one side while you prepare the fish.

Drizzle some extra virgin olive oil over your mackerel fillets and add a generous pinch of salt – putting extra oil on the skin side of each fillet to prevent the fish sticking to the grill or pan. Put the fillets, skin side down, on your hot grill or pan and cook for 2 minutes. Turn over and give them another 2 to 3 minutes, until cooked through. Pop your 4 tortillas on the grill next to the fish, or in a hot dry frying pan for a few seconds to warm them.

To serve, spoon a quarter of the avocado mixture into the middle of each tortilla and top with a spoonful of sour cream. Break each of the mackerel fillets in half – removing any bones you see as you go – and divide between your tortillas. Toss the salad one last time and put some on top of the fish. Scatter over some cilantro leaves, your remaining chile, and a few drizzles of hot chile sauce if you fancy. Definitely give each one a good squeeze of your remaining lime, then roll your tortillas up (make sure you close the ends so it doesn't all drip out!).

For the wrap
1 ripe avocado, halved and pitted
2 limes
2 mackerel fillets, pinboned
4 small flour tortillas
¼ cup sour cream
a few sprigs of fresh cilantro, leaves picked
optional: hot chile sauce, to serve (see page 240)

For the salad
1 green or yellow zucchini
4 asparagus spears
2 large scallions, trimmed and thinly sliced
2 radishes, cut into matchsticks
1 fresh red chile, seeded and minced
juice of 1 lime
extra virgin olive oil
sea salt and freshly ground black pepper

Wine suggestion:
French dry white – a Riesling from Alsace

SEVEN SEAS SOUP

While we were fishing, Rigo told me about this *caldo de siete mares* or "seven seas soup," which he used to love as a kid. That conversation, combined with all the wonderful flavors and ingredients around me in LA, inspired me to make my own version of this soup. There's a long list of ingredients, but if you ask your fishmonger to prep everything for you when you pick them up, you'll find this a really simple dish to make.

Serves 6

★　　★　　★　　★　　★　　★

For the salsa soup base

1 red onion, peeled and quartered
4 fresh tomatoes, quartered
1 x 14-oz can diced tomatoes
juice of 4 limes
a good pinch of sea salt
a small bunch of fresh cilantro
1 fresh jalapeño chile (or other green chile), stalk removed
1 or 2 dried chiles (I used a large smoked ancho), stalk removed
optional: a slug of tequila

For the soup

1½ cups white rice
2 x 15-oz cans black beans, drained
olive oil
4 cloves garlic, peeled and thinly sliced
2 large handfuls of clams, washed
2 large handfuls of mussels, debearded and washed
12 raw large shrimp, shell on
14 oz white fish fillets, such as halibut, pinboned and sliced into 1-inch strips
14 oz red snapper fillets, pinboned and sliced into 1-inch strips
4 squid, cleaned and sliced into 1-inch strips
¼ pound crabmeat, picked

For the garnish

½ red onion, peeled and minced
2 fresh red or green chiles, thinly sliced
a small bunch of fresh cilantro, leaves picked
extra virgin olive oil
2 limes, halved or quartered

Wine suggestion:
Spanish dry sherry – a chilled Fino

Make your salsa soup base by whizzing all the ingredients in a food processor or liquidizer until you have a purée. Add a generous ⅔ cup of water and whiz again. Season to taste.

Cook your rice following the package instructions, then drain and cover with aluminum foil to keep warm while you heat your beans in a small pan on a medium heat. Let your rice and beans tick away while you start your soup. Put your biggest saucepan over a medium heat and add a few lugs of olive oil and your sliced garlic. When the garlic is just starting to turn lightly golden, add your clams and mussels, discarding any that are not closed, and pour over your soupy salsa base. Sprinkle in the rest of your seafood and fish, reserving the crabmeat. Give it a stir, place the lid on, bring everything to a boil, then turn the heat down and let it tick over for 7 minutes. After this time your mussels and clams should have opened (throw away any that haven't), so stir through your picked crabmeat and you're ready to serve.

Check the consistency and taste and add a bit more salt and pepper – it should have a bit of attitude before you garnish it, so don't be afraid to go nuts. When you're happy, get the garnishes in the middle of the table.

By now your rice will be drained and ready to go. Have a taste of the beans and season them with salt and pepper if needed, then put a good spoonful of rice and a spoonful of beans in the bottom of each bowl. Add a ladleful of soup, making sure everyone gets a couple of shrimp and a good mixture of all the different types of fish. Or put it into a large dish in the middle of the table and let your guests build their own. Garnishes are really important touches in any Mexican meal, so adding that fresh crunch with a scatter of red onion and thinly sliced chile, then tearing over your picked cilantro leaves, is a brilliant way to kick it all off. Finish with a drizzle of extra virgin olive oil and serve with lime wedges on the side for squeezing over. What a celebration.

My friend Rigo made me a roasted salsa and I loved it so much that I'm going to show you how to make a roasted vegetable salsa with an incredible depth of flavor to it. It's a great alternative if you've got a little more time on your hands. Really good sustainable tuna is always best when seared quickly and served with fresh flavors, so the zucchini, mint, and lemon salad is perfect alongside this, and it's really quickly made.

You'll have quite a lot of salsa left over, but you can keep the rest in the refrigerator and serve it with roast chicken, tortilla chips, or whatever you fancy!

First get your salsa going. Prick your chiles all over, then, on a hot grill or grill pan, blacken and blister all your salsa vegetables Once nice and black all over, pop them into a large bowl, cover with plastic wrap, and put to one side. Halve and seed your bell peppers and chiles, then peel the skins off your charred veggies. Don't wash any of these veggies under the tap or you'll wash away their wonderful flavors.

At this point, get your tuna out of the refrigerator so it has time to come up to room temperature. Put all your charred vegetables into a food processor. Add your lime juice, cilantro, a generous pinch of salt and pepper, and a few good lugs of olive oil, and pulse until it's the right consistency for you. Have a taste – it's important to get the flavors right, so add more salt, pepper, or lime juice until you're happy. Put the salsa into a bowl and set aside. Remember to check the seasoning later, as the flavors may well change.

Using a speed peeler, peel the zucchini or squash lengthways into thin ribbons. If you've got big zucchini, avoid the fluffy center. Put these ribbons into a bowl with the mint leaves, then drizzle with a good lug of extra virgin olive oil and the lemon juice and toss until nicely coated.

Put your grill pan on a high heat and let it get screaming hot. Drizzle the tuna with olive oil and season well with salt and pepper on both sides. Lay it in the hot pan and sear for 2 to 3 minutes on each side if you like it blushing like I do, or for a little longer if you prefer.

Put a big spoonful of salsa on each of your plates and lay a piece of tuna on top. Give your zucchini salad a good squeeze of lemon juice and another drizzle of extra virgin olive oil, taste it for seasoning, then plonk a nice handful of ribbons over each piece of tuna. Such fresh flavors.

TUNA ON ROASTED SALSA

Serves 4

4 x 7 oz (1 inch thick) pieces of sustainably caught (sushi-grade) tuna
extra virgin olive oil
sea salt and freshly ground black pepper

For the salsa
2–3 fresh green chiles
2 green bell peppers
1 red onion, peeled and halved
8 cloves garlic, unpeeled
3 medium red tomatoes
juice of 3 limes
a large handful of fresh cilantro
olive oil

For the zucchini salad
2 zucchini or yellow squash
a handful of fresh mint, leaves picked and chopped
extra virgin olive oil
juice of 1 lemon

Wine suggestion:
American red – a young
Pinot Noir from Oregon

MEXICAN STREET SALAD

This simple little salad can be quite extraordinary, but you've got to season it with that Mexican spirit by being brave with the lime juice, salt, and chiles, until it's singing in your mouth. It does a great job of waking up the other things it's served with – a few spoonfuls of this next to a grilled chicken breast or pork chop would be an absolute celebration.

Vegetable-wise, the onion, cilantro, and white cabbage are non-negotiable; they form the base of this salad. But feel free to have a play with the other ingredients: Use things like fennel or asparagus. Basically whatever's in season and available should be a nice addition.

Serves 4–6

★　　★　　★　　★　　★　　★

½ a small white cabbage
½ a small red cabbage
a small bunch of radishes (about 10), trimmed and thinly sliced
2 carrots, peeled and thinly sliced
a large bunch of fresh cilantro, leaves and stalks finely chopped
2 large jalapeño chiles (or other green chiles), to taste, thinly sliced
1 red onion, peeled and thinly sliced
extra virgin olive oil
juice of 2–3 limes
sea salt

Wine suggestion:
French white – an unoaked Sauvignon Blanc from the Loire Valley (such as Quincy) or, if serving with chicken or pork, French red – a young red Bourgogne Pinot Noir

The easiest and quickest way to make this is to use a food processor with a slicer attachment or a mandolin. If you don't have either of those, use a speed peeler, or simply grate everything finely.

Shred your white and red cabbage into two separate piles. Put just the white cabbage into a large bowl with the radishes, carrots, and most of the cilantro. Mix everything together really well, then kick up the flavors by adding almost all the chopped chiles, the sliced red onion, and a good few lugs of extra virgin olive oil. Add most of the lime juice and a good pinch of salt, then toss together and have a taste. Just keep adjusting everything, adding more fragrance with the cilantro, heat with the last of the chiles, and acid with another squeeze of lime juice, until it's just right for you.

When you're happy, fold in the red cabbage right before serving so it doesn't stain everything, and tuck in.

Who would have believed a cactus farm would have been right in the middle of LA? They're used raw in salads, pickled or chopped up and cooked in so many different ways, like a vegetable

FIERY SHRIMP COCKTAIL

We Brits love our "prawn" cocktails, so you can imagine how excited I got when I tried an American-style shrimp cocktail at an LA "swap meet" (outdoor market). I'd never really seen it made this way before; it's got a tomato sauce with real attitude and chili kick that's been spiked with a dressing. Obviously, no matter what sort of seafood you use, be it cooked squid, mussels, lobster, crab, whatever you fancy, you want to get the freshest stuff you can so that this tastes as incredible as possible. I like to serve my version by ripping up some lettuce, sprinkling over some sprouts, adding a few chunks of ripe avocado, then spooning over the seafood and delicious juices.

Serves 4

★ ★ ★ ★ ★ ★

For the shrimp cocktail

1 lb cooked or raw large shrimp, shell-off
olive oil
sea salt and freshly ground black pepper
1 cup tomato sauce
juice and zest of 1 lemon
juice of 3 limes, zest of 1
1 garlic clove, peeled and minced
1–2 red or green chiles, to taste, sliced
2 scallions, trimmed and sliced at an angle into ½-inch pieces
a handful of soft, fresh herbs (such as basil, dill, cilantro, or a mixture of all three), leaves picked and roughly chopped
optional: 1 tablespoon Worcestershire sauce, such as Lea & Perrins
optional: tequila
1 cucumber

For the garnish

1 small romaine heart or round lettuce, quartered
2 avocados, halved and pitted
2 handfuls of mixed sprouts (try alfalfa, mung beans, sunflower, onion seeds, to name but a few)
a few limes, halved or quartered

Wine suggestion:
Australian white – a Viognier from the Eden Valley

If you've got fresh raw shrimp, pour a lug of olive oil into a large pan on a medium heat, let it heat up, then add your shrimp with a pinch of salt and pepper. Fry and toss around for a couple of minutes, until the shrimp are starting to color slightly and cooked through.

Put your cooked shrimp into a large bowl and pour in your tomato sauce. Add the lemon and lime zest and juice, the garlic, most of your chiles, the scallions, and most of your soft herbs. Stir, and season with salt, pepper, another squeeze of lemon or lime juice if needed, and a bit more chile to get the sauce as fiery as you dare. If you're inclined to add some Worcestershire sauce or even a splash of tequila at this point, it could be quite nice, but I'll leave that up to you.

Use a fork to really scrape down the length of your cucumber so it gets grooves around the outside – this increases the surface area and gives the sauce more places to get into. Cut the cucumber into thick slices and add to the bowl. Give it a stir, then cover with plastic wrap and pop it into the refrigerator while you get your garnishes prepped. So often, seafood wants to be served warm or hot, but I think this particular dish works best chilled, especially if the weather's warm.

When you're ready to eat, spoon the mixture into a serving bowl and put it on a platter along with your garnishes and some lovely crusty bread or tortillas. Scatter over the reserved soft herbs to finish it off, and let your guests help themselves. Nice served with some hot bread.

I decided to name this salad as a salute to an old favorite of mine: the classic Green Goddess salad dressing, famous on the west coast of America.

When you set out to make a really amazing salad, it's worth putting the effort into having a good look for some interesting leaves of different shapes, textures, and colors. I've added a few edible flowers to my salad because I think they look good, taste nice, and make people talk. Flowers like marigolds, pansies, and violas are totally edible, delicious, and colorful, but don't go picking any old thing, because some are also poisonous!

GREEN GOD SALAD

Serves 4

Get a liquidizer or hand blender for your dressing. Scoop the avocado flesh into the liquidizer and add half the chile, the juice of 2 of your limes, and 3 times as much extra virgin olive oil as lime juice (about ⅓ cup). Add the rest of the dressing ingredients and a pinch of salt and pepper, pop the lid on, and whiz until you get a smooth, shiny liquid. Add a splash of water or tequila to get it to the right drizzling consistency if you like, then have a taste. It's up to you to give it attitude, so add a bit more of anything you think it needs. I like to make my dressing slightly saltier and more acidic than it needs to be, because when it's added to the salad the flavor gets toned down a bit.

Next make your crunchy topping. Pour the vegetable oil into a large sturdy pan and heat it to 350°F. If you don't have a thermometer, just add a small piece of potato to the oil. When it turns crisp and golden and floats to the top, the oil is ready. Make sure you concentrate and are very careful, though, because hot oil can burn badly. Remove the piece of potato and carefully lower in the tortilla strips. Move them around a bit and fry them for a few minutes. When golden and crisp, use a perforated spoon to remove them to a plate lined with paper towels to drain. Toss the onion slices in the flour to lightly coat them, then carefully lower them into the hot oil and deep-fry until golden and crispy. Move them to the paper towels and sprinkle with a pinch of salt.

Put your mixed salad leaves into a bowl with the radishes, peas, pea shoots if you have them, and just enough of the dressing to lightly coat the leaves. Toss together using your hands, then pile on a big platter or bowl in the middle of the table with some edible flowers scattered on top. Plonk your jug of incredible dressing and bowl of crunchy topping down next to it and let your guests get stuck in and assemble their own. Delicious. This salad is great on its own, but amazing with some fish or chicken.

For the salad
5 large handfuls of interesting salad leaves, such as butterhead lettuce, oakleaf lettuce, radicchio, arugula, mizuna, and dandelion
a bunch of small radishes, trimmed
2 handfuls of freshly shelled peas
optional: 2 handfuls of pea shoots if you can get them!
optional: a few edible flowers, such as marigolds, pansies, or violas

For the dressing
1 ripe avocado, halved and pitted
1 fresh red chile, seeded
juice of 2–3 limes
extra virgin olive oil
6 sprigs of fresh dill
6 sprigs of fresh mint, leaves picked
6 sprigs of fresh cilantro, leaves picked
1 tablespoon sour cream
sea salt and freshly ground black pepper
optional: a small splash of tequila

For the crunchy topping
1 quart vegetable oil
3 soft tortillas, rolled up and thinly sliced into ¼-inch strips
1 red onion, peeled and thinly sliced about ¼ inch thick
1 heaping teaspoon all-purpose flour

Wine suggestion:
French dry white – a Chenin Blanc from Anjou in the Loire Valley

The idea here was to big up the zucchini by surrounding them with their best friends: mint, garlic, chiles, and salty cheese. Farro is a really interesting grain to use, but pearl barley or couscous would work well in its place. The salad is absolutely gorgeous on its own, but would also make a pretty incredible stuffing for roasted bell peppers, a boned shoulder of lamb, the baked tortillas on page 214, or as a sweet little side with some lovely grilled meats.

I use beautiful baby zucchini for my salad, but medium or large ones would still definitely work. Zucchini over 5 inches long will need to be halved and the fluffy seedy inside scooped out, as otherwise they will taste bland and slightly bitter. To make this salad even more beautiful, have a look around for different varieties of zucchini – including yellow or mottled squash.

Soak the farro in a bowl of cold water for 2 hours or, preferably, overnight. Drain, then add to a saucepan of salted boiling water with the chicken bouillon cube. Bring back to a boil and cook for 20 minutes, until the farro is cooked but still has a slight bite, then drain and put to one side.

When the farro has been cooking for 10 minutes, put a large nonstick trying pan on a medium heat and add a drizzle of olive oil. When the oil is really hot, add the zucchini, garlic, and most of your chiles, and cook for a few minutes, until the zucchini are lightly golden but still have freshness and a bit of crunch. Add half your chopped mint, half your scallions, and a good pinch of salt and pepper. Finely grate in the zest of 1 lemon, then squeeze in the juice of both. Add a lug of olive oil, stir, and have a taste to make sure the seasoning is really good and the acid and oil are balanced.

Add the drained farro to the pan and toss everything together. Taste and season again if needed, then take the pan off the heat and leave it to cool to room temperature before folding in the remaining mint and the feta. Transfer to a platter or a large bowl and sprinkle over the reserved chiles, the small mint leaves, and the rest of the scallions.

I love this served at room temperature, but feel free to pop it into the refrigerator for later. If you do, just remember to taste again before serving, as the flavors develop and it might need a bit more seasoning.

PS: A few tablespoons of yogurt, a teaspoon of harissa, and some chopped, salted lemon will give this a Moroccan twist.

ZUCCHINI, MINT, & FARRO SALAD

Serves 4

scant 1¾ cups farro
1 organic chicken bouillon cube
olive oil
1lb baby zucchini, trimmed and sliced at an angle about ¼ inch thick
8 cloves garlic, peeled and thinly sliced
2 fresh red chiles, seeded and minced
a bunch of fresh mint, leaves picked, larger ones finely chopped, smaller ones reserved
4 scallions, trimmed and thinly sliced
sea salt and freshly ground black pepper
2 lemons
½ lb feta cheese, crumbled

Wine suggestion:
Italian dry rosé – Vinruspo Rosato

GORDITAS & SALSA

Gordita means "little fat girl" in Spanish and is meant as a sort of cute, cuddly term of endearment. It's also the name for these sweet little puffy tortillas, which are often made around Easter and other special occasions. Look at the gorditas as a tasty spoon for carrying all kinds of big exciting flavors. Mexicans put all sorts of things, from beans, to meat, to salsa, on them. I've gone for quite a delicious and delicate apple salsa here – give it a try.

★   ★   ★   ★   ★   ★

For the gorditas

4 cups masa harina (a cross between cornmeal and corn flour)
½ level teaspoon sea salt
1 heaping teaspoon baking powder
scant 3 cups hot water
all-purpose flour, for dusting
olive oil

For the salsa

1 red apple, halved and cored
3 large, ripe tomatoes, quartered and seeded
2 scallions, trimmed
1 red chile, seeded
a small bunch of fresh cilantro
1 tablespoon pumpkin seeds
1 tablespoon sunflower seeds
1 lime
sea salt and freshly ground black pepper

To serve

½ lb Don Francisco Mexican cheese, or feta (which is similar)
optional: 1 fresh red chile, very thinly sliced
1 lime, cut into wedges

Wine suggestion:
French dry white –
a Gewürztraminer from Alsace

Put the masa harina and salt into a large bowl and make a well in the center. Mix the baking powder into the hot water and pour this into the well. Using a fork, mix the masa harina into the liquid, and when it starts to come together use your hands to knead it. Divide the dough into 16 equal squash ball–sized pieces and dust them lightly with flour. Roll each piece around in your hands, then pat and flatten into a small round roughly the size of the base of a wineglass. Put these on an oiled cookie sheet, dust with flour, and put aside while you make your salsa.

Dice your apple, tomatoes, and scallions, and thinly slice your chile. Put them all into a bowl. Pick the leaves from your cilantro and put them into a bowl of ice water until you're ready to serve. Chop the cilantro stalks up nice and fine and add to the bowl with the other salsa ingredients. Put a large frying pan on a medium heat and add your pumpkin and sunflower seeds. Toss them around for a few minutes and toast them. Add them to your salsa with the juice of your lime, a good lug of olive oil, and a pinch of salt and pepper. Mix well, then have a taste and add a little more seasoning, lime juice, or chile if you think it needs more attitude.

Put the frying pan back on a medium heat and add a couple of good lugs of olive oil. Cook as many gorditas as will comfortably fit into the pan for about 2 to 3 minutes on each side, or until they're golden and puff up a little.

Serve the gorditas warm out of the pan with a tablespoon of your beautiful salsa, a little hunk of cheese, a couple of your drained cilantro leaves, and a few slices of chile, if you fancy, and with lime wedges on the side for squeezing over.

This is one of those dishes that could absolutely convince any non–chickpea lovers out there to change their minds. I love the combination of the different parts of the chicken: quick-cook breasts with slower-cooked thighs taste completely different from each other but work so well at the same time. Any other white poultry, such as turkey, guinea fowl, or pheasant, will be equally delicious cooked this way.

CHICKEN ON CHICKPEAS

Serves 4

Boil the garlic cloves for the marinade in a small pan of water for around 8 minutes, until soft. While they're cooking, lay your chicken breasts on a board, cover them with plastic wrap, and bat out each one with a pan to flatten the chicken so it cooks evenly. Drain the garlic cloves, then put them into a bowl and mash them with a fork. Stir in the parsley, lemon zest and juice, a pinch of salt and pepper, and a good lug of extra virgin olive oil.

Use your fingers to carefully make a pocket between the skin of all your chicken pieces and the meat, making sure you don't tear the skin. Push your marinade inside each hole so it flavors the meat under the skin, then press the skin flat. Rub any leftover marinade all over the skin. Put the chicken into a bowl, cover it with plastic wrap, and pop it into the refrigerator to marinate for at least 2 hours.

When you're ready to cook, preheat the oven to 400°F.

Get a large frying pan on a medium heat. Add a good lug of olive oil and the chopped onion, garlic, and paprika. Cook gently for 10 minutes, until softened but not colored, then add your sliced grilled peppers to the pan, along with the juices they came in. Add the tomatoes, drained chickpeas, a lug of vinegar, the chile, and a good pinch of salt and pepper. Give everything a good stir, bring to a boil, and simmer for half an hour. Check the seasoning, then put to one side.

Put your chicken thighs onto a large hot grill pan or grill, turning them every minute or so for 10 minutes until golden and lovely, then move them to a roasting pan and pop them into your hot oven for 15 minutes. Immediately add the chicken breasts to the griddle pan, skin side down, and cook for 10 minutes or so, turning every minute until they're golden and beautiful. Add them to the roasting pan with the thighs for the last 5 minutes of cooking.

Serve your chickpea stew topped with slices of your chicken. Drizzle with a little extra virgin olive oil and sprinkle with a few fresh basil leaves to finish.

4 single chicken breasts, preferably free-range or organic, skin on
4 small boneless chicken thighs, preferably free-range or organic, skin on
a few fresh basil leaves, to serve

For the marinade
4 cloves garlic, peeled
a bunch of fresh Italian parsley, finely chopped
finely grated zest and juice of 1 lemon
sea salt and freshly ground black pepper
extra virgin olive oil

For the chickpea stew
olive oil
1 onion, peeled and diced
4 cloves garlic, peeled and minced
½ teaspoon smoked paprika
1 x 10-oz jar grilled peppers in olive oil, roughly sliced
8 red and yellow tomatoes, seeded and roughly chopped
1 x 15-oz can good-quality chickpeas
white or red wine vinegar
1 or 2 fresh green chiles, seeded and minced

Wine suggestion:
Californian red – a Pinot Noir from Santa Barbara

STUFFED TOMATO TORTILLAS

This recipe can be taken in two different directions: either rolled up and served straightaway, or baked and served hot. A lovely lady, Maria, taught me how to make it the first way at her party on the night I arrived in Los Angeles. I had never tried dipping tortillas in tomato sauce to flavor them before, and I thought that was a great way of doing something a bit different with them. Maria and her family filled their dipped tortillas with the avocado mixture and ate them right away. They were delicious and tasty, but I wanted to take the idea a bit further, so I decided it would be interesting to bake the wraps in the tomato sauce, a bit like cannelloni in Italy. The result was also delicious, full of fresh and lovely Mexican flavors.

Serves 4

★　★　★　★　★　★

For the tomato sauce
olive oil
2 cloves garlic, peeled and finely sliced
1 x 14-oz can diced tomatoes
1 lime
sea salt and freshly ground black pepper

For the tortillas
3 ripe avocados
2 limes
8 corn tortillas
1 fresh red chile, seeded and very thinly sliced
a small bunch of fresh cilantro, leaves picked, stalks finely chopped
1 cup freshly grated Manchego or Cheddar cheese
generous 1 cup sour cream, plus extra to serve
a bottle of chile sauce

Wine suggestion:
Italian red – a young Chianti

Preheat the oven to 400°F. Get a saucepan on a medium heat and add a couple of lugs of olive oil. Add the garlic and gently fry for a couple of minutes until lightly golden. Add your canned tomatoes, squeeze in the juice of your lime, and bring to a boil, then turn the heat right down, season to taste with salt and pepper, and simmer for 10 minutes, until the sauce has slightly thickened.

While that's ticking away, halve, peel, and pit your avocados, then chop the flesh and mash it with the juice of 1 lime and a pinch of salt and pepper. At this point you can try them Maria's way: dip the tortillas in your tomato sauce for 5 seconds, move to a plate, and spoon in some avocado mixture, a sprinkling of chile, cilantro, and cheese, then roll up and eat right away with a dollop of sour cream and a few sprigs of cilantro. Delicious – and everyone at the party thought so – but I also love them baked and hot. To try them that way, take an appropriately sized baking dish and pour in some of your tomato sauce so that it coats the bottom. Divide the avocado mixture between your tortillas, and top with a sprinkling of chile, cilantro, and cheese. Roll them up, and arrange them snugly in your dish on top of the tomato sauce. Pour any leftover sauce on top, then spoon over your sour cream and any leftover cheese and chile.

Bake in the oven for 15 minutes, until golden and crisp on top. Serve with a fresh green salad, and have a bit more sour cream and some wedges of lime on the table, with a bottle of extra chile sauce in case you fancy a bit more heat.

CALIFORNIA SPROUT SALAD

This salad is something I knocked up after walking from one end of the Beverly Hills farmers' market to the other. In California it's really common for people to talk about the health benefits and nutritional value of the food they sell. Sprouts have all sorts of things going for them: they're packed with vitamins, minerals, and proteins and, amazingly, even keep growing after they've been harvested, so their vitamin content actually increases! The dressing here is insanely good. Crispy chorizo and garlic just taste absolutely heavenly together. Once it's drizzled over the salad, you've got something that's going to be frankly fantastic in a pitta or on a flatbread.

Serves 4   ★   ★   ★   ★   ★   ★

¾ lb mixed shoots and sprouts (try alfalfa, mung beans, sunflower, pea shoots, onion seeds, to name but a few)
1¼ cups freshly shelled peas
1 fresh red chile, seeded and minced
a small handful of fresh mint leaves
4 handfuls of watercress or arugula

For the dressing
olive oil
6 oz chorizo sausage, finely chopped
2 cloves garlic, peeled
¼ cups balsamic vinegar
¼ cup extra virgin olive oil
sea salt and freshly ground black pepper

Wine suggestion:
Spanish red – a young Tempranillo

Start by making your dressing. Pour a lug of olive oil into a frying pan and put it on a medium heat. Add your chopped chorizo and fry for 3 or 4 minutes until dark, golden, and crispy. Remove the pan from the heat and using a perforated spoon transfer the meat to a plate lined with paper towels.

Finely grate your garlic into the hot chorizo oil left behind in the pan, give the pan a good shake, then add your balsamic vinegar, extra virgin olive oil, and a good pinch of salt and pepper. Mix it up quickly, angling the pan in different ways as you go so you collect all the awesome flavors from the chorizo. This will give you the most fantastic warm dressing.

Once you've got a nice mixture, have a taste and add more vinegar or salt if needed until it is absolutely delicious. Put the pan to one side and let the dressing cool a bit. If you want to make it look a bit prettier, you can reserve some of the crispy sausage, garlic, chile, and mint leaves to fling over the top and help your guests realize what's in your tasty salad. You can dress your salad whenever you want, but, like any warm salad, it's only going to look good for the first 2 minutes so it's best to dress the vegetables right before you serve it. Toss everything together in a big bowl, then transfer it to a nice serving platter. It will be incredible to eat right away.

Sunday Morning at the
Beverly Hills farmers' market

By simply grilling a whole load of different vegetables until they're nicely charred, then dressing them beautifully, you can create a fantastic antipasti selection where every single mouthful pops and explodes in your mouth. This method of grilling really brings out wonderfully nutty flavors in the vegetables. Each of the dressings here goes really well with its vegetable. What more could you want on a sunny day?

CALIFORNIAN ANTIPASTI

★ ★ ★ ★ ★ ★

Serves 6

Start by making your different dressings: line up 5 bowls and whack one of the different sets of ingredients into each one. For all of them you'll need to season to taste with salt and pepper and add the same amount of extra virgin olive oil as you have of acid, whether this is juice or vinegar. Give each dressing a quick stir and put aside.

Trim and wash the vegetables you'll be using to get them ready for grilling. The only vegetables that are slightly fussy to prep are the artichokes, but it isn't nearly as difficult as you might think. Just trim the stalk off about 1¾ inches from the base, then slice the top 1¾ inches off the head. Quickly click back the outer leaves to reveal the tender light green leaves. Peel the stalk and the base of the artichoke with a knife and a peeler, and right away rub it all over with a lemon half to stop it going black. Cut it in half, and get rid of the furry "choke" in the center and any fluffy bits. Rub the heart that's left behind with lemon too. If you still feel you need a bit of extra help with this process, go to www.jamieoliver.com/how-to and you'll find a video of this being done.

Get your grill nice and hot, or heat a large dry grill pan on a high heat. Grill the vegetables so they get little bar marks on all sides, keeping an eye on things. Use your instincts – when the vegetables look beautiful and cooked but still have some bite to them, they're perfect, so get them off the grill and toss them in their preferred dressings.

Serve with grilled meats, seafood, or as part of a simple antipasti like I've done here, with some toasted bread rubbed with raw garlic, a selection of cured meats and beautiful cheeses like Manchego or Gorgonzola. Just get your head in the right place and you'll be able to rattle this out in no time.

2 zucchini, halved lengthways and seeded
2 yellow squash, halved lengthways and seeded
6 baby or violet artichokes
1 lemon, halved
a bunch of thin asparagus
a bunch of large scallions
1 large fennel bulb, trimmed and cut into 8 wedges, leafy tops reserved for the dressing
a loaf of ciabatta or sourdough bread, to serve
1 whole head of garlic, sliced in half across the middle

For each of the dressings
extra virgin olive oil
sea salt and freshly ground black pepper

For the zucchini and yellow squash
a few sprigs of fresh mint, leaves picked and finely chopped
½ lemon

For the artichokes
a few sprigs of fresh oregano, leaves picked and finely chopped
juice and zest of ½ orange

For the scallions
a few sprigs of fresh basil, leaves picked and finely chopped
2 tablespoons white wine vinegar

For the asparagus
a few sprigs of fresh dill, leaves picked and finely chopped
½ lemon

For the fennel
finely chopped fennel tops
zest and juice of 1 lime

Wine suggestion: a Californian dry rosé

HOMEBOY

When I was in East LA, I went to visit an incredible project called Homeboy Industries. It is a social, entrepreneurial, and visionary masterpiece, aimed at getting kids away from gang culture, teaching them a useful trade, and giving them some stability. From my experience of running my Fifteen Foundation charity restaurants, I could see it was fantastic, reassuring, and a little emotional to see a similar thing happening in LA: proceeds from an exceptional business going toward training people who need a break in life. The two main parts of the Homeboy business are a restaurant and a bakery, but attached to these are a tattoo-removal place and a counselling office, as well as all sorts of other brilliant businesses. It's a magnet for people who want to make changes in their life.

The restaurant, Homegirl Café, was run by the girls, and the team had a great family feel to it. They were making incredible salads, all named after different members of staff or their customers. The food was Mexican, but completely out of the realms of Mexican food as I knew it – there were no clichés here, and watching them in the kitchen gave me all sorts of ideas for killer salads and dressings, some of which are in this chapter.

The heavily tattooed boys in the Homeboy bakery looked incredibly menacing, and some of the stories I heard (murder, drugs, etc.) sent shudders down my spine. But I soon forgot all that because they were cranking out some of the best breads and most delicate and beautiful cakes I'd ever seen, and were filled with pride in their work.

If you're in the LA area, I urge you to jump in a cab and get down to Homeboy. You'll leave inspired, having eaten an amazing lunch. I firmly believe that projects like Homeboy, Fifteen, or Delancey Street in San Francisco are invaluable. They give people who really need it a second chance to find love and pride in a safe place. If you're interested in finding out more about these organizations, visit the following websites: www.homeboy-industries.org, www.fifteen.net, or www.delanceystreetfoundation.org.

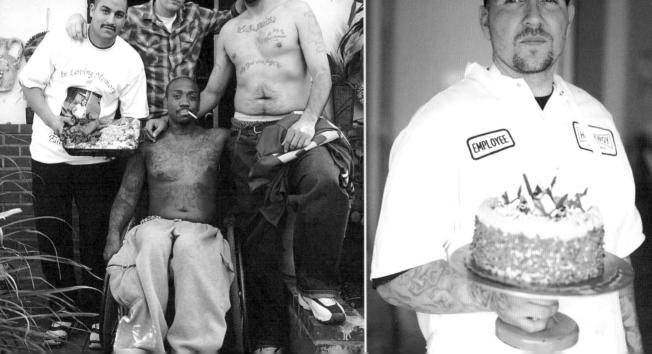

1 STEAK 2 SAUCES

As a lover of good steak, I had quite a few conversations with people in LA about how they liked to eat theirs. This dish is a result of me soaking up all those vibes. I'm pairing a cooked sauce, made with peanuts and spices, with a fresh green salsa that is going to send your taste buds into orbit. If you notice that your peanut sauce is lighter than mine, don't worry. The peanuts I used in LA were just darker. It will still taste delicious.

Serves 4

★   ★   ★   ★   ★   ★

For the steak
4 x ½-lb toploin (strip) or rib-eye steaks (approx. 1 inch thick)
olive oil
a sprig of fresh rosemary
1 clove garlic, halved

For the peanut sauce
¼ lb roasted peanuts in the shell, shelled, skins removed
¼ cup sesame seeds
1 teaspoon dried oregano
1 teaspoon cumin seeds
a few sprigs of fresh thyme, leaves picked
1 smoked chipotle chile, crumbled (or 1 teaspoon smoked paprika)
3 cloves garlic, peeled and thinly sliced
scant ½ cup extra virgin olive oil
a slug of rum
juice of 1 lime
1–2 fresh green chiles, stalks removed, seeds left in
sea salt and freshly ground black pepper

For the Mexican salsa verde
a small bunch of fresh cilantro
a small bunch of fresh mint, leaves picked
1 clove garlic, peeled
1–2 fresh red or green chiles, seeded
4 large scallions, trimmed
2 tomatoes, roughly chopped
juice of 1–2 limes

Wine suggestion:
French red – a Syrah such as Crozes Hermitage or Saint-Joseph from the northern Rhône Valley

Take your steaks out of the refrigerator and let them get up to room temperature while you make your peanut sauce. Put a dry frying pan on a medium heat and toast the nuts and sesame seeds for a few minutes, until lightly browned. Add the oregano, cumin seeds, thyme, chipotle chile, and garlic and cook for another minute or so. Tip into a liquidizer with the extra virgin olive oil, rum, lime juice, fresh chiles, salt and pepper, and just over ¾ cup of water. Whiz until shiny and smooth, then have a taste and adjust with a bit more salt, chile, or lime juice if needed. Put to one side.

To make your salsa, get yourself a good knife and a big cutting board. Set aside a few of the cilantro leaves, then chop the top of the bunch, stalks and all, with the mint leaves, garlic, chiles, scallions, and tomatoes until it's all very fine – watch your fingers here! Sprinkle over a generous pinch of salt and pepper, then add most of the lime juice and a good lug of extra virgin olive oil. Mix together on the board, taste it, season with more salt, pepper, lime juice, or chile, and put it into a bowl ready to go.

Get a frying pan, grill pan, or grill screaming hot and season both sides of your steaks with salt, pepper, and a good drizzle of olive oil. Add the steaks to the pan or grill. Turn every minute and cook to your liking. I'm going to give you some rough timings, but use your intuition: a ½ lb steak about 1 inch thick wants about 2 minutes each side for medium rare and 3 minutes each side for medium. As it cooks, whip the meat with the sprig of rosemary and rub it with the cut side of the garlic clove for some extra flavor.

When the steaks are perfectly cooked to your liking, move them to a plate to rest for a few minutes. Cut them into ½-inch-thick slices, spread the peanut sauce all over a large serving platter or divide between your plates, and gently put the slices of steak on top. Finish with a few dollops of salsa, and scatter over your remaining cilantro leaves. Drizzle over any resting juices and let everyone tuck in. This goes beautifully with the Mexican street salad (see page 198).

TUNA TARTAR

If beautiful fresh fish inspires you like it does me, this is something you have to try. You'll get small, dainty portions, but each bite will be a real wake-up for the senses. Tartare is seen as a really cheffy thing to make, because most people, unless they're quite foodie, won't eat raw meat or fish at home. But if you get some insanely fresh sustainable tuna that looks the business – purply pink and glossy with a fresh smell of the sea – this will be heaven.

Serves 4 as an appetizer

★　　★　　★　　★　　★　　★

olive oil
2 cloves garlic, peeled
and very thinly sliced
a small bunch of fresh cilantro
1 scallion
1 fresh green chile, stalk removed
3 limes
sea salt and freshly
ground black pepper
½ lb sustainably caught
(sushi-grade) tuna
2 blood oranges, peeled and
sliced into rounds, pips removed
10 red or yellow cherry or
grape tomatoes, quartered
4 heaping teaspoons sour cream

Wine suggestion:
Australian dry white – a Riesling

Pour a few good lugs of olive oil into a small saucepan over a medium heat. Gently fry the garlic slices until they are lightly golden crisps; don't let them burn. Remove them to some paper towels to drain. Pick 8 cilantro leaves and put them to one side in a little cup of cold water.

This is best served right away while the flavors are all super fresh, so when you're ready to eat, put half your bunch of cilantro, half your scallions, and half your chile into a liquidizer and blitz with the juice of 1 lime and about the same amount of olive oil. Season and balance so it's got attitude and a kick. If it needs to be loosened, add a tiny splash of water. Finely chop the remaining half of your cilantro, scallion, and chile on a board with the tuna until the mixture is as chunky or fine as you like.

At this point you're nearly ready to go, so lay 2 or 3 of your orange slices in the middle of each of 4 little plates and spoon your blitzed green sauce around them. Toss the tuna mixture in a bowl with the juice of the second lime and the same amount of olive oil. Have a taste, season it really well, then spoon your tuna tartare over your orange slices. Top with a few tomato quarters and a dollop of sour cream, then sprinkle over some of your garlic chips and your pretty cilantro leaves. Serve right away with wedges from your third lime. If you want to add some more sliced chile or a pinch of paprika, rock on!

THESE HOMEBOYS SURE KNOW HOW TO BAKE A GOOD CAKE

This is a serious indulgence of the senses. I took some inspiration from the savory mole sauce that Mexicans serve with their meat. Mole (pronounced mo-lay) uses thirty-seven spices, so I took elements of that and turned it into a chocolate dusting for this incredible chocolate filling. Once it sets, you'll have this dark and outrageously sexy filling that's silky and heavy in your mouth. Make this for someone special and they'll want to marry you!

CHOCOLATE MOLE TART

Serves 10–12

Follow the sweet pastry recipe on page 122, leaving your oven on at 350°F when you take your tart crust out to cool.

Spread the hazelnuts out on a sheet pan and place in your hot oven for 6 to 8 minutes, until golden. Remove from the oven and leave to cool, but leave the oven on.

Heat 1 inch of water in a pan over a low heat and put a large heatproof glass bowl over the top of it, making sure the bottom of the bowl doesn't touch the water. Put your bashed-up chocolate into the bowl with a pinch of salt. When it starts to melt, add the butter and give it the occasional gentle stir. Keep the heat low or the chocolate will split. Turn the heat off once everything is smooth and melted.

Pour 5 tablespoons of cold water into a clean pan on a low heat with ¾ cup of the sugar and whisk gently. When all the sugar has dissolved and you have a smooth syrup, set aside.

You want the eggs to get really fluffy, so put them into the bowl of an electric mixer or use an electric hand mixer and add the remaining ¼ cup of sugar. Mix for about 4 minutes, until pale and frothy. At this point, slowly pour in your warm sugar syrup, mixing as you go. Turn the mixer off, pour in the melted chocolate, then mix again for 10 seconds, no longer.

Use the back of a spoon to spread the dulce de leche around the entire base of the cooled tart crust until evenly coated. Bash up your roasted hazelnuts and sprinkle them all over the dulce de leche. Pour over the chocolate filling mixture, using a spoon to even it out. Put the tart on a sheet pan and bake in the hot oven for 17 minutes, until the chocolate has set around the edges but is quite wobbly in the middle (have faith!). Put to one side and let it cool for 2 hours (if you can bear it!) – the filling will settle a little as it cools.

When ready to serve, use a pestle and mortar to bash all the spicy dusting ingredients together until fine. Sieve this over the tart for the finishing touch and serve with a dollop of crème fraîche. You won't believe what's happening in your mouth. Store any leftover chocolate dust in the refrigerator and use it to jazz up ice-cream or hot chocolate.

1 x sweet pastry recipe (see page 122)
optional: 1 blood orange, peeled and sliced into rounds, to serve
optional: crème fraîche, to serve

For the filling
heaping ¾ cup hazelnuts
2 x 4-oz bars good-quality bittersweet chocolate (70% cocoa solids), bashed up
sea salt
11 tablespoons unsalted butter, chopped into cubes
1 cup superfine sugar
3 large eggs, preferably free-range or organic
4–5 tablespoons dulce de leche or caramel sauce

For the spicy dusting
1 level teaspoon ground cinnamon
2 whole cloves
1 level teaspoon coriander seeds
1 dried red chile
zest of ½ orange
4 heaping teaspoons unsweetened cocoa powder
2 heaping teaspoons confectioners' sugar
a few pinches of sea salt

Wine suggestion:
Spanish sweet sherry – Pedro Ximénez

This is a lovely recipe for shortcake, which is a bit of a cross between a cookie and a cake, making it perfect to serve as a dessert. In the picture I served it with California peaches and a sort of vanilla cream. But since making it back home, I've found stirring bashed-up chocolate through the cream gives it a sort of chocolate chip vibe that works brilliantly too, so I'm giving you that recipe here. But, depending on what's in season where you are, you can certainly play around with this and serve it with apricots, plums, strawberries, or raspberries. The key to it being delicious is to use perfectly ripe fruit. From the Highlands of Scotland to the sprawling mass of Los Angeles, things like shortbread and shortcake are not a million miles away from each other. People need their biscuits, man!

PEACH SHORT CAKE

Serves 8–10

Preheat the oven to 400°F. Put all the dry shortcake ingredients into a food processor, grate in the zest of your oranges, and pulse until combined. Add the butter and pulse again until the mixture starts to look like coarse meal. If doing this by hand, simply rub the butter into the dry ingredients using your fingertips until the mixture resembles coarse meal. Add the cream a splash at a time and pulse quickly or stir until you've got dough, then stop. Dust a clean surface with flour, tip the dough onto it, and use your hands to knead it a little and bring it together into a round shape roughly the size of a salad plate (about 8½ inches) and about ½ inch thick.

Cover a sheet pan with a piece of parchment paper, dust it with a little cornmeal, and put your round of dough on top. Using the back of a knife, score the top of the dough into 8 wedges to pre-portion it and place the sheet pan in the oven. Bake for 18 to 20 minutes, until lightly golden and spread out, then remove from the oven, sprinkle with a little sugar and put to one side to cool.

While the shortcake is cooking, halve and pit the peaches and cut each half into 4 wedges. Place these in a bowl and squeeze over the juice from the zested oranges. Roughly tear the mint leaves and add most of them to the bowl along with the sugar. Give it all a good stir and put to one side until ready to serve.

To make the chocolate chip cream, lightly whip the heavy cream to soft peaks with the sugar. Bash up most of the chocolate into very small pieces, reserving a piece for grating over later, and stir these into the cream. Add the vanilla extract and gently fold everything together.

Serve the shortcake with a good dollop of the chocolate cream, a few peaches, and any leftover juices drizzled over. Sprinkle with your remaining mint leaves, finely grate over the reserved chocolate, and dive in.

For the shortcake
1½ cups all-purpose flour, plus extra for dusting
scant ½ cup cornmeal
1 tablespoon baking powder
a pinch of sea salt
½ cup superfine sugar, plus extra for dusting
2 oranges
7 tablespoons chilled butter, cubed
¾ cup heavy cream

For the peaches
4 ripe peaches
4 sprigs of fresh mint, leaves picked
2 heaping teaspoons sugar, to taste

For the chocolate chip cream
¼ cup heavy cream
1 teaspoon superfine sugar
½ x 4-oz bar good-quality bittersweet chocolate (70% cocoa solids)
1 teaspoon vanilla extract

Wine suggestion:
sweet light white pudding wine
– such as a Moscato d'Asti

CHOCOLATE ROCKY ROAD

Makes 12 chunky pieces

2 x 4-oz bars good-quality bittersweet chocolate (70% cocoa solids)
½ fresh red chile, seeded and diced
heaping 1 cup mixed unsalted nuts, such as almonds, hazelnuts, pistachios, or pecans
1 tablespoon sunflower or pumpkin seeds
¾ cup mixed dried fruit, such as golden raisins, dried mango, dried sour cherries, or cranberries, larger bits chopped

Wine suggestion:
a glass of chilled Tawny Port

I remember those chocolate refrigerator cakes from back in the day that had meringue, oatmeal, and other bits and pieces in them. This delicious treat has a similar vibe. In California they use all sorts of lovely dried fruits like salted mango, nuts, and even red chiles, which might sound a bit scary but is actually quite subtle and delicious. It's damn good, and if you're a parent, setting fruit and nuts in a lava flow of chocolate is as good as it gets.

In California, I made a really big slab of this for everyone to enjoy. If you have got a lot of mouths to feed, feel free to double or even triple this recipe to suit your needs.

★   ★   ★   ★   ★   ★

Preheat your oven to 400°F. Smash up the chocolate and melt it in a heatproof glass bowl over a saucepan of simmering water, making sure the bowl doesn't touch the water. Once the chocolate is smooth and melted, remove the bowl from the heat and put to one side. While the chocolate is melting, put the chile on a sheet pan with the mixed nuts and the seeds. Place in the hot oven for 5 minutes, until the nuts are toasted and shiny. Leave to cool for a few minutes, then roughly chop everything together on a board and mix with the dried fruit in a bowl.

Put a large handful of this fruit and nut mixture to one side, and tip the rest into the bowl of chocolate. Stir well until everything is completely coated. Line a baking tray with a piece of parchment or wax paper and spoon the chocolate mixture onto it, using the back of a spoon to smooth it out to the sides. Sprinkle the reserved fruit and nuts evenly over the top, and leave in a cool place or in the refrigerator for 30 minutes to set.

Once the rocky road has set, smash it up into bite-size or larger pieces and pile up on a serving plate. Lovely with a cup of coffee, or even finely bashed up over some good-quality vanilla ice cream. Any leftover bits will keep happily for up to a week in an airtight container but you'll struggle to keep them around for that long!

THE AMAZING DATE SHAKE

Makes 2 shakes

This milk shake is a shout-out to all the date producers in California. It's delicious and dead simple. Just chuck 20 pitted dates into a liquidizer with a cup of milk and blitz until smooth. Add a small handful of ice cubes and a pinch of ground cinnamon and whiz again. Serve straightaway in tall glasses.

Fill a regular coffee mug with superfine sugar and pour it into a small saucepan with 2 fresh bay leaves, a small handful of fresh basil leaves, and 1 cinnamon stick. Fill the same mug again with water, add that to the pan too, and bring everything to a boil, stirring gently. Once the sugar has completely dissolved and it's clear, pour immediately through a strainer into a large earthenware dish, discarding the herbs and cinnamon. Pour in 1 quart of freshly squeezed blood orange juice (or any other citrus juice you fancy). Stir, then cover with plastic wrap and place in the freezer. After a few hours use 2 forks to scuff it up into fluffy frosty shards, and serve.

BLOOD ORANGE GRANITA

CHILE VINEGAR

Makes 1½ cups

1 x 12-oz bottle of red or white
wine vinegar or cider vinegar
2 or 3 fresh red or green chiles
2 fresh bay leaves
optional: 2 teaspoons sugar

Flavoring vinegar is a really cool thing to do. Simply squashing a few chiles, spices, or different herbs into a bottle of white or red wine vinegar or apple cider vinegar turns it into something much more interesting and special. It's dead cheap, looks good, and will make salad dressings, marinades, sauces, and salsas taste better. Use this in place of regular vinegar in any of the recipes in this book. I first tried this drizzle over Miss Betty's collard greens in Georgia (page 269) and it was genius.

★　　★　　★　　★　　★　　★

Take your bottle of vinegar and decant about a quarter of it into a jug to use with salads or anything else you fancy another day. Prick your chiles with a fork and scrunch up the bay leaves to get their flavors going, then shove them into the bottle along with a bit of sugar if you like. Pop the top on the bottle and give it a good shake to chuff everything up and help the flavors mix. Keep the chile vinegar in your refrigerator, ready to be sprinkled over everything from collard greens, to stews, to root vegetable salads, and even used in dressings.

HOT CHILE SAUCE

Makes ½ cups

2 medium onions, peeled
2 cloves garlic, peeled
12 fresh red chiles, stalks cut off
olive oil
2 teaspoons chili powder (depending
on how hot you like it)
6 tomatoes, chopped
⅔ cup apple cider vinegar
2 tablespoons sugar
1 cup apple juice
sea salt and freshly ground
black pepper

Even though you can definitely buy great chile sauces these days, it's loads of fun making your own. You can usually find two or three types of fresh chiles in supermarkets or grocery stores, and frankly, the more the merrier! Aside from being a great condiment to have on hand, chile sauce is integral to quite a few recipes in this book.

If you're going to make this, I'd multiply the recipe by four and make a year's worth. Put it into small sterilized jars or bottles (see page 296 for sterilizing instructions), then immerse them, with the lids on, in boiling water and simmer for 10 minutes or so to get them ready for storing or for giving away to friends who could use a bit of excitement in their lives.

★　　★　　★　　★　　★　　★

Blitz your onions, garlic, and chiles in a liquidizer or food processor, or chop them up roughly. Heat a good lug of olive oil in a large frying pan and gently fry the onions, garlic, and chiles on a low heat for around 10 minutes, until softened but not colored. Add your chile powder and fry for a further 1–2 minutes. Add the tomatoes, vinegar, sugar, apple juice, scant ½ cup of water, and a good pinch of salt and pepper. Bring to a boil, then reduce to a low heat and simmer for around 10 to 15 minutes, stirring occasionally. You want it to be a pouring consistency and not too thick, so add a splash of water to help it along.

Allow your chile sauce to cool, then blitz until smooth. Pass twice through a fine strainer to get a lovely smooth consistency, then have a taste, adjust the seasoning, and add a splash more vinegar if needed. If you're going to use your sauce quickly, you can just put it into the refrigerator in a bowl and you'll have about a week to use it up. If you want to keep it for longer, simply divide it between your sterilized jars or bottles (see page 296) and store it in a cool, dark place or the refrigerator until you need it.

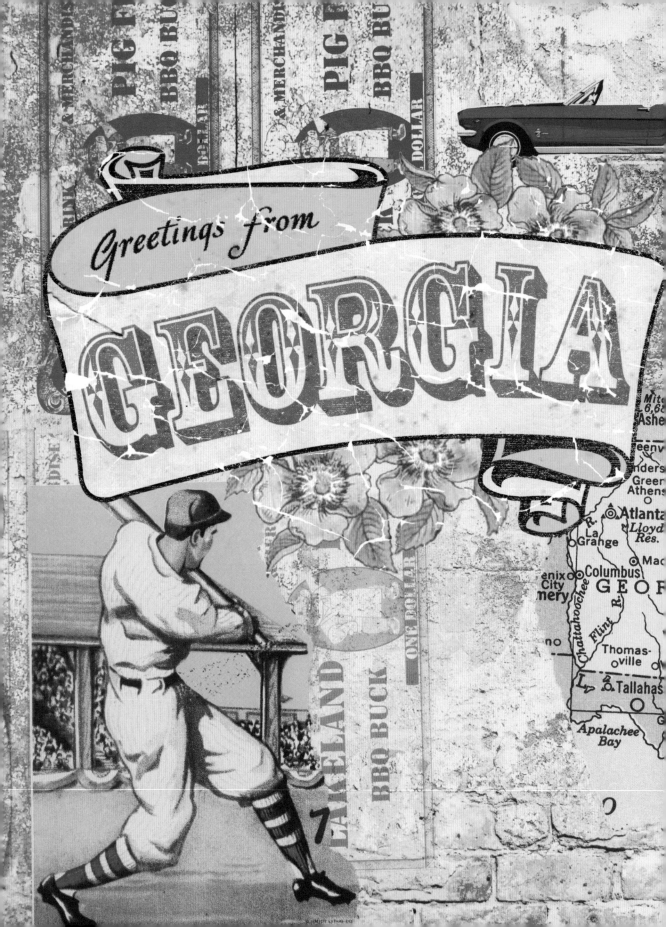

Because I'd always wanted to do a proper American-style road trip, I decided to rent an RV and drive myself through the lovely state of Georgia. From what I saw, it had a bit of everything going for it. The Atlanta nightlife was very cool and buzzy, as was the city, and Savannah was absolutely gorgeous – full of old-world charm, big beautiful houses, and trees dripping with Spanish moss. The smaller towns along the highway all seemed to have that quaint American "Main Street" feel to them and were surrounded by plenty of lovely countryside.

Not only did this road trip give me a chance to explore the towns and cities in Georgia, it also meant I got to meet all sorts of wonderful people. I'm here to tell you that the reason Southern hospitality is so legendary is because it's real! I visited a Baptist church, a family homestead, a roadside barbecue joint, and a Savannah soul food restaurant, and ate posh desserts with some proper Southern belles, and everyone, without exception, threw the door open and welcomed me with plenty of warmth and plenty of food!

I'm happy to say that family and community seemed to be very important everywhere I went; the way all the age groups shared time is not too far away from what goes on in the quaintest villages in Europe. Whether I was hanging out at a black community event or eating dinner with "white folk" in the country, one thing seemed pretty consistent: everyone had a healthy respect for their "mama" and "papa," which unfortunately isn't always the case elsewhere. I found everyone incredibly well mannered and didn't catch anybody swearing (which was a bit of a shock to me – I had to mind my p's and q's!). If you're a total stranger, that doesn't matter, people from the South will just use terms of endearment like "sugar" or "darlin'" until they get to know you better. That easy familiarity with people is, to me anyway, a real talent, and everyone's open, friendly attitude put me right at ease.

In Gray, Jones County, I met one of the nicest families, headed up by a wonderful mum and dad. Lonnie Senior was a retired pastor, and his lovely wife, "Miss Betty," really knew her way around the kitchen. To introduce me to Southern-style cooking, Miss Betty served up the most incredible array of food. She said it was something she always did for family gatherings so that there was plenty of choice, but she must have been cooking for days! Some of the delicious dishes in this chapter, like the comforting turkey stew (page 255), were inspired by things I tried at her table. Lonnie Senior very kindly gave me some of his personal store of venison, left over from the hunting season, for my venison and creamy beans dish (page 247) – I was nervous about cooking for them after eating all their wonderful food, but they loved it, and Miss Betty even said it was good enough to be considered a Southern dish.

Their son, Lonnie Junior (aka Bubba), was head of the local barbecue association and an absolute expert in all things grilled. He competed in various big barbecue competitions with his team, "Bubba Grills," and when he invited me to cook at a huge competition in Florida called Pig Fest, it seemed like too good an opportunity to pass up. There were going to be seventy-six professional barbecue experts competing and up to 30,000 people visiting, so it was a pretty big deal. I was a bit worried what the rest of his team would make of a British boy joining them, but his sons and friends were absolutely fantastic people and really included me. Pig Fest turned out to be a good laugh, and I'm happy to say that we didn't do badly!

Because lima beans aren't as common in Britain as they are in Georgia, I decided to use the wonderful broad bean for my Southern creamy beans. The marinade I've used here is absolutely amazing, and although for beef the flavors would probably be a bit too strong, venison, quail, pigeon, and lamb are all bold enough to handle them.

Venison is such an underrated meat, and in the supermarkets people will often pass it by. In the UK, whatever you're allowed to hunt can also be bought by the public, but in Georgia, buying game is illegal, so they rely on the hunting season to stock up for personal use. You can also check farmers' markets for farm-raised venison.

★　　★　　★　　★　　★　　★

Make your marinade first by chopping up your thyme leaves and garlic very finely, or bashing them up in a pestle and mortar. Put them into a bowl with your balsamic vinegar, extra virgin olive oil, and a good pinch of salt and pepper and mix, then pour half this mixture into a large sandwich bag and add your pieces of venison. Seal the bag, then rub the bag all over, to massage the flavors into the meat, and put to one side.

Put a large frying pan on a medium heat and add a drizzle of olive oil. Add the bacon and cook until golden and crispy, then add the rosemary, diced onion, celery, and carrot and cook for 15 minutes, stirring occasionally, until the vegetables have softened. Add your lima and corn to the pan with the broth and cream, then give it a good stir and cook with the lid on for 5 minutes. Season well with salt and pepper, and if it's thick and creamy, it's ready. If it's watery, carry on simmering with the lid off until it thickens. Set aside.

Put another large frying pan on a high heat and let it get screaming hot. Add the marinated venison and keep turning it every 30 seconds for 5 to 8 minutes, until cooked to your liking. For the last 30 seconds of cooking, pour all the reserved marinade into the pan. Shake it all around, then tip the venison and all the juices onto a plate and let the meat rest for about 3 minutes.

While your meat is resting, check on the beans and, if you want, pop them back on the heat for a couple of minutes. Move the meat to a board and slice it fairly thickly at an angle, then put your creamy beans on a big platter and serve the venison slices on top. Drizzle over any juices from the board or plate, and tuck in right away.

VENISON & CREAMY BEANS

Serves 4–6

4–6 x ½-lb pieces of trimmed venison loin
olive oil
4 slices of smoked bacon, the best quality you can afford, finely diced
4 sprigs of fresh rosemary, leaves picked
1 onion, peeled and diced
1 celery stalk, trimmed and diced
1 carrot, peeled and diced
2⅓ cups frozen broad or lima beans
2 cups frozen corn
1½ cups chicken broth, preferably organic
scant ½ cup heavy cream
a pat of butter

For the marinade
a small bunch of fresh thyme, leaves picked
4 cloves garlic, peeled
½ cup balsamic vinegar
½ cup extra virgin olive oil
sea salt and freshly ground black pepper

Wine suggestion:
French red – a Fronsac, St-Emilion, or Pomerol from Bordeaux

SOUTHERN PECAN & APPLE SALAD

I've noticed that Southern women put plenty of time and care into their food, so it's nice to respect that by taking a bit of time to slice the apples for this salad delicately and make them look beautiful. This is such a light and colorful salad, but it's also a wonderful base, which you can manipulate into a more substantial meal by adding things like crispy bacon, shredded pork, blue cheese, slices of clementine, chervil, tarragon, or basil. Any of these things stirred through will build on what is already an absolutely delicious salad.

Spend a bit of time washing and preparing your salad leaves and dry them either in a spinner or by swinging them around in a dish towel above your head like a lunatic. This will make a big difference to the way the dressing sticks to the salad leaves, so it's well worth doing.

Serves 4   ★   ★   ★   ★   ★   ★

olive oil
2 tablespoons butter
⅓ cup (packed) light brown sugar
scant 1 cup pecan halves
2 red or green apples
2 heads Belgian endive, leaves removed, washed and spun dry
a couple of handfuls of mixed leaves, such as arugula and radicchio, washed and spun dry

For the dressing
zest and juice of 1 orange
1 teaspoon Dijon mustard
1 tablespoon white wine vinegar
3 tablespoons extra virgin olive oil
sea salt and freshly ground black pepper

Wine suggestion:
Italian dry rosato – a Montepulciano d'Abruzzo Cerasuolo

Lightly rub a sheet pan with some olive oil and put to one side. Put a large saucepan on a low heat and add your butter and sugar. Leave on a gentle simmer for a couple of minutes, stirring occasionally to stop it catching, until the sugar has completely dissolved and the mixture starts to darken. Gently stir in your pecans until they're well coated in the caramel syrup. Be careful not to splash yourself, and don't be tempted to have a taste because hot caramel can burn quite badly. Once coated, tip the nuts onto the oiled pan and use the back of a spoon to separate them out into one layer. Leave them to cool so the caramel can harden on the nuts.

Meanwhile, make your dressing. Put your orange zest and juice, Dijon mustard, and white wine vinegar into a large salad bowl and add a good lug of extra virgin olive oil. Whisk them, then have a taste – you want to get a nice balance between the sharpness of the vinegar and the smoothness of the oil, so add a little more oil if needed, then season carefully with salt and pepper.

Core, quarter, and thinly slice your apples and add to the bowl with all your leaves. Break the cooled pecans apart, add half of them to the bowl, and use your hands to delicately toss and dress everything. Serve on one big platter, or divide up between plates, and finish by crumbling over the rest of your beautiful caramel pecans.

This is a scrumptious little recipe with big flavors and big attitude. I've used quail, which I asked the butcher to spatchcock (cut along the backbone, leaving the breastbone attached, then flatten out) for me, but you'll also get amazing results with chunks of rabbit or other birds such as spatchcocked cornish hens or pigeons. If you do use different birds, just bear in mind that they'll be a bit bigger than these little quail and will want longer in the pan to cook through. At its heart this is simply cooked meat with smashed veggies, it's what happens in the last few minutes when you're making the sauce that puts the magic into it. Good fun to make and gorgeous to eat. If you want to cook this for more than two people, simply up the number of quail (along with your other ingredients) and roast them in an oven preheated to full whack until crispy and delicious while you make your sauce. Toss them in the pan to coat them, then pop them back into the oven to glaze and set for a minute or two. Dead easy!

GLAZED QUAIL & TURNIP SMASH

Serves 2

Put the turnips into a pan with some cold salted water and bring to a boil. Once boiling, add the potatoes and continue to boil for 10 to 14 minutes, until a small knife goes through them very easily. Drain in a colander, leave to steam dry, then return them to the pan and add a large pat of butter and a good pinch of salt and pepper. Crush with the back of a spoon so the veg are smashed, but still quite rustic and chunky. Have a taste to make sure you've got the seasoning perfect, then cover with a lid or some foil to keep warm while you cook your quail.

Put a large thick-bottomed frying pan or skillet on a high heat. Toss the quail in some olive oil, a pinch of salt and pepper, and a pinch of cayenne. Rub the flavors all over the meat, inside and out, then lay your oiled quail in the hot pan. Cook for about 8 minutes, skin side down, until golden and crispy, then flip them onto the other side for a minute or two more.

After the quail have been cooking for a few minutes, add the bacon. It's your job to keep turning things and watching the meat, so use your instincts and turn the heat up or down if you think it needs it. When the quail and bacon are golden and gorgeous-looking all over, turn the heat down to low. Add a pat of butter, ¼ teaspoon of cayenne, and the sugar. Pour in the Worcestershire sauce and ¼ cup of water, and stir and jiggle it about to create a wonderful glazy, spicy sauce. Keep turning the meat so it gets nicely coated, and after about 2 minutes have a taste of the sauce. It should have a fine balance of sweet and spicy, so add another pinch of cayenne if you like a bit of a kick, as I do. If you think it's a bit dry, feel free to add a splash more of water.

To serve, divide the smash between 2 plates or spread it over a platter, with your quail on top. Roughly chop your parsley leaves, sprinkle them over with a little hit of cayenne pepper, and serve with some simple boiled greens. Absolutely delicious.

For the smash
½ lb turnips, peeled and cut into 1-inch pieces
sea salt and freshly ground black pepper
½ lb potatoes, such as Yukon Gold, peeled and cut into 2-inch chunks
a large pat of butter

For the quail
4 spatchcocked quail
olive oil
cayenne pepper
8 slices of smoked bacon, the best quality you can afford, roughly chopped into 1-inch pieces
a pat of butter
2 heaping tablespoons dark brown sugar
½ cup Worcestershire sauce, such as Lea & Perrins
a small bunch of fresh Italian parsley

Wine suggestion:
New Zealand red – a Pinot Noir from Marlborough

THE SMITHS HAD A CHARMING HOME,
A BACKYARD SHED FULL OF QUIRKY GEAR,
AND FREEZERS FULL OF BEAUTIFUL VENISON

I was treated to some seriously delicious Southern food at a family get-together in the town of Gray. The mother of the household, Miss Betty, made a bloody tasty and comforting stew, and this is my take on it. Miss Betty let me in on a little secret: she'd used leftover roast turkey, a can of mushroom soup, and a box of dumpling mix for hers. I've tried to achieve those flavors by making mine from scratch and am really pleased with the results. For those of you used to round dumplings, let me introduce you to flat rolled dumplings ... they remind me a bit of pappardelle and are rather delicious!

COMFORTING TURKEY STEW

★　　★　　★　　★　　★　　★

Serves 6–8

Put a large frying pan on a medium high heat and add your diced onions and a lug of olive oil. Fry gently for 10 minutes or so, but don't let the onions color. Add your sliced turkey and pour in 1 quart of chicken broth to cover the turkey completely. Don't worry if it looks like a lot of liquid, because your dumplings will soak up a fair amount. Bring to a boil, then turn down the heat and simmer gently for 30 minutes with the lid on.

Meanwhile, make your dumplings. Put your flour into a mixing bowl, make a well in the middle and crack in your egg. Add a good pinch of salt and pepper and 5 or 6 gratings of nutmeg. Mix together with a fork, add 2 to 3 tablespoons of the simmering broth from the pan, a splash at a time, and knead until you have a smooth dough. Cover the bowl with plastic wrap and pop the bowl into the refrigerator.

When the turkey is ready, shred the meat apart with 2 forks, then add the mushrooms to the pan with the cream and stir. Have a taste and season to your liking with salt and pepper, then let it tick away while you get on with finishing the dumplings.

Dust a clean worktop and a rolling pin with flour and roll the dough out until it's roughly the size of this open book and the thickness of a quarter. Slice into 18 to 20 ribbons about ¾ inch wide and stir these into your stew. They suck up quite a bit of moisture, so add a splash more broth if and when needed. Bring back to a boil, then turn down and simmer gently for 10 minutes.

At this stage your dumplings should be soft and cooked through, so roughly chop your parsley leaves and add them to the stew. Finely grate over the fragrant lemon zest and ½ clove of garlic right at the end. Stir, then check the seasoning one last time. Divide everything between your bowls and serve right away with a fresh green salad and some hot crispy bread.

3 onions, peeled and diced
olive oil
1¾ lbs skinless turkey breast, preferably free-range or organic, cut into ½-inch slices
1¼ quarts chicken broth, preferably organic
½ lb small white or crimini mushrooms, thinly sliced
⅔ cup heavy cream
a small bunch of fresh flat-leaf parsley
1 lemon
½ clove garlic, peeled

For the dumplings
1¼ cups all-purpose flour, plus extra for dusting
1 large egg, preferably free-range or organic
sea salt and freshly ground black pepper
whole nutmeg

Wine suggestion:
French dry white – a Côtes du Rhône, from either the Marsanne or Roussanne grape or a blend

CRAB BALLS WITH SALSA

I always think crab balls or cakes are much tastier and more delicate if you use as few bread crumbs in the filling as you can get away with. That way, when you get through that golden crust, the inside will be full of beautiful crabmeat, totally amazing, and great served with lovely lemony salads and a kicking salsa. Add a little chopped shrimp or lobster through the mix if you want to make yours a little different . . . delicious!

Serves 4 ★ ★ ★ ★ ★ ★

¾ cup all-purpose flour
3 cups bread crumbs made from stale bread
3 large eggs, preferably free-range or organic
14 oz good-quality picked white crabmeat
1 lemon
sea salt and freshly ground black pepper
a small bunch of fresh Italian parsley, very finely chopped
1 or 2 fresh red chiles, to taste, seeded and minced
1 quart vegetable oil
cayenne pepper, to serve
1 lemon, cut into wedges, to serve

For the salsa
10 ripe tomatoes
2 fresh red chiles, seeded and minced
½ red onion, peeled and diced
sea salt
2 tablespoons red wine vinegar
1 tablespoon extra virgin olive oil
a small bunch of fresh basil, leaves picked and roughly chopped, smaller leaves reserved

Wine suggestion:
Sicilian dry white – from Inzolia

Get 3 large plates and put the flour on one and the bread crumbs on another. Separate the eggs, putting the whites on your third plate and the yolks into a bowl. Add the crabmeat to the bowl of egg yolks, grate in the zest of your lemon, add a pinch of salt and pepper, the chopped parsley and chiles, and use your hands to scrunch everything together really well. Take a small handful of bread crumbs from the plate and sprinkle into the bowl. You don't want too much, just enough to bind everything together. Divide the mixture into 4 piles.

Take one of the piles, cup it in the palms of your hands, and really squeeze and shape it until you've got a clementine-size ball. Do the same with the other 3. Roll each ball carefully in the flour, then in the egg white, then around the plate of breadcrumbs, sprinkling the crumbs over to completely cover the crab. If one of the balls happens to break, that's OK – just pat it back together again, and repeat the steps.

Although you can cook them right away, I prefer to put them on a plate in the refrigerator for an hour so they firm up a bit. Once they're nicely chilled, pour the vegetable oil into a large, sturdy, deep saucepan and put it on a medium heat. You want the oil to reach 350°F, but if you don't have a thermometer just put a piece of potato in the pan – when it turns golden and crispy and floats to the top, you'll know the oil is good to go, but be careful.

Make your salsa while your oil heats up. Seed 4 of your tomatoes and pop them into a food processor with your chiles, red onion, and a pinch of salt. Whiz up to a fairly fine slurry and pour into a bowl. Seed the remaining 6 tomatoes, then dice them and stir them into the slurry with the vinegar, olive oil, and chopped basil. Have a taste and check the seasoning.

When your oil is hot enough, remove the piece of potato, then carefully lower in your crab balls and fry for 4 to 5 minutes. Keep an eye on them and turn them as they cook so they get evenly golden. Use a perforated spoon to move them onto a plate lined with paper towels to drain, and serve right away on a bed of your tomato and basil salsa, with a pinch of salt and cayenne sprinkled over, a few of your reserved basil leaves scattered on top, and lemon wedges for squeezing over.

RED PEPPER SUMMER SOUP

It gets pretty damn hot in the South, and sometimes a bowl of delicious cold soup is a really welcome break from the heat. This is a classic soup from Savannah, which I've tweaked to suit my tastes. It's lovely served hot, but also really gorgeous like this, ice cold, on a summer's day. If you've never tried cold soup, don't turn your nose up at it before you've given it a try. Since getting back from Georgia, I've added fresh basil to this recipe because I think it adds some brilliant flavor. So if your soup looks a bit greener than the one in the picture, no worries.

Serves 4–6

★   ★   ★   ★   ★   ★

2 onions, peeled and roughly chopped
4 cloves garlic, peeled and roughly chopped
4 red bell peppers, seeded and roughly chopped
1 fresh red chile, halved, seeded, and roughly chopped
¼ cup olive oil
1 quart chicken broth, preferably organic
a small bunch of fresh basil, leaves picked
3 tablespoons red wine vinegar
sea salt and freshly ground black pepper
¼ cucumber
1 stalk celery
extra virgin olive oil
cayenne pepper

Wine suggestion:
Spanish dry sherry – a manzanilla

Put your chopped onions, garlic, bell peppers, and chile into a large saucepan with the olive oil and fry gently on a medium heat with the lid on for about 20 minutes. Give it a stir every 3 or 4 minutes, and once everything is starting to soften and turning sweet and delicious, pour the chicken broth into the pan. Bring to a boil, then turn back down to a medium heat and cook for a further 10 minutes with the lid on.

Pour your soup into a liquidizer or food processor – you may need to do this in a couple of batches – and add your basil leaves and red wine vinegar. Give it a good whiz, then have a taste and correct the seasoning with a pinch of salt and pepper. Really concentrate on the seasoning and try to get it perfect for your taste. Pour into a bowl and let cool. Once completely cool, cover the bowl and pop it into the refrigerator until it's really nice and cold.

About 10 minutes before you're ready to serve your soup, prepare the garnish. Peel, seed, and dice your cucumber, then peel away any stringy bits from your celery, trim, and dice it very small. If your celery has yellow leaves on it, keep those for garnish too because they're really nice.

You can either serve your soup in one large bowl on a tray of ice in the middle of the table or divide it up between 4 bowls. Drizzle over a bit of extra virgin olive oil, top with your chopped celery, cucumber, and any celery leaves you've saved, then sprinkle with a little cayenne pepper and enjoy!

Peaches grow in abundance in the South, which is why they have so many great uses for them: in cocktails, in cobblers, in pickles, . . . and, of course, in ice cream. I had the pleasure of making this particular ice cream in Lonnie Senior's old-fashioned machine.

This is pretty much one of the most delicious things going, and one of the reasons to live, so it ain't a bad thing to learn. It's absolutely perfect for my taste because to my mind this much sugar combined with canned peaches in syrup is more than sweet enough. However, the locals said it wasn't sweet enough for them, so feel free to have a taste and increase the sugar if your sensibilities are a bit more "Southern." You could also give this a bit of an exciting angle by whizzing up a few teaspoons of chopped ginger in syrup with your peaches. It's absolutely delicious and a little goes a long way.

★　　★　　★　　★　　★　　★

Roughly chop the peaches into ¼ inch chunks and use a fork to mash up half of them. Put the chopped peaches into one bowl and the mashed ones into another and pop both into the refrigerator to chill.

Put the egg yolks and sugar into a bowl and mix until creamy and smooth. Add your milk, cream, and vanilla seeds and mix again. Pour this mixture into a thick-bottomed saucepan on a very low heat, and stir continuously with a spatula until you've got a wonderful thick custard that coats the back of a spoon. It's important to keep the heat very low and keep stirring, otherwise your eggs will scramble. Once the custard is thick, smooth, and lovely, take the pan off the heat, immediately pour it into a large bowl, and let it cool completely.

Once its cooled, you've got two options: you can use an ice-cream machine, if you've got one, or you can go down the traditional route and let the ice cream freeze over several hours.

If using an ice-cream machine, add your mashed peaches to your cooled cream mixture, then follow your machine's instructions and let it do all the work! When the mixture starts to thicken and look a bit like ice cream, add your chopped peaches, let it whiz a couple more times, and put it into the freezer.

If you're making this by hand, tip both bowls of peaches into your cooled cream mixture, give it a good stir, then transfer to a large bowl or Tupperware container, cover, and put it into the freezer. It should set in 6 to 8 hours, but you'll need to give it a good churn with a fork every 30 minutes to 1 hour to stop ice crystals forming. Whichever way you do it, the result will be delicious!

OLD-FASHIONED PEACH ICE CREAM

Makes 1 quart

1 x 15-oz can peaches in heavy syrup, drained
6 large egg yolks, preferably
free-range or organic
½ cup plus 2 tablespoons sugar
1⅔ cups whole milk
¼ cup heavy cream
1 vanilla bean, halved and seeds scraped out

Wine suggestion:
French sweet white –
a Muscat de Beaumes-de-Venise

Religion plays a major role in the lives of many Americans, so when I arrived in Atlanta on a Sunday, I headed down to the local church for the evening service. The pastor at Rainbow Park Baptist Church, Steven Dial, was an incredibly inspiring character who talked a lot of sense. With the recession on everyone's mind, he managed to make religion really relevant and helpful. After the service, the congregation spilled out into a huge canteen-style kitchen for their weekly "potluck supper," where everyone contributes a dish made at home to create a massive feast. It's a chance to sit down together, to laugh, tell jokes, and talk about life, and to "break bread" in the truest sense of the word. I joined in, and it was a wonderful way to be welcomed to the state of Georgia.

Since the congregation was almost entirely black, it was also my first chance to eat the classic soul food dishes. Delicious stuff like collard greens, smoked turkey stew, red rice, grits, and biscuits – some of which you'll find in this chapter. I'd always thought "soul food" was a black slang term for food with attitude. But later, in Savannah, I got a real education about its true origins, and I couldn't have been more wrong. At a wonderful restaurant called Mom & Nikki's, I got to cook with the owner, Nikki, an absolutely beautiful girl who wore her heart on her sleeve, and her family. Nikki explained that back in the bad old days, black slaves were given the bits of food that the white man didn't want: stuff like bones, ribs, neck, and variety meats. So they used their imagination and resourcefulness to make those things as delicious as possible. The term "soul food" actually came about because the people cooking it were putting every little bit of their hearts into turning those meager scraps into delicious meals that would nourish their body and soul. It was about survival.

I looked around Nikki's restaurant on Martin Luther King Boulevard, in a city that was hugely important to the civil rights movement, and about half the people lining up were white. Everyone, from soldiers to little kids, was sitting together and tucking in, and it made me think that, even though soul food came from a sad place, it now feels like a celebration and a testament to the dignity and strength of the black community. Ultimately, I felt proud and lucky to be there, learning about this incredible food, just one week after President Obama had moved into the White House.

RICH GRITS

When I made this at my friend Nikki's soul food restaurant, she named it "rich grits" because she thought shrimp were getting a bit pricey to be included in a dish during a recession. In my defense – if you live somewhere like Savannah, which is near the coast, you should be able to get shrimp at a pretty fair price. Grits are a delicious base for all sorts of wonderful things in Southern cooking, and their buttery, cheesy texture and the lightly spiced sausages and shrimp make a fantastic combo.

Serves 4   ★   ★   ★   ★   ★   ★

For the grits
2 cups medium ground grits, fine cornmeal, or white polenta
3 tablespoons butter
1 cup freshly grated Cheddar cheese
sea salt and freshly ground black pepper

For the prawns and sausage
6 good-quality pork sausages
olive oil
¾ lb raw shrimp, shells off
2 cloves garlic, peeled and minced
½ teaspoon smoked paprika
a pat of butter
1 lemon
a small bunch of fresh Italian parsley, finely chopped

Wine suggestion:
Italian red – a Dolcetto d'Alba

Bring a quart of water to the boil in a large saucepan. Pour in your grits or cornmeal and cook following the package instructions. If you're using polenta, check the package to make sure the ratio of water to polenta is the same. Be sure to stand over the pan and stir constantly to make sure there are no lumps and it doesn't catch. When your grits are ready, add the butter and grated cheese, and stir and beat in really well. Have a taste and add some seasoning to the point where it's delicious. Pop the lid on the pan to keep the grits warm while you crack on.

Get a large frying pan on a medium heat. Squeeze the sausages out of their skins bit by bit and roll the meat into little ¾-inch balls. Don't go getting fancy, just pack them into roundish shapes. Once you've done that with all your sausages, turn the heat up under the pan and add the meatballs to the pan with a few lugs of olive oil.

Shake the pan every now and then, and after 4 or 5 minutes the meatballs should be looking gorgeous all over. Add your shrimp and minced garlic and sprinkle in your smoked paprika. Give everything a good shake and within about 2 minutes the shrimp will be perfectly cooked, so add a pat of butter and cook for another minute or two, shaking and stirring every 10 seconds or so. Take the pan off the heat, squeeze in the juice of your lemon, add your chopped parsley, and season to taste with a pinch of salt and pepper. Let everything mix together, and stir around to pick up any flavors from the bottom of the pan. Have a taste and check you're happy with it. Stir a splash of boiling water into your grits to bring them back to life, and divide between your plates. Spoon over the lovely meat and shrimp, drizzle over any leftover juices, and serve right away. So easy!

Collard greens are an absolute soul food classic with a funny connection to my country: the word "collard" is actually an old English word for cabbage. When you talk to people in Georgia about collard greens, you discover that they all have their own favorite bits: some like the greens, some like the broth, some like the meat – and I love that. I think it's fair to say that soul food is famed for being deep-fried or on the heavy side, but these greens are one of the lighter dishes; so if you choose your bits and pieces of soul food wisely, it's not bad for you.

Normally you use vegetables to make meat taste good, but here you're using meat to make the greens taste good, and the results are fantastic. When I first tried this dish, it was served with an amazing chile vinegar. The flavors worked so well together that I made my own version (see page 240).

COLLARD GREENS, TURNIPS, & PORK

Serves 6

Get a saucepan large enough to hold all your ingredients and add your pork knuckle, bay leaves, and 2½ quarts of your finest tap water. Simmer on a medium heat with the lid on for 2½ hours, adding more water during cooking if you think it needs it. If you're lucky enough to have small, hand-ball–sized turnips, great. If not, you might have to cut them in half so they're roughly that size before adding them to the pan with the carrots, celery, collard greens, and a good pinch of salt and pepper. Cook for a further 35 minutes.

Wash your other greens, cut them into roughly 2-inch slices, and add them to the pan. Squash them down and give them a good stir so they fit in. Stir after the first 5 minutes, then cook for about 20 minutes more, or until they're tender and a pleasure to eat, but still quite green and exciting.

Take the pan off the heat and use tongs to move the pork bones from the pan to a board. Shred the meat off the bones with a fork, then return the meat to the pan and get rid of the bones and any fat. Have a taste and season carefully with salt and pepper. I think a little vinegar at this point helps to lift this dish, so either add a slug of white wine vinegar or, if you feel adventurous, make the spicy hot chile vinegar (see page 240) and drizzle some of that on top. Serve with a good drizzle of extra virgin olive oil.

2¼ lbs pig's knuckle, the best
quality you can afford
2 fresh bay leaves
1 lb turnips, scrubbed clean
2 carrots, peeled and roughly chopped
2 celery stalks, trimmed
and roughly chopped
sea salt and freshly ground black pepper
1 lb collard greens or Swiss
chard, cavolo nero, kale, Brussels
tops, or a mixture of these
optional: white wine vinegar
extra virgin olive oil, to serve

Wine suggestion:
French red – a young Beaujolais, such
as a Morgon Côte de Py, slightly chilled

FRIED CHICKEN & SALAD

I just couldn't bring myself to leave this recipe out, because it's an absolute classic and it's something that you'll find wherever you travel in the South.

And listen, if you like KFC (and I know a lot of you do), you'll love this. Next time you find you've got that craving for salt and crunch, why not try making it yourself? Have it as a treat with something light and simple like this kick-ass salad to balance it out, and you're laughing. If you're going to cook for the kids, or if you want to make smaller pieces, you can use 4 thighs and 4 drumsticks instead of 4 whole legs, and it will still be delicious.

Serves 4

 ★ ★ ★ ★

For the chicken
4 chicken legs, preferably free-range or organic, skin on
1¼ cups buttermilk
1 fresh red chile, seeded and minced
1 heaping teaspoon dried thyme
1 clove garlic, peeled and finely grated
juice of 1 lemon
sea salt and freshly ground black pepper
1 quart vegetable oil
2¾ cups all-purpose flour
1 tablespoon smoked paprika
cayenne pepper

For the salad
1 cucumber
a small bunch of fresh basil
4 tomatoes
½ red onion, peeled and thinly sliced
red wine vinegar
extra virgin olive oil

Wine suggestion:
Italian red – a Barbera
d'Asti or d'Alba

Run a small, sharp knife along all of the bone of each chicken leg and thigh so the meat really splays open. This will help it to cook and marinate a bit faster. Pour your buttermilk into a large mixing bowl and add the chopped chile, thyme, grated garlic, lemon juice, and a good pinch of salt and pepper. Add the chicken legs and leave to marinate for at least 1 hour or in the refrigerator overnight.

Get a large, sturdy, deep thick-bottomed saucepan or skillet, pour in your vegetable oil, and put it on a high heat. Keep an eye on the oil, as it can burn you badly if you're not in control. You want the oil to reach 350°F – it's best to use a thermometer, but if you don't have one, get a piece of potato and drop it into the oil. When it is crisp and golden and floats to the top, you'll know the oil is about the right temperature for you to add the chicken.

Put your flour on a large plate and season it with a pinch of salt, pepper, and the paprika. Toss your pieces of chicken in the flour, shake off any excess, then dunk them quickly back in the buttermilk again and straight back into the flour to create two layers that will turn golden and delicious once fried. Use a perforated spoon to lower each piece of chicken into the hot oil. Cook the chicken legs for 15 to 20 minutes, turning carefully with tongs every couple of minutes so they cook evenly on all sides. You can check the chicken is cooked by cutting open the thickest part of it and having a look. If it's at all pink, put it back in the oil for a few more minutes.

Meanwhile, make your salad. Use a fork to really scrape down the length of your cucumber so it gets grooves around the outside. This will give the dressing more places to get into. Thinly slice the cucumber into rounds and put it into a large bowl with the basil leaves. Cut 2 of your tomatoes into wedges, slice the other 2 into rounds, and add to the bowl with your sliced onion. Pour a splash of red wine vinegar and 3 times as much extra virgin olive oil into the bowl, season with a good pinch of salt and pepper, and toss everything together until perfectly dressed.

Once your chicken is wonderfully golden and cooked through, drain it on paper towels. Sprinkle over some salt, hit it with a pinch or two of cayenne, and serve it right away while it's wonderful and crispy.

I think this is a really simple way to make a lovely flatfish like flounder, lemon sole, gray sole, or turbot look, and taste, really exciting. If you want to, you can ask your fishmonger to run a knife down the back of the fish and make a pocket for you to stuff. If not, it's dead easy to do at home. If you need some guidance, check out www.jamieoliver.com/how-to to watch a video of it being done. Once you've tried it this way, you can stuff the fish with whatever you fancy: lobster or crabmeat, small fish, herbs, tomatoes ... just let your imagination go wild! Getting a nice big fish isn't hard, but you might want to order it in advance from your fishmonger. It's equally delicious with individual portions though, so look at this as a principle as well as a recipe.

SHRIMP-STUFFED FLATFISH

Serves 4

Preheat your oven to 400°F. If you look at the head and the tail of your fish, more often than not there's a secret line between them that the Big Man upstairs has drawn. Using this as your guide, carefully cut into one side of the line near the head, push down gently, angle the tip-end of your knife toward the bone, and score between the flesh and the bone to peel away that beautiful fish fillet. Run the knife down to just above the tail and part the fillet from the bone – 1¾ to 2 inches deep on both sides. Even if you don't get it perfect, you'll be stuffing this pocket with shrimp, so no one will know if your knife work was a bit shabby.

Get a sheet pan that snugly fits your fish and sprinkle your thinly sliced onions around the base of the pan. Season both sides of your fish with salt and pepper and lay it on top of the onions. Try to sweep most of the onions under the fish so they sweeten as they cook. Put the butter into a small pan on a low heat, and once it's melted pour it into a bowl and leave to cool for 5 minutes.

Add a pinch of salt and pepper, the grated garlic, and a pinch of cayenne to the butter, then grate over the zest of half your lemon. Toss the peeled shrimp through this mixture until nicely coated, then stuff them loosely inside the fish, pouring over any flavored butter left behind in the bowl. Before putting the fish into the oven, drizzle over some olive oil and a splash of white wine, then halve your lemon and add both halves to the pan. Adjust the cooking time depending on the size of your fish: a large fish will want 25 minutes, 2 small fish about 12 minutes. You'll know it's beautifully cooked when the flesh flakes away from the bone.

Finely chop your parsley leaves and sprinkle them over the fish once it's out of the oven. Squeeze over the juices from your roasted lemon halves, and serve. I like to put this in the middle of the table with something propping up one end of the pan so that the delicious milky juices run out of the fish and mingle with the butter, olive oil, and lemon juices at one end of the pan. Spoon this over clumps of your fish and shrimp, and anything else you're serving it with, like baby potatoes, mashed potatoes, or simple steamed greens – it will taste wonderful.

either 1 x 2 ¾–3½ lb or 4 x ½-lb flatfish, such as flounder, lemon or gray sole, or turbot
2 medium onions, peeled and thinly sliced
sea salt and freshly ground black pepper
5 tablespoons butter
2 cloves garlic, peeled and finely grated
cayenne pepper
1 lemon
½ lb medium raw shrimp, shells off
olive oil
a splash of white wine
a small bunch of fresh Italian parsley

Wine suggestion:
Austrian dry white – a dry Grüner Veltliner

HAM HOCK ON GREEN GRITS

Serves 4–6

★　★　★　★　★　★

Grits really are absolutely delicious. The word "grit" actually comes from us Brits – from the old English word "grytt," meaning a sort of coarse meal, or something ground. Perhaps we have more in common with Southern folk than we thought! You can also make this with beef or lamb shanks or any other stewing cut of meat – although personally, I think the fact that the ham is smoked gives this dish a wonderful extra dimension of flavor. Stirring puréed greens through grits isn't a very American thing to do: it's more Tuscan. But it gives them some attitude and added flavor – the Americans I served it to gave it their seal of approval!

For the meat and broth

1 x 3½ lb smoked ham hock,
the best quality you can afford
2 celery stalks, trimmed
and roughly chopped
1 onion, peeled and roughly chopped
2 tomatoes, roughly chopped
1 green bell pepper, seeded
and roughly chopped
3 cloves garlic, peeled
and roughly chopped
a small bunch of fresh thyme, leaves picked
a small bunch of fresh sage, leaves picked
3 or 4 fresh bay leaves
sea salt and freshly ground black pepper

For the grits

2 cloves garlic, peeled
¾ lb mixed kale, cavolo nero,
or chard, roughly chopped and
any thick stems removed
2 cups grits, fine cornmeal, or polenta
3 tablespoons butter
1 cup freshly grated Cheddar cheese

Wine suggestion:
Italian red – Primitivo from Puglia or
its Californian cousin, Zinfandel

Put your smoked ham hock into a large pot and cover with cold water. Bring to a boil, then drain off all the water to remove some of the excess saltiness from the ham. Add enough fresh water to cover the ham again by a few inches, and add the rest of the ingredients for the meat. Bring to a boil, then turn down the heat and simmer for about 3 to 4 hours, or until the meat comes away from the bone. Keep an eye on the water level to make sure the meat stays covered, and skim away any fat from the top every now and then. Once the ham is tender and poached to perfection, turn the heat off and leave with the lid on so it stays moist and warm while you start on the green grits.

Bring another large pan of water to the boil. Add your 2 peeled garlic cloves and boil for a few minutes. Add your greens and cook for 2 to 3 minutes, until they are just tender but still full of color. Drain, reserving the cooking liquid, then put the greens and garlic into a liquidizer or food processor with a few ladles of the cooking liquid. Liquidize until smooth, season to taste with a pinch of salt and pepper, and put aside.

Making grits is dead simple – basically you're going to use 1 quart of liquid to 2 cups of grits, cornmeal, or polenta, but follow the package instructions as a guide. You can use water, but I like to use the cooking liquid from the ham. If you want to do that, drain 1 quart of liquid from the pan – add some water to make it up to a quart if you don't have quite enough. Bring it to the boil in another large pan, then add the grits and cook following the package instructions. Stir occasionally and let it blip away until thick and oatmeal-like.

When your grits are ready, stir in the butter and grated Cheddar and season to taste. Pour your lovely green purée over the grits and use a spatula to gently fold it into the mixture so you get a nice marbled effect. Drain your ham, reserving any cooking liquid and all those lovely veg, and get rid of any skin. You can either serve the meat in one piece or shred it into different-sized chunks. Pour the grits onto a large warmed platter, pop the ham on top, spoon over a little of the reserved cooking liquid and veg, and serve in the center of the table.

This is a delicious recipe that feels exciting and hits all the right spots. Yes, it's deep-fried, but if you use fresh oil, cook it quickly, and blot it with paper towels once you're done, you'll be surprised how non-greasy it can be. To contrast with the crispy texture and the meatiness of the fish, I've dry-grilled the corn and used it to make this zingy salsa. The salsa gets better the longer it sits, and if you've got any left over it will also be incredible with white meat like pork. Feel free to use a mixture of scaled, pinboned fillets of white fish, such as branzino, snapper, pacific cod, turbot, pollock, haddock – most fish or shellfish like scallops are good cooked like this, just avoid oily fish.

CRISPY FISH & CORN SALSA

Serves 4

½ cup buttermilk
4 x ½-lb meaty white fish, scaled and pinboned and cut into ¾-inch-thick slices
sea salt and freshly ground black pepper
1 quart vegetable oil
1⅔ cups fine cornmeal or plain flour
2 lemons, cut into wedges, for serving

For the corn salsa

2 fresh ears of corn, husked
1 fresh red chile, seeded and minced
2 ripe medium-sized tomatoes, diced
½ yellow bell pepper, seeded and diced
2 scallions, peeled and minced
½ clove garlic, finely grated
1 tablespoon soy sauce
juice of 1 lemon
¼ cup extra virgin olive oil
a small handful of mint leaves, roughly chopped
smoked paprika

Wine suggestion:
Spanish dry white – Albariño

Pour your buttermilk into a bowl. Season the fish pieces with salt and pepper and then soak them in the buttermilk for about an hour – this will do really nice things to the fish's texture.

Meanwhile, make your salsa. Put your corn into a hot dry grill pan and lightly char it all over; this will take about 20 minutes. Remove the corn to a plate and let it cool a little, then carefully run a small sharp knife from top to bottom to remove those beautiful kernels of corn. Discard the cobs and put the kernels into a bowl with all the other salsa ingredients and a pinch of salt, pepper, and paprika. Stir it all up and have a taste to get the seasoning right – you want heat from the chile, freshness from the mint, and salt to cut through it all.

Get a large, sturdy, deep saucepan over a high heat, pour in your vegetable oil, and heat it to around 350°F. Ideally you want to use a thermometer to check this, but if you haven't got one, you can put in a small piece of potato, and when it rises to the top and turns crispy and golden, you know the oil's ready. Just make sure you haven't got any kids or pets running around the kitchen, as hot oil can burn badly.

Put your cornmeal or flour onto a large plate and add a good pinch of salt and pepper. Take a piece of fish out of the buttermilk – let the excess drip off, then roll it in the cornmeal or flour. Do the same thing with all of the fish, then carefully lower into the pan of oil using tongs or a perforated spoon. Deep-fry the fish for 2 to 3 minutes, until golden, crisp, and brown, then remove to a plate lined with paper towels and sprinkle with sea salt. As soon as the last batch is ready, divide most of your salsa between your plates, pop the pieces of fish on top, and finish with a touch more salsa. Serve with arugula or a crisp green salad, and wedges of lemon for squeezing over.

BBQ!

Roadside "hog roast" restaurants are quite common in Georgia, and the concept behind them is brilliant. A "pit master" preps whole pigs, then stays up all night carefully turning them over a huge pit of coals and roasting them to absolute perfection. In the morning, he brings the pigs off their wire racks, rips off all the incredible crispy rind, then chops and pulls the meat apart, ready for the cook to use in all sorts of delicious ways for the customers. I stopped by one of these places, Neal's Bar-B-Que, off the highway in Thomson, one night to see how it was done. The pit master was a big, handsome, strapping man called Barry. When I saw him I expected him to be as hard as nails, but of course he turned out to be absolutely lovely.

After working with Barry, and seeing the attention to detail that went into barbecuing those hogs, I realized he had the same care and pride you'd find at an Italian prosciutto house or French cheesemaker. At Neal's the pork was served with coleslaw and little savory doughnuts called hush puppies. It was all so delicious that I've made my own versions of the same things and included them in this chapter (see pages 283 and 284).

Once I got a taste for this sort of cooking I couldn't wait to get down to Pig Fest in Florida and get stuck in with the Bubba Grills team, who were competing there. I figured Barry knew his stuff, so I persuaded him to hop into my van and come along for the ride to help out, along with my new friend, Nikki, from the soul food restaurant. The competition itself was completely bonkers in the best way possible: an absolute celebration of the great American barbecue and all things pig!

The Bubba Grills team also stayed up all night to "mind their meat." To them, and to barbecue aficionados in general, this isn't seen as a hassle; it's a ritual and something they take real pride in. I was honored to be invited to sit up with one of the lads, Larry. We huddled in our sleeping bags and stayed up until dawn feeding the fire, watching the ribs, and having a few beers.

I definitely wasn't feeling too sparky in the morning, but those ribs were bloody amazing and the energy and excitement of the competition, combined with some strong coffee, soon got me fired up again.

PREPARING AND ROASTING HOGS OVER HOT COALS FOR SEVEN OR EIGHT HOURS IS SERIOUSLY PHYSICAL WORK – BUT BARRY MADE IT LOOK EASY AND DID IT WITH A SMILE

Slow-roasting a whole "hog" is a big deal in the South, and roadside restaurants will use that pork in all sorts of delicious ways. I've made a deconstructed version of a roadside restaurant meal here by roasting half a shoulder of pork, dressing it with fresh flavors, and serving it with my take on their traditional coleslaw. I wasn't really into all the added sugar so I swapped it for slices of apple, which works brilliantly and serves the same purpose, but in a much fresher way. Put these things together on a plate and throw in a few hush puppies (see page 284) like they do in Georgia and you've got yourself a proper Southern-style meal.

★　　★　　★　　★　　★　　★

Preheat your oven to full whack. Score the pork skin about ½ inch deep all over with a sharp knife. Drizzle a little olive oil over the pork and season generously with salt, pepper, and paprika. Rub the flavors all over the skin, then put your pork in a roasting pan in the middle of the oven and immediately turn the temperature down to 320°F. Cook for about 4 hours, basting occasionally with the juices from the pan, then turn the oven down to 300°F and continue to cook for another 2 hours, or until you can pull the meat apart really easily. Remove the rind and put it to one side, then remove any fat from the pan. Pull all the pork apart, discarding any bones and fat as you go, and use 2 forks to sliced the meat into small- and medium-sized pieces. Cover with aluminum foil until needed.

To make your coleslaw, finely slice your veggies and apples or use a food processor or box grater. Put them into a large bowl and season with a pinch of salt and pepper. Add your mayonnaise, a drizzle of extra virgin olive oil, a pinch of cayenne, and the red wine vinegar. Mix everything together until you've got a perfect coleslaw texture. Have a taste; it should be fresh and lovely, so season and put it to one side while you dress your meat.

Pick your mint leaves and finely chop them on a large board. Seed and mince your chiles on the same board as your mint. Drizzle the olive oil and red wine vinegar all over the chiles and mint and add a good pinch of salt. Add this to your pan of pulled pork and mix it all together. Serve the dressed pork in a pile on a plate next to the crispy rind and a good portion of that wonderful coleslaw. Finish the whole plate off with a little salt and a hit of paprika and tuck in with a lovely cold beer.

SOUTHERN-STYLE PORK & SLAW

Serves 10–12

For the pork
½ shoulder of pork, neck end with bone in (approx. 11 lbs), the best quality you can afford
olive oil
sea salt and freshly ground black pepper
2 heaping teaspoons smoked paprika, plus a little extra for sprinkling over
a handful of fresh mint
1 or 2 fresh red chiles
⅓ cup olive oil
3 tablespoons red wine vinegar

For the collard greens and apple slaw
½ white cabbage, thinly sliced
1 red onion, peeled and coarsely grated
3 carrots, peeled and coarsely grated
2 big handfuls of collard greens, washed and spun dry
3 crunchy apples, very thinly sliced
sea salt and freshly ground black pepper
2 tablespoons mayonnaise
extra virgin olive oil
cayenne pepper
4–5 tablespoons red wine vinegar

Wine suggestion:
Italian red – a Rosso di Montalcino from Tuscany

HUSH PUPPIES

Makes 25–30

scant 2½ cups fine
cornmeal or polenta
heaping ¾ cup self-rising flour
1 x 12-oz bottle of beer
scant 1 cup fresh or frozen corn
4 scallions, trimmed and thinly sliced
¼ lb Cheddar cheese, finely grated
sea salt and freshly
ground black pepper
1 quart vegetable oil
smoked paprika

Wine suggestion:
French dry rosé from the
Languedoc, or a cold beer

Hush puppies are little savory doughnuts and I think they're quite cool. I was told their name comes from the time of the Great Depression, when loads of people were going hungry. When they did get a bit of food, their hungry dogs would hang around whining, so they'd throw these little buns to them to keep them quiet. That might be an old wives' tale, but if it is, I don't care because I like the story. OK, they're not the healthiest things on the planet, but every now and then ... they're not going to hurt you.

★   ★   ★   ★   ★   ★

Put the cornmeal and flour into a bowl, add your beer, and leave to sit for a few minutes. Add the corn, sliced scallions, grated cheese, and a pinch of salt and pepper and use a fork or a spoon to mix it up really well. Once your batter is ready, pour your vegetable oil into a large, sturdy saucepan and put it on a high heat. Please make sure you don't move the pan about and that no one is running around the kitchen while you're doing this, as hot oil can burn quite badly.

You want the oil to reach about 350ºC, so if you don't have a thermometer get a small piece of potato and drop it into the pan. When it turns crisp and golden and rises to the top, the oil is ready to go. Get a tablespoonful of mix and carefully drop it into the hot oil. In Georgia they roll their batter into round balls, but I say just let it drop off the spoon: a bit scruffy and rustic feels right to me. You'll need to cook them in batches.

Keep your eye on them and let them fry for about 3 to 4 minutes, then remove with a perforated spoon and drain on a plate lined with paper towels. Sprinkle over a tiny bit of sea salt and a hit of paprika to finish them off, and serve right away, either on their own or, as they do at roadside restaurants, as part of a meal with the amazing pork and slaw (page 283). Naughty but nice!

SURF 'N' TURF

You really want to cook this recipe on a grill, where you'll have space to cook the meat and the lobster together. It's undoubtedly one of the most luxurious things you can eat: half a lobster and filet mignon steaks served with an absolutely kick-ass homemade potato salad. Come on! The good news is that you can achieve this – no matter how experienced a cook you are. A glass of white wine and life doesn't get much better than that.

Serves 2

★　　★　　★　　★　　★　　★

1 x 2¼–2½ lb uncooked lobster
4 x filet mignon steaks (approx. ¼ lb each)
olive oil
1 lemon, halved
a large pat of butter
1 clove garlic, peeled and minced
paprika

For the potato salad
¾ lb baby or creamer potatoes, red- or white-skinned, washed and scrubbed, larger ones halved
½ red onion, peeled and diced
red wine vinegar
a pinch of sugar
2 heaping tablespoons mayonnaise
a small bunch of fresh Italian parsley, leaves picked and roughly chopped
sea salt and freshly ground black pepper

Wine suggestion:
Californian white – an oaked Chardonnay from Monterey or the Russian River Valley

You can ask your fishmonger to kill and halve the lobster for you, and remove the stomach sac and the big vein that runs through the tail. Cover the halved lobster with a dish towel and put to one side. Take your steaks out of the refrigerator so they can come up to room temperature while you make your potato salad and get your grill screaming hot.

Boil the potatoes in salted water for 15 to 20 minutes, until a knife goes through them easily. Drain, and while still hot slice them to whatever thickness you like. While the potatoes are cooking, toss your diced onions in a bowl with 2 tablespoons of vinegar and a pinch of sugar. Let them soak for a few minutes, then drain. Toss your sliced potatoes in a large bowl with the mayonnaise, drained onions, most of your chopped parsley, a pinch of salt and pepper, and 2 tablespoons of vinegar, and put to one side.

Pull the 2 big claws from the lobster and give each of them a light bash with the bottom of a saucepan to crack them open slightly – this will help the heat get inside and cook the flesh. Rub both lobster halves all over with olive oil. Season the steaks really well on both sides and rub them with olive oil. Put the lobster halves on the grill, shell side down, with the big claws, and cook for about 4 minutes, then flip over and cook the halves flesh side down for 2 minutes. Add your steaks and the lemon halves at the same time as your lobster and cook the steaks for about 3 minutes per side for medium, slightly less for rare, and longer for well done (use your intuition!).

When the steaks are cooked to your liking, put the butter on a plate with the minced garlic and put your steaks on top to melt the butter. Put the chargrilled lemons on the plate too, add a drizzle of olive oil, and leave to rest while you give your lobster claws another minute or two on the grill.

Put a lobster half on each serving plate and lean 2 steaks against it. Drizzle over all the melted butter, oils, and juices from the steak plate and sprinkle over the rest of your chopped parsley. Serve with a few spoonfuls of your potato salad, your lemon halves, and a dusting of paprika, and enjoy!

COMPETITION MORNING: I MIGHT HAVE LOOKED
A BIT ROUGH ON NO SLEEP BUT OUR TEAM'S
BARBECUED MEAT WAS WORTH IT!

BEER BUTT CHICKEN

Serves 4

1 large whole chicken (approx. 3½ lbs),
preferably free-range or organic
1 can of Budweiser or other beer

For the rub
1 heaping teaspoon fennel seeds
1 level teaspoon cumin seeds
1 level teaspoon smoked paprika
1 heaping teaspoon light brown sugar
1 level teaspoon mild chili powder
sea salt and freshly ground black pepper
olive oil

Wine suggestion:
Italian red – a Chianti Rufina from Tuscany

I've never seen this done in Britain, but it's a really fun and effective way to cook chicken. I'm giving you two methods, one in the grill and one in the oven – both will give you tasty, moist chicken. You need a standard kettle-style grill with a cover and a thermostat. Make sure it's tall enough to hold the upright chicken. The steam from the beer cooks the inside of the bird, so the meat ends up lovely and juicy.

★　　　★　　　★　　　★　　　★　　　★

Preheat your grill or oven to 400°F. Take your chicken out of the refrigerator while you make your rub. In a pestle and mortar, bash up your fennel and cumin seeds and mix with the paprika, brown sugar, chili powder, salt, and pepper. Stir in about 3 tablespoons of olive oil until you get a nice paste. Drizzle this rub all over the chicken, inside and out, using your hands to make sure you get it into all the nooks and crannies.

Crack your beer open, have a couple of good gulps so your can is just about half-full, then lower your chicken's cavity onto the top of the can so it looks as though the chicken is sitting on the can. A bit undignified, I know, but trust me – it's going to be delicious.

If you're using the grill, try to strategically move a small amount of coals to the sides rather than directly underneath the chicken, so the heat radiates around it and cooks it from all angles rather than grills it. The same principle applies to roasting.

Carefully sit the chicken on the bars of your grill or in a roasting pan on the very bottom of your oven. Cook for 1 hour 10 minutes to 1 hour 30 minutes or until it's golden and delicious and the meat pulls away from the bone and the juices run clear. If this isn't the case (all grills and ovens are slightly different), just cook for a bit longer.

Once done, remove the can and loosely cover your chicken with aluminum foil and a dish towel while you get some grilled vegetables, salad, or warm breads together – but trust me, it tastes so good you won't need much else.

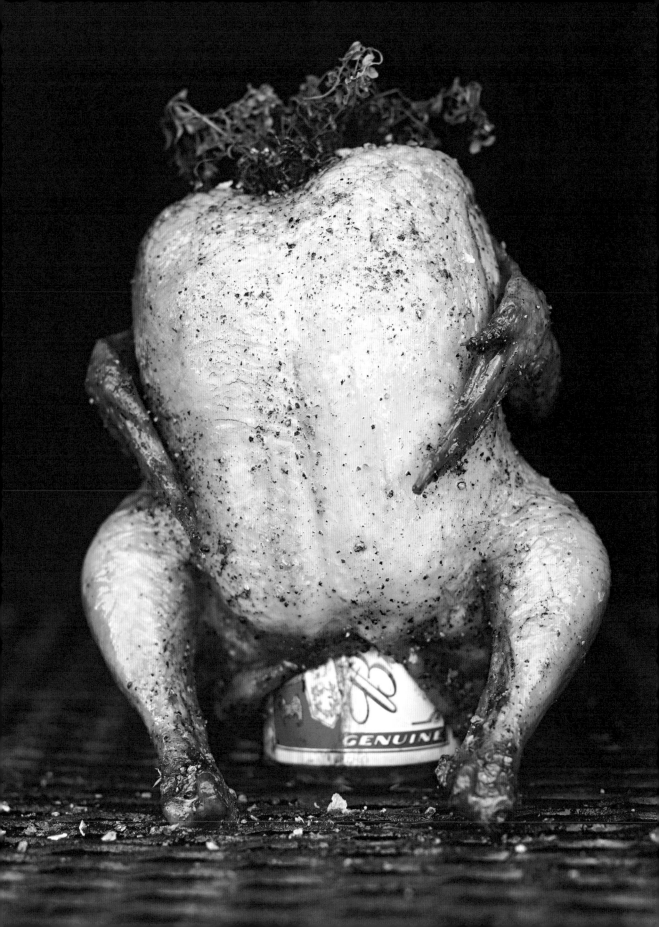

COMPETITION CHICKEN

When it comes to chicken on the barbecue, legs are where it's at – barbecue aficionados ain't interested in the breast. The legs work hard, but if you cook them slowly they'll repay you with sticky melt-in-the-mouth meat, and skin that's really crispy and super delicious. Give this recipe a go in the oven, or on a grill with a lid and a thermostat using the same method, and you won't look back.

Serves 4

★　　★　　★　　★　　★　　★

1 x barbecue rub recipe (page 297)
apple cider vinegar
olive oil
8 fat chicken thighs, preferably free-range or organic, skin on, bone left in
2 cloves garlic, peeled
a few small pats of butter
scant ½ cup water or chicken broth, preferably organic
½ x barbecue sauce recipe (page 296)
sea salt

Wine suggestion:
French red – a young
Côtes du Rhône, or a cold beer

It's nice to marinate these overnight, or at least a good few hours before you are going to cook them. So make your barbecue rub first and put it into a bowl with a splash of cider vinegar and a few lugs of olive oil. Toss the chicken in your rub mixture and really massage the flavors into each piece until you feel the granules turning into a paste. Cover the bowl with plastic wrap and pop it into the refrigerator. About an hour before you're ready to cook them, bring them out of the refrigerator so they get up to room temperature.

Preheat your oven to 275°F. Pick each thigh up and tuck the skin underneath it to make it look pert and tidy so it stays that way as it cooks. Put the thighs on a rack over a sheet pan and pop them into the oven skin side up for 30 minutes.

Thinly slice your garlic. Remove the chicken from the oven and add a few small pats of butter and the water or broth, then scatter over the garlic. Take the chicken off the rack and put it skin side down in the pan. Cover tightly with aluminum foil and put back into the oven for 30 minutes.

While all that's happening, make your barbecue sauce. Put half of it into a large bowl and the other half into the refrigerator to use another time.

Remove the chicken from the oven and discard the foil. Turn each piece skin side up and return the pan to the oven for another 20 minutes to dry out the skin a bit.

When the chicken comes out of the oven, use tongs to dunk each piece into your barbecue sauce. Let any excess sauce drip off, then put the thighs back onto the pan skin side up. To get the skin really melt-in-the-mouth, turn the oven up to 400°F. Put the chicken back into the oven for 20 minutes, but watch it like a hawk so it doesn't burn.

Serve straightaway with a pinch of sea salt and some nice fresh greens.

WOODYS
A SURFING TRADITION SINCE
1956
LONG BEACH, CALIFORNIA

These are truly incredible ribs – the method for which was inspired by the barbecue team I joined in Georgia, "Bubba Grills." Two of the guys, Lonnie Junior (aka Bubba) and Larry, were kind enough to share their secret method with me. I can assure you it will give you the most ridiculously tender, delicious meat. Loads of love to their posse. I've adjusted their method for home cooking and flavored these ribs with my own rub and sauce, which I'm really proud of.

Because Britain doesn't have as much sunshine as somewhere like Georgia or Florida, I've created an oven method for this that rocks. But if you've got a grill with a lid and a thermometer, by all means give this a go. All the same timings apply. Good ribs do take time, so give them a bit of attention.

5 ★ PORK RIBS

Serves 4

1 x barbecue rub recipe (page 297)
2 cups apple juice
apple cider vinegar
4 racks of baby back pork ribs (approx. 14 oz each), the best quality you can afford
½ x barbecue sauce recipe (page 296)
sea salt

Wine suggestion:
Italian red – a full Valpolicella, such as a Ripasso

Make the barbecue rub the night before. Once that's done, get a bowl wide enough to hold a rack of ribs and fill it with your apple juice and a splash of vinegar. Sprinkle the barbecue rub onto a board. Dunk each rack in the bowl, then put it on a board and toss and generously dust and cover it with the barbecue rub until it's well coated (cover your bowl of apple juice and pop into the refrigerator to use later). Massage the rub into the meat really well. The Bubba Grills guys say that when you feel the granules in the rub turning into a smooth paste, you know it's changing the flavor of the meat. Wrap each rack in plastic wrap, and put into the refrigerator overnight.

The next day, take your racks out of the refrigerator an hour or two before you want to cook them so the meat can come up to room temperature. Preheat your oven or grill to 250°F. Put your ribs curved side down – or frowney-face down, as Larry would say – on a sheet pan and cook them for 1½ hours.

Remove the racks of ribs from the oven or grill. Get 4 big pieces of aluminum foil, just over double the size of your ribs, in front of you, and lay a rack, smiley-face up, on each one. Bring the edges of the foil up, and divide your reserved apple juice between them. Bring the corners of the foil together and fold them to make a tight package. Carefully return the parcels to the sheet pan and put back into the oven or grill to cook for another 1½ hours. Make the barbecue sauce while you're waiting – half the quantity will do, so put the rest into the refrigerator to use another time.

When the time is up, take the packages out of the oven or grill, carefully unwrap them, pour away the liquid, and discard the foil. Put the ribs back in the pan and into the oven to help them dry out for about 15 minutes. After that, take them out and generously brush them on both sides with the barbecue sauce. Return them to the oven for 30 minutes so the glaze has time to set. At this stage the meat will be incredibly tender but will also have some wonderful texture to it. I like to serve this on a board, cut into nice big chunks with a sprinkle of sea salt on top. Absolute heaven.

MY EPIC BBQ SAUCE

I really love this barbecue sauce. There are loads of layers of flavors that make it truly insane. Although there are lots of ingredients, it doesn't take long at all to whip up. I think if you're going to make this you may as well make a lot so that it's in the refrigerator and on hand when you next need a huge flavor kick. The results are incredible, so it's worth the time and effort to get it right.

Makes approx. 2 cups

★　　★　　★　　★　　★　　★

For the paste
1 medium onion, peeled and quartered
10 cloves garlic, peeled
2 fresh red chiles, stalks removed
olive oil

Herbs and spices
10 sprigs of fresh thyme or lemon thyme, leaves picked
10 sprigs of fresh rosemary, leaves picked
a small bunch of fresh cilantro
10 bay leaves
1 teaspoon cumin seeds
2 tablespoons fennel seeds
2 tablespoons smoked paprika
6 whole cloves

To finish
zest and juice of 2 oranges
1 heaping cup (packed) light brown sugar
⅓ cup balsamic vinegar
generous ⅔ cup ketchup
2 tablespoons Worcestershire sauce, such as Lea & Perrins
2 teaspoons English mustard
generous ⅔ cup apple juice
1 teaspoon sea salt
1 teaspoon freshly ground black pepper

Blitz the onion, garlic, and chiles together in a food processor until you've got a really fine paste. Pour a lug of olive oil into a saucepan and gently fry this paste for 5 minutes on a low heat to really get the flavors going.

While that's happening, add all your herbs and spices to the food processor, then peel in strips of orange zest using a speed peeler (you don't want any white pith) and blitz up really well. Add this puréed mixture to the pan and cook for another minute. Add the sugar, stir in well, and cook for a few more minutes, until it begins to dissolve and you get a thick brown paste. Pour in 1¼ cups of water and cook for 2 more minutes, then squeeze in the juice of both your oranges and add all the remaining ingredients. Stir well and bring everything to a boil, then turn down the heat a touch and simmer for 5 to 10 minutes, until the mixture starts to thicken slightly.

Pour the sauce slowly through a fine strainer into a large bowl and get rid of any larger bits left behind in the strainer. Rinse the strainer and pass the sauce through the strainer again so it's really silky.

Let cool completely, then either divide the sauce between jars or get marinating straightaway. Once it's in the refrigerator, you'll have about a week or so to use up the rest of the sauce. If you want to keep it for longer, you'll have to sterilize some jars. It's dead easy. Either put them in the sink along with their lids and cover them completely with boiling water from the kettle; or fill a really large saucepan with water, bring it to the boil, then immerse the jars and lids and continue to boil for 10 minutes; or, if you've got a good dishwasher with a really hot cycle, run them through that.

Pour the sauce into your sterilized jar, screw the lid on tightly, and immerse the jar completely in a large suacepan of boiling water for 10 minutes. Let it cool, then put it into the refrigerator or a cool dark cupboard until you need it. It should keep for about 6 months, no problem.

MY BARBECUE RUB

1 tablespoon fennel seeds • 2 teaspoons smoked paprika • zest of 1 orange • 1 teaspoon dried thyme • 1 tablespoon light brown sugar • a good pinch of sea salt and freshly ground pepper • 2 cloves garlic, peeled and finely grated

Bash up the fennel seeds in a pestle and mortar and mix with all the other ingredients until you have a lovely deep red paste. Simple!

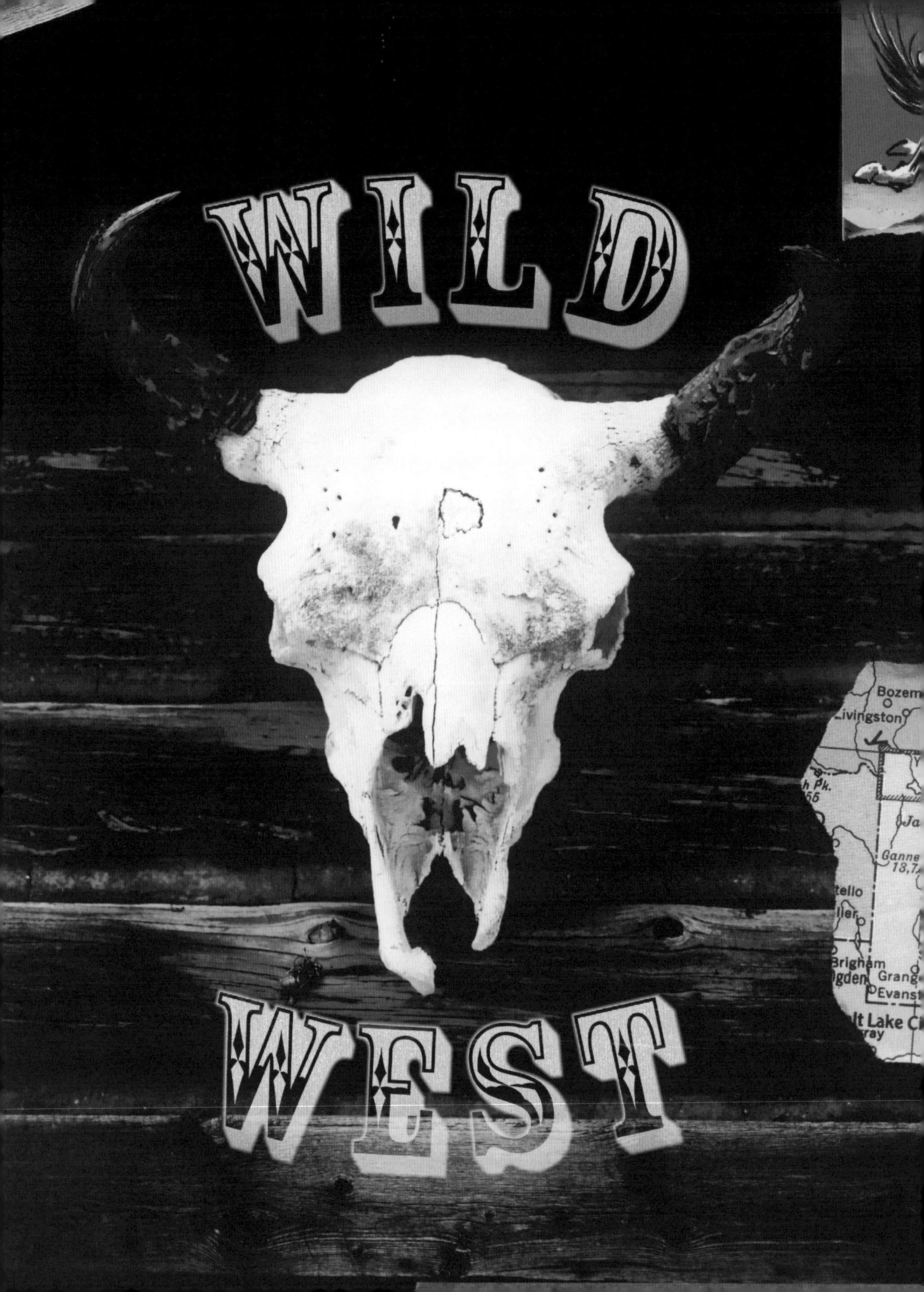
WILD
WEST
Livingston
Brigham
Ogden

ike a lot of kids, I grew up loving the idea of being a cowboy. I'd run around the garden with my cap gun, use my poor sister as a bucking bronco, and watch Western movies like *Butch Cassidy and the Sundance Kid*, *Young Guns*, and even *Blazing Saddles* (especially that classic campfire scene! "How 'bout some more beans, Mr. Taggart?"). I still love the idea of all that, so leaving America without tracking down that great American icon – the all-American cowboy – wasn't an option.

After a bumpy ride through Wyoming's unpredictable weather system, my tiny windup plane landed in a frontier town founded by Buffalo Bill: Cody, Wyoming. I had so many questions running through my head: Did the sort of cowboys I was thinking of still exist? (The answer is yes.) Did they really wear hats and spurs all the time? (Yes.) Were they really a hit with all the girls? (Yes.) Was there more to their cooking than tinned beans and steak? (Thankfully, yes!)

The state of Wyoming is sandwiched between six other states, smack bang in the middle of America in an area once known as the Wild West. Montana is to the north of Wyoming, and both these states are bigger than England, not to mention full of natural resources, like oil and cattle.

From Cody I headed into the Pryor Mountains to experience real cowboy living. A wonderful couple, "Hip" and Loretta Tillett, took me across the state line into Montana to "Dead Man's Camp," where they run their cattle during the spring and summer. I wanted to look the part when I got there, so I embraced my inner six-year-old and "duded up" with chaps, belt, boots, hat – the whole lot. With all that gear on I hardly recognized myself!

This part of America is known as Big Sky Country, and when you're sitting on a horse, with mountains and open country as far as the eye can see, the landscape really commands your attention. Life at the Tilletts' cow camp was like it would have been 100 years ago: wooden outhouses, no running water or electricity, tents with wood fires in them, and a small wooden cabin for communal dinners. The days were full of good old-fashioned manual labor and I mucked in with the cooking, branding, and even castrating duties (talk about being thrown in at the deep end!). Of course the by-product of castration is the unusual but tasty Rocky Mountain oysters (aka deep-fried bull's testicles – recipe not included!). I was filthier by the end of these few days than I've ever been, but I had such an incredible time it didn't matter.

I'm convinced that some of the best cooking is a result of resourceful people making the best of the situations and surroundings they find themselves in, and I was pleasantly surprised to find that cowboy cooking includes all sorts of brilliant examples of that. I had recipe ideas running through my head all week, and the food in this chapter is inspired by conversations and memories people shared with me, as well as ingredients I found in the small towns I passed through. All of it reflects real cowboy cooking and my take on it.

The life of a cowboy is definitely not an easy one – but if you like hard work, open country, and running into the occasional grizzly … it might be right up your street. I'll definitely be hanging on to all my gear. You never know, I might feel like a change of career one day.

WILD WEST

BEST BAKED BEANS

Serves 8

★　　★　　★　　★　　★　　★

olive oil

4 red or white onions, peeled and thinly sliced

1 heaping teaspoon smoked paprika

2 to 3 dried chiles (such as ancho or chipotle), stalks removed

2 tablespoons butter

6 x 15-oz cans pinto or cannellini beans

2 x 14-oz cans diced tomatoes

3 or 4 dried bay leaves

sea salt and freshly ground black pepper

white wine vinegar

2 tablespoons molasses

8 slices of smoked bacon, the best quality you can afford

2 sprigs of fresh rosemary, leaves picked

a large handful of freshly grated Parmesan or Cheddar cheese

4 or 5 slices good-quality stale bread

Wine suggestion: Californian or Australian red – a Grenache

Back in the pioneer days, feeding a group of hungry cowboys from a chuck wagon traveling through the Wild West was all about being resourceful and making the few dried ingredients you had in your mobile pantry stretch until you hit the next ranch or town. Baked beans are a real cowboy staple, and this is my version, which I've tweaked by using fresh ingredients and adding a delicious, crunchy topping.

If you really want to make this special, it's well worth buying interesting dried chiles – they add wonderful heat and flavor and they'll keep happily in your cupboard for ages – ready to add some excitement to all sorts of dishes.

Put a few lugs of olive oil into a large Dutch oven or similar pan on a medium heat. Add your sliced onions and smoked paprika and fry for around 10 to 15 minutes, or until softened and lightly colored, stirring often. While that's happening, put your dried chiles into a bowl and cover them with 1¼ cups of boiling water to rehydrate them and release their flavors. Add the butter to the pan of onions, and once it's melted, add the beans, along with any juices from their cans. Add the canned tomatoes, bay leaves, and a good pinch of salt and pepper, then take the dried chiles out of their soaking water, slice them thinly, and add them to the pan with the chile water left behind in the bowl.

Give everything a good stir and bring to a simmer, then turn the heat down to low and cook the beans slowly for 1½ hours – you want it just blipping away so the beans don't split and go mushy. Have a taste and correct the seasoning with salt and pepper, adding a little slug of vinegar and the molasses to bring out the flavor and give the beans a beautiful sheen.

While the beans are simmering, preheat your oven to 350°F. Put the bacon, rosemary leaves, and grated cheese into a food processor. Tear in the bread, and pulse until you have fine flavored bread crumbs. Sprinkle this mixture over the beans and put the pan into the oven for 40 minutes to an hour, until the topping is golden, crunchy, and delicious. Frankly, it's a meal in itself, but it will also go really nicely next to meat or fish.

Wyoming is landlocked, so really the only fish you can get that tastes delicious is from the rivers and streams. Certain varieties of trout were plentiful, which was brilliant for me, as it's one of my favorite things in the world to eat. People in Wyoming love their trout, but unfortunately it tends to be a very underrated fish elsewhere. If you're into your fly-fishing, this recipe is a great excuse to get out there – just make sure you check the fishing regulations before you do!

When buying the trout, ask your fishmonger to scale and gut them for you, and ideally get him to score each fish on both sides for you too. The scores should be ½ inch apart and about ⅛ inch deep. Most fish sold in supermarkets is unscaled, so if you need to do it yourself, don't worry, it takes literally 3 or 4 minutes of going over the skin with a blunt knife to work your way against the grain of the scales, from the tail to the head of the fish, flicking off the scales as you go. If you feel you need a bit more guidance for this, check out my website, www.jamieoliver.com/how-to, and I'll show you how to scale, gut, score, and fillet a fish so you'll know for next time.

Put your trout into a roasting pan and add all the marinade ingredients. Toss the trout in the marinade and really rub the flavors all over the fish, making sure you get it into all the cavities – this will give it amazing flavor. Cover the tray with plastic wrap and put into the refrigerator to marinate for 1 to 2 hours, no longer.

While your fish is marinating, put all the chopped vegetables and herbs for the salad into a bowl. Toss with the juice of 1 lemon and an equal amount of extra virgin olive oil, season well with salt and pepper, and put aside while you cook your fish. Get your fish out of the refrigerator, then drain and pat dry with paper towel. Season really well with salt and pepper.

You can cook the fish in a screaming hot grill pan or grill, or broil them in the oven at full whack. Rub the fish with olive oil, season with salt and pepper, then either place the trout on the hot grill pan or grill to cook for 4 to 5 minutes on each side, or pop onto a sheet pan and place under the broiler, at full whack, for about 12 minutes, turning over halfway. When the trout are golden and crisp on the outside and the meat flakes easily away from the bones, they're ready.

Once cooked, serve on individual plates or a big platter with that fresh lovely salad and lemon wedges on the side for squeezing over.

Serves 4

4 whole trout (approximately 14 oz each), scaled and gutted
1 lemon, cut into wedges, to serve

For the marinade
1 heaping teaspoon Kosher salt
1 heaping teaspoon freshly ground black pepper
2 tablespoons olive oil
¼ cup cider vinegar
¼ cup bourbon or whiskey
zest and juice of 1 lemon

For the salad
4 tomatoes, halved, seeded, and thinly sliced
1 cucumber, halved lengthways, quartered, and sliced
4 scallions, trimmed and thinly sliced
1 red, yellow, or orange bell pepper, seeded and finely chopped
a small bunch of fresh Italian parsley or basil, finely chopped
a small bunch of fresh dill, finely chopped
juice of 1 lemon
extra virgin olive oil

Wine suggestion:
American dry white – a Riesling from Washington State

IN THE OLD DAYS, COWBOYS, OUTLAWS, AND GUNSLINGERS WOULD STOP BY THE FRONTIER TOWNS, LIKE CODY, TO FILL UP ON FRESH SUPPLIES FOR THE WEEKS TO COME AND HAVE A LAUGH IN THE LOCAL SALOON

MOUNTAIN MEATBALLS

Rocky Mountain oysters, which are deep-fried calves' testicles, are a Wild West delicacy. Although fairly tasty, I wasn't sure it would be the most popular recipe to include in this book, so I made up my own cowboy meatball dish instead. These monster meatballs are so delicious: they're stuffed with cheese and smothered in a rich chile sauce. I hereby dedicate these balls to all the bulls in the Wild West losing theirs!

Serves 8

★　　★　　★　　★　　★　　★

olive oil
2 red onions, peeled and diced
2½ lbs good-quality ground meat
(beef, buffalo, or a mixture)
1 heaping teaspoon Dijon mustard
1 teaspoon dried oregano
a pinch of cumin seeds, bashed
up in a pestle and mortar
1 teaspoon coriander seeds, bashed
up in a pestle and mortar
2 handfuls of bread crumbs
2 large eggs, preferably free-range or organic
sea salt and freshly ground black pepper
1 cup freshly grated Cheddar cheese

For the chile sauce
1 large red onion, peeled and diced
2 red or yellow bell peppers,
seeded and roughly chopped
10 cloves garlic, peeled and thinly sliced
1 to 2 fresh red chiles, seeded
and minced, to taste
½ teaspoon smoked paprika
⅓ cup Worcestershire sauce,
such as Lea & Perrins
heaping ⅓ cup ketchup
⅓ cup apple cider vinegar
⅓ cup molasses or dark brown sugar
2 tablespoons Dijon mustard
1⅔ cups hot coffee
3 plum tomatoes, quartered
a small bunch of fresh Italian parsley

Wine suggestion:
French red – a ripe Côtes du Rhône

Preheat your oven to full whack. Put a large frying pan on a medium heat and add a good lug of olive oil. Add the 2 diced onions and fry for 10 minutes or until softened, then remove from the heat and let cool completely. Put your ground meat into a bowl with the mustard, oregano, cumin, coriander, bread crumbs, eggs, a good pinch of salt and pepper, and the cooled onions. Use clean hands to really scrunch it all together well, then divide the mixture into 8 patties.

Pick each patty up, one at a time, and roll into a baseball-sized ball. Stick your thumb deep into the ball to make a pocket, then stuff in a good pinch of grated cheese. Cup, pack, and pat the meat around the cheese, using your hands to mold it back into a ball. You'll soon get the hang of it. Place the balls in a large oiled Dutch oven or roasting pan, drizzle over a good lug of olive oil, then bang into the oven for 25 to 30 minutes, until golden and sizzling.

Meanwhile, crack on with your chile sauce. Use paper towels to wipe out the pan you cooked your onions in, and put it back on a medium heat with a few lugs of olive oil. Add the onion, bell peppers, garlic, fresh chiles, and paprika and fry gently for about 15 minutes. Stir in the Worcestershire sauce, ketchup, vinegar, molasses or sugar, mustard, coffee, and tomatoes, and bring everything to a boil. Turn the heat down to medium-low and simmer for 20 minutes, until the sauce has thickened. It should be thick and delicious, but if you'd like it a bit thicker, just turn the heat up and cook for a few more minutes.

Remove the cooked meatballs from the oven when they're ready and spoon away as much of the fat from the pan as you can. Pour your chile sauce over the top, and return the pan to the oven for 5 more minutes. Finely chop your parsley, sprinkle over, and serve with a spoonful of rice or mashed potatoes and a lemony green salad. The cowboys I met could easily nail two of these in one sitting, but if you aren't going to be roping cattle all day I'd say one is probably plenty!

One of the cowgirls I met said she struggled for ideas at mealtimes because the men weren't overly keen on eating veggies. However, she did say one of the things they would eat was broccoli salad. Every diner and restaurant in Cody seemed to have one on the menu, so I created this version, which is absolutely delicious and hits all the right spots. When I cooked it for a group of ranchers, there was none left by the end of the night. Success!

Use a small knife to remove the broccoli florets and cut them up into smaller ones. Basically, this is your opportunity to make the broccoli really delicate and more salady-looking, so spend a bit of time doing this. You'll be left with the stalk, so discard the thick, dry base, then cut the remaining stalk in half lengthways and thinly slice.

Blanch your broccoli florets and sliced stalks really quickly in boiling salted water for 60 seconds, just long enough to soften the broccoli but still leave it with a bit of a bite. Drain it in a colander, then spread it around a clean dish towel to steam dry (this is important because it will help the dressing cling to the broccoli). Once completely dry, transfer to a serving dish.

Fry the bacon on a medium heat with a small splash of olive oil, until crisp and golden, then spoon most of the bacon bits over your broccoli. Any leftover fat in the pan can be used in your salad dressing. Pour it into a mixing bowl with all the other dressing ingredients and whisk.

Add the sliced tomatoes and chopped chives to your broccoli and bacon bits. Dress it all really well, and check the seasoning. If it needs tweaking, add a splash more vinegar. If you've got any chive flowers, sprinkle those over the top and serve straightaway. It's beautiful on its own or served next to any grilled or roasted meat or fish.

PS: I also like to toss things like diced feta cheese or chopped fresh chiles through this salad. Different-colored cherry or grape tomatoes are really nice too.

BROCCOLI SALAD

Serves 6 as a side

2 large heads of broccoli
8 slices of smoked bacon, the best quality you can afford, cut into small pieces
olive oil
3 firm red tomatoes, halved, seeded, and thinly sliced
a small bunch of fresh chives (with flowers if you can get them), finely chopped, flowers reserved

For the dressing
½ clove garlic, peeled and finely grated
2 teaspoons Dijon mustard
⅓ cup extra virgin olive oil
2 tablespoons white wine vinegar
sea salt and freshly ground black pepper

Wine suggestion:
Italian white – a Falanghina from the south

PITCHFORK FONDUE

Back in 1922 one of Cody's restaurants, Cassie's, used to make its money as a brothel. These days it's much more respectable, and the only breasts you can pay for are on the grilled chicken! On the night I was there a guy named Del Nose had a "pitchfork fondue" going on in the parking lot. I'd never seen steak being skewered onto pitchforks, then dipped into a cauldron of boiling pork fat – it put the *petits fondues* of the French Alps to shame.

I have to say the simple steak sandwiches Del was churning out were damn tasty. But it was interesting to see that these steaks were completely unseasoned. In every other state I'd visited, people piled on the seasoning and even said I wasn't seasoning my food enough. In Wyoming, everyone seemed adamant that you had to respect the natural flavors of the meat. It was a great introduction to cowboy cooking and gave me a chance to have a beer and a chat with some young rodeo riders.

On this trip I learned that there are actually two kinds of cowboy: rodeo cowboys and "cowmen." Rodeo cowboys are the athletes of the cowboy world, and without doubt they are the craziest, bravest whippersnappers around. Rodeo started out as a way for cowboys to showcase their skills, and has grown to become part of the American tradition, one that I can't see disappearing, regardless of health and safety.

The cowboys I met at Cassie's were only in their late teens and early twenties, and were fantastically passionate in their quest to reach their ultimate adrenaline high: staying on a very pissed-off bucking horse or bull for more than eight seconds. All had lost teeth and nursed broken bones – but were still doing pretty well, all things considered.

What those rodeo boys do on a nightly basis is miles away from what cowmen, like my new mates Hip and his young ranch hand, Poncho, do. These guys are cowboys in the traditional sense of the word. As well as moving huge herds across steep, crumbling landscapes that a Land Rover would struggle with, they also brand the cattle, deliver calves, and protect the herd from "cattle rustlers." Truly epic farming ... cowboy style!

WORCESTER STEAK 'N' MUSHROOMS

The Wild West just wouldn't be the same without its man-sized steaks. When I was there, I'm embarrassed to admit that I ordered a cowgirl-sized steak in the local restaurant because the cowboy ones were huge! Wild mushrooms like these morels grow in the mountains and are such a treat, especially with steak. This is an unusual way of marinating and glazing the meat using the wonderful flavor of Worcestershire sauce. Purists think steak should be cooked simply, and they're right: beautiful steaks, cooked simply, are a joy. That said, using rich intense flavors, like I've done here, is incredibly delicious and makes a great change from your everyday steak.

Serves 4

4 x ½-lb steaks, filet mignon, rib-eye, or top loin (strip)
½ lemon

For the marinade
¼ cup Worcestershire sauce, such as Lea & Perrins
¼ cup olive oil
1 clove garlic, peeled and minced
2 sprigs of fresh rosemary, leaves picked and finely chopped
2 fresh bay leaves, finely chopped
a good pinch of freshly ground black pepper

For the potatoes
1¾ lbs baby potatoes, washed and scrubbed clean
sea salt and freshly ground black pepper
a pat of butter
juice of ½ lemon

For the mushrooms
a pat of butter
olive oil
1 onion, peeled and diced
½ lb morels or wild mushrooms, trimmed, cleaned, and torn into bite-sized pieces (if using morels, give them a quick wash and dry them in a salad spinner or dish towel)
2 cloves garlic, peeled and thinly sliced

For the glaze
2 pats of butter
¼ cup Worcestershire sauce

Wine suggestion:
Californian red – a Zinfandel from Sonoma County

Mix all the marinade ingredients together in a large bowl, add the steaks, and really rub the marinade into them. Cover the bowl with plastic wrap and pop into the refrigerator to marinate for 3 to 4 hours. If you're short on time, an hour at room temperature will do. Take your steaks out of the refrigerator 20 minutes before you want to cook them, to allow them to come up to room temperature.

Boil the potatoes in salted water. Once done, drain them, then return them to the pan, add a pat of butter, squeeze in the lemon juice, and add a pinch of salt and pepper. Toss to coat them, then put to one side with the lid on to keep warm. Meanwhile, get a frying pan on a high heat and add a pat of butter, a good lug of olive oil, and the diced onion. Fry for about 4 minutes, then add the mushrooms and garlic to the pan and cook for about 3 minutes, stirring regularly. Have a taste and correct the seasoning with salt, pepper, and a few drips of lemon juice. Remove from the heat and set aside.

Preheat a large, thick-bottomed pan or griddle pan on a high heat until screaming hot. Add the steaks, turning them every minute until cooked to your liking. As a rough guide, a ¾ inch thick steak will take about 2 minutes per side for medium rare, 3 minutes for medium, and 4 minutes for well done, but use your instincts. Once you're happy, remove the steaks to rest on a warm plate. Turn off the heat and add the butter and Worcestershire sauce to the pan you cooked your steaks in, with a small splash of water to create a kinda Worcestershire glaze. Use a wooden spoon to scrape all the goodness from the bottom of the pan.

Once rested, return the steaks and their juices to the pan, tossing quickly so they get shiny. Either leave the steaks whole, or slice them up and divide between the plates, pouring over the lovely glaze. Gently crush some of the potatoes with the back of a spoon, and add to the plates. Scatter over the mushrooms, slice the remaining lemon half into wedges, and serve. Delicious!

Marcy Tatarka, an absolutely lovely cook I met in Wyoming, was full of all sorts of local food knowledge. She told me that people in this part of America are really into their pasties! Turns out that in the 1920s and '30s, miners from Cornwall came over to work in Montana and it wasn't long before the locals developed a taste for the good old Cornish pasty. Their recipes haven't evolved radically since, but they do embrace local ingredients like chicken, squash, and sage. Pastry isn't exactly health food, but a delicious pasty once in a while won't hurt you. If you like, you can make a slightly "skinnier" pasty by reducing the butter to 1¾ sticks and adding 3 tablespoons of olive oil. But frankly, if I'm making these, I just go for it old-school style.

CORNISH COWBOY PASTIES

Serves 8

★ ★ ★ ★ ★ ★

Preheat the oven to 350°F. Bring your butter and water to a boil in a large saucepan, then take the pan off the heat. Stir the flour and salt into the mixture bit by bit with a spatula, until you've got a dough. Tip it onto a floured surface and use your hands to shape it into a smooth ball. Put the ball of dough into a floured bowl, dust the top with flour, then cover with plastic wrap and chill in the refrigerator for about 30 minutes while you make the filling.

Meanwhile, get a large frying pan and fry your chopped onion in a lug of olive oil for 10 minutes or until softened. Add the diced chicken and fry for 5 minutes until brown, then add the rest of the chopped vegetables and herbs. Fry for another 5 minutes, then add 3 or 4 good gratings of nutmeg. Season well with salt and pepper, then pour in the chicken broth and Worcestershire sauce. Stir in the flour and simmer on a medium heat for 15 to 20 minutes, until most of the stock has cooked away and you're left with nice thick gravy.

Dust a clean surface and a rolling pin with flour, then divide your pastry dough in half and roll each half out until it's slightly thinner than ¼ inch. Use a cereal bowl (about 6 inches in diameter) to cut 4 circles out of each half, so you end up with 8 circles. You may need to cut out 2 or 3 circles from each half first, then re-roll the remaining pastry to make the rest. Dust the circles with flour, and spoon your filling into the middle of each one. Brush the edges of the pastry with some of the beaten egg, then fold each circle in half over the filling and crimp the edges with your finger and thumb to seal them. If you want to see how this is done, check out the video on www.jamieoliver.com/how-to.

Line 2 baking trays with parchment paper, scatter a handful of cornmeal or polenta over the paper, and place your pasties on top. Brush the pasties all over with more of the beaten egg and sprinkle over a little more cornmeal. Bake in the hot oven for 30 to 35 minutes, or until golden, and serve straightaway with a fresh green salad. A taste of Cornwall in the Wild West – who'd have thought it!

For the pastry
2 sticks plus 2 tablespoons butter
1¼ cups hot water
4½ cups all-purpose flour,
plus extra for dusting
1 teaspoon salt
1 large egg, preferably
free-range or organic, beaten
a handful of medium ground
cornmeal or polenta

For the filling
1 red onion, peeled and diced
olive oil
4 skinless, boneless chicken
thighs, preferably free-range or
organic, cut into ¾ inch dice
½ a small butternut squash
(approx. ½ pound), peeled
and cut into ½ inch chunks
1 carrot, peeled and roughly chopped
1 medium potato, peeled and
cut into ½ inch chunks
6 sprigs fresh sage or thyme,
leaves picked and chopped
nutmeg
sea salt and freshly ground
black pepper
1¼ cups chicken broth,
preferably organic
2 tablespoons Worcestershire
sauce, such as Lea & Perrins
1 tablespoon all-purpose flour

Wine suggestion:
Italian red – a Barbera d'Alba

Bulls and broncos are seriously powerful animals and they hate having passengers. I stayed well clear and let the rodeo boys do their thing - exciting, but madness!

WYOMING

HOME ON THE RANGE!

COMMITTEE OF THE YEAR

PROFESSIONAL RODEO COWBOYS ASSOCIATION

99
98

ARGE OUTDOOR RODEO

Cody Nite RODEO

WILD WEST RICE

As in many other parts of America, there are Native American reservations in and around the beautiful mountains I visited. I was told that a popular Native dish was hollowed-out pumpkin stuffed with rice and other delicious things. I got excited by the possibilities, so decided to play around with the idea and use flavorings like cinnamon, chiles, and fresh dill, which are fairly common in this area, to create this little number. I also kept with the cowboy vibe of using dried ingredients by adding dried cranberries.

Frankly, I think it's great as a meal in itself with a spoonful of natural yogurt and a fresh little salad, but it would also make a vegetable and rice side to any meat or fish dish.

Serves 8–10

★ ★ ★ ★ ★ ★

olive oil
2 onions, peeled
and thinly sliced
8 cloves garlic, peeled
and crushed
2½ cups wild black or red rice
sea salt and freshly
ground black pepper
a large bunch of fresh dill
1 quart chicken broth,
preferably organic
2¼ lb acorn or
butternut squash
ground cinnamon
2 fresh red chiles,
deseeded and finely chopped
2½ cups basmati rice
1½ cups dried cranberries
zest and juice of 1 lemon

Wine suggestion:
French white –
a Crozes Hermitage

Preheat your oven to 350°F. Get a wide and fairly shallow Dutch oven or similar pan on a medium heat and add a lug of olive oil, your onions, garlic, wild rice, and a good pinch of salt and pepper. Fry for around 10 minutes, or until the onions have softened and the nutty flavors in the rice have had a chance to come out. Finely chop the dill stalks and roughly chop the leaves. Add the stalks to the pan, reserving the leaves for later, then pour in your chicken broth and bring to a boil. Put a lid on the pan and simmer for around 10 minutes, stirring occasionally.

While that's happening, carefully halve your squash and seed it. Quite often with butternut or acorn squash the skin is so thin and delicate you don't need to peel it, as it goes really soft when cooked and is a pleasure to eat. However, if it looks thick or tough in places, it is worth peeling it. Slice the squash into ¾ inch wedges and toss them in a large bowl with a good lug of olive oil, a big pinch of cinnamon, the chopped chiles, and the reserved dill leaves. Season well with salt and pepper.

Remove the lid from the rice and stir in the basmati rice, dried cranberries, and the zest and juice from your lemon. Gently push your wedges of squash down into the rice so they're sort of half-in, half-out, replace the lid or cover with aluminum foil, and put into the hot oven to bake for 45 minutes. After this time, the rice and squash should be lightly golden and soft. You can serve them now or, if you want a bit of crispiness, simply take the lid off and pop it back into the oven for another 10 minutes to let it brown up a bit. And there you have it – a delicious dish inspired by cowboys *and* Indians. Brilliant!

TRAYBAKED CHICKEN

Serves 4

★　　★　　★　　★　　★　　★

In this part of America they make a beautiful *al forno* or oven-baked dish with sliced sweet potatoes, Yukon potatoes, sage, and onion. I took that delicious base and turned it into a great one-pan meal by adding supremes of chicken. You might think it's unusual to marinate the chicken in brine, but it makes it outrageously soft and juicy. Give it at least 2 hours to marinate, but if you really want the full benefit, overnight is best.

For the brine
1 quart water
2 tablespoons kosher salt
⅓ cup honey
3 cloves garlic, peeled and crushed
2 sprigs of fresh sage, leaves picked
¼ cup apple cider vinegar
juice and zest of 1 lemon

For the bake
4 chicken breasts/supremes of chicken, wing bone attached, skin on
2 slices of smoked bacon, the best quality you can afford, finely chopped
3 sweet potatoes, scrubbed and thinly sliced
4 medium potatoes (such as Yukon Gold – soft and fluffy is best), scrubbed and thinly sliced
1 medium onion, peeled and thinly sliced
4 cloves garlic, peeled and thinly sliced
2 sprigs of fresh sage, leaves picked and shredded
olive oil
sea salt and freshly ground black pepper
1⅔ cups chicken broth, preferably organic
⅔ cup heavy cream
1 cup freshly grated Parmesan cheese
a few pats of butter

Wine suggestion:
Portuguese red – an Alentejo

Mix all the brine ingredients together in a large bowl and add your chicken breasts. Cover the bowl with plastic wrap and leave in the refrigerator for at least 2 to 8 hours – or overnight.

When ready to cook, take the chicken out of the refrigerator so it can come up to room temperature, and preheat your oven to 350°F. Get yourself a wide Dutch oven or similar roasting pan and add the chopped bacon, all the sliced veggies, the garlic, and the sage. Add a lug of olive oil and a good pinch of salt and pepper and toss everything together. Pour in the chicken broth, then put into the oven for 30 minutes so the potatoes can begin to soften and soak up the broth.

Drain your chicken breasts, discarding the brine, and pat them dry with paper towels. Take the potatoes out of the oven and pour over the cream. Sprinkle over a little more black pepper and the Parmesan, then use a spoon to make little nests in the vegetables for the pieces of chicken to sit in. Put the chicken in these nests and dot little pats of butter on and around the breasts. Return the pan to the oven to cook for 35 minutes, or until the chicken is golden and cooked through and the potatoes are delicious. To check if your chicken is cooked through, simply stick a sharp knife into the thickest part. If the juices run clear, you're laughing. Serve straightaway with nice simple greens or a salad and enjoy.

PS: You could also use supremes of pheasant, or even pork, in the same way. Just remember to adjust the cooking times if necessary.

Hip and Loretta's cow camp was all about simple, authentic living and mucking in. I'd leave my tent at sunrise, do some cooking, then spend the rest of the day herding with Hip and the guys. By the end of my time there my cowboy gear was properly broken in!

FIRE ENTERTAINMENT, YELLOWSTONE PARK.

HAYNES·

CAMPFIRE COOKING

One of my days in Cody was spent cooking around a campfire with Judy, Jeff, and Rawhide. The three of them shared some of the history of the cow trails with me, while Judy, who loves her Dutch oven cooking, made us a delicious lunch. Dutch oven cooking was developed by (unsurprisingly) the Dutch. They shoveled coals over the lids of durable cast-iron pots, as well as underneath them, and created miniature ovens. What's amazing is that you can boil, steam, casserole, braise, and even bake beautiful little cakes with nothing more than these pots and a campfire. It's easy to see why Dutch oven cooking became so popular in the American West.

Cattle drives were big business in the mid to late 1800s, and cowboys would head off in crews, sometimes for months at a time, to drive thousands of cattle from Texas, where they had more than they needed, up into states like Wyoming and Montana. Chuck wagons were basically the grandfathers of the modern day RV or trailer, and a brilliant way to move gear and food around the trail. One thing that was essential on the trail was a good cook!

The crew's "cookie" would often be an injured cowboy who couldn't ride with the others, and his wagon would be stocked up with loads of dried and canned foods and perhaps a secret bottle of whiskey (for medicinal purposes). He'd cook for the whole camp from his tiny mobile pantry and would have to be frugal, clever, and incredibly resourceful to avoid running out of supplies. If he was lucky, someone might shoot a rabbit, elk, or buffalo, but if not, he'd have to wait to stumble across a town or ranch before he'd be able to give his food attitude with fresh ingredients.

Most of the cooking I did on this particular trip was done outside, around a fire. And that got me thinking: it's only in the past century that we've traded the heat and smoke of the fire for the reliability and convenience of modern ovens. For me, the smoky earthy flavors that fire shares with food are a forgotten but wonderful seasoning. There's something about sitting around a campfire that's magical, something that stops it ever becoming boring. Everyone says the kitchen is the heart of the home, but the heart of the heart of the home is the fire ...

CHILI CON JAMIE

Everyone should know how to make a really good chili, and this one's a right cracker. I've been working on it for a while, and cowboy-land helped me pull it together. The cut of meat is really affordable and delicious, and gives the chili a gorgeous texture, similar to a beef stew. I wanted to make sure this had real attitude, so I achieved a brilliant depth of flavor by mixing dried chiles with fresh ones and adding fresh herbs. I made this the cowboy way, over a fire, and when you're cooking like that, one of the best ways to control the temperature is to add liquid. The cowboys had plenty of coffee on hand, so I used that and it ended up adding to the wonderfully unique flavor.

Serves 10–12

★   ★   ★   ★   ★   ★

4½ lbs beef brisket, trimmed and sliced into 1-inch-thick pieces across the grain

2 cups hot coffee

3 large dried chiles (ancho, chipotle, or poblano)

olive oil

2 heaping teaspoons ground cumin

2 heaping teaspoons smoked paprika

1 heaping teaspoon dried oregano

2 fresh bay leaves

2 red onions, peeled and diced

3–4 fresh chiles

2 cinnamon sticks

10 cloves garlic, peeled and thinly sliced

sea salt and freshly ground black pepper

4 x 14-oz cans diced tomatoes

3 tablespoons molasses or dark brown sugar

3 red, yellow, or orange bell peppers, seeded and sliced

2 x 15-oz cans beans (kidney, butter, or pinto), drained

optional: sour cream, to serve

Ask your butcher to trim and slice your brisket for you. If you're doing it yourself, carefully trim the meat by discarding any fat or silver skin. Cut the meat against, rather than with, the grain into 1-inch-thick pieces.

Make your coffee and, while it's hot, soak the dried chiles in it for a few minutes to let them rehydrate. Meanwhile, put your largest Dutch oven or similar pan on a low heat and add a few lugs of olive oil, the cumin, paprika, oregano, bay leaves, and onions. Fry for 10 minutes, until the onions have softened. Seed and chop half your fresh chiles. Slice up the rehydrated chiles and add them to the onion mixture along with the chopped fresh chiles, the cinnamon sticks, sliced garlic, a good pinch of salt and pepper, and a splash of the chile-infused coffee. Stir, then add the rest of the coffee, the canned tomatoes, and the molasses or sugar. Add the pieces of brisket and another good pinch of salt and pepper, cover with a lid, and simmer for around 3 hours, stirring occasionally.

After a few hours use 2 forks or a potato masher to break the meat up and pull it apart. Once you've done this, add the sliced bell peppers and canned beans and leave to simmer, stirring occasionally, for 30 minutes with the lid off until the meat is completely falling apart and delicious. Have a taste and season well – if you require a bit more heat (like I would), this is the time to seed and chop the rest of your fresh chiles and stir them in. Dollop a big spoonful of sour cream over the chili if you fancy it, and serve straight from the pan, with fluffy rice, flatbreads, or potatoes and a really nice fresh lemony green salad. Don't forget multiple cold beers! Enjoy.

While I was cooking with Judy at the Old Trail Town in Cody, I saw her preparing a really colorful potato dish in a Dutch oven. She called it Painted Hills potatoes, and said she'd evolved it from her friend's baked potato recipe. Since he lived on a ranch in the Painted Hills, and this dish had so many lovely colors in it, she named it after them. That sharing and gradual developing of recipes is something I'm really into, so I'm keeping with the spirit and I've evolved Judy's dish once again to my own tastes. Funnily enough, when I was a kid I used to make a "potato dish special" almost exactly the same as this, but I'd dice the bell peppers and potatoes. It's an absolute cracker.

PAINTED HILLS POTATOES

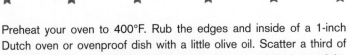

Serves 6–8

Preheat your oven to 400°F. Rub the edges and inside of a 1-inch Dutch oven or ovenproof dish with a little olive oil. Scatter a third of your sliced onions, potatoes, and bell peppers around the base of the dish, and season from a height with a good pinch of salt and pepper, a pinch of oregano, and a third of your rosemary. Sprinkle over a third of the grated cheese, then repeat the layers twice more until you've used everything up. Dot the cubes of butter over the top and pour the broth into one corner. Carefully press the whole lot down with your hands to really compress and flatten it.

Cover with aluminum foil or a lid and put into the middle of your hot oven for 1½ hours. After this time, remove the lid or foil and put the dish back into the oven for a further 20 minutes, so the top gets golden and delicious. This dish is man enough to have as a light supper during the week with a lovely green salad, but is equally delicious served alongside a roast dinner or lovely grilled fish or meat.

PS: In the past, I've added sliced parsnips, celery root, or fennel to this dish, and they work a treat.

olive oil
3 red onions, peeled and thinly sliced
2¾ lbs potatoes, washed, scrubbed, and thinly sliced
3 red bell peppers, seeded and thinly sliced
3 yellow bell peppers, seeded and thinly sliced
sea salt and freshly ground black pepper
dried oregano
3 sprigs of fresh rosemary, leaves picked and finely chopped
1½ cups freshly grated Parmesan or Cheddar cheese
3 tablespoons butter, cubed
2 cups chicken broth, preferably organic

Wine suggestion:
dry French white – a crisp white Valençay from the Loire Valley

COWBOY SCRAPPLE

Scrapple is a really clever cowboy dish that makes great use of leftover grits and meat – usually sausage meat or ground beef – from the previous day. These are flavored, then fried to make a kind of crisp patty. It's brilliant for breakfast topped with an egg. Just use it as you would a piece of toast or crostini. It will be the hero, but also the base of the dish. It would also make a great lunch served with mozzarella and a lovely herby salad.

Serves 6 hungry cowboys

★　　　★　　　★　　　★　　　★　　　★

2 cups grits, cornmeal, or polenta
½ lb pork sausages (approx. 4 sausages), the best quality you can afford
8 slices smoked bacon, the best quality you can afford, finely chopped
2 heaping teaspoons fennel seeds, bashed up in a pestle and mortar
2 dried chiles
3 sprigs of fresh rosemary, leaves picked and finely chopped
sea salt and freshly ground black pepper
olive oil
6 large eggs, preferably free-range or organic, to serve

Wine suggestion:
Spanish red – a chunky Yecla from the southeast

Bring a quart of water to a boil in a large pan. Add the grits, cornmeal, or polenta and cook for 10 minutes, stirring constantly, until the grains have dissolved and you have a very thick mixture. If you're using polenta, check the package to make sure the ratio of water to polenta needed is the same, and bear in mind that polenta often takes a bit longer to cook so may need a few extra minutes.

While this is cooking, get a large pan on a medium-high heat. Using a small sharp knife, slit your sausages open and squeeze all the meat into the pan. Add the chopped bacon and bashed-up fennel seeds and crumble in the chiles. Use a wooden spoon to squash the sausage meat flat in the pan. Fry everything until beautifully golden and crunchy, breaking up the meat as you go. Pour any excess fat into a small bowl and put aside.

Add the chopped rosemary to the pan and cook for another minute, then remove the pan from the heat until your cornmeal is ready. Spoon the cornmeal into the pan and mix everything together nicely. Turn the heat down to low and continue to cook until it's almost too thick to stir. Have a taste, and add a pinch of salt and pepper as required. Get yourself a deep loaf pan or other container approximately 5 x 9 inches and rub the pan with the reserved fat from the bowl. Tip in the scrapple and pack it down tightly, then cover and place in the refrigerator for 2 to 3 hours so it firms up.

When you're ready to cook, heat a nonstick frying pan on a medium heat. Run a knife around the edge of the container and turn the scrapple out onto a board in one piece. Slice it into ¾-inch-thick pieces – you should get 12 nice slices out of it. Fry the scrapple with a little olive oil for 3 or 4 minutes per side, or until really crispy and golden on both sides – you may need to do this in batches, or in 2 pans. When it's nearly perfect, fry or poach your eggs in a separate pan. Serve the scrapple and eggs together, with a little ketchup or hot chile sauce (see page 240).

AWESOME APPLE PANCAKES

Makes 6 cowboy-sized pancakes

butter, for cooking
natural yogurt, to serve
honey, to serve

For the pancake batter
1 apple, coarsely grated, core and all
1 large egg, preferably free-range or organic
1 cup self-rising flour
1 cup milk or water
a good pinch of sea salt
1 tablespoon honey
a pinch of ground cinnamon,
plus extra for serving

Without question these are some of the tastiest pancakes you can make, and definitely something to rattle out quickly and consistently at the weekend. I love the principle of this recipe: you literally have to read it once and you should be able to make it from memory for the rest of your life. I've grated the whole apple here, core and all, as the core is one of the most nutritious parts of the fruit and you really don't notice it. I've also made these with sliced bananas, grated pears, small cubes of mango, and even tablespoons of shredded or fresh coconut. Blueberries, raspberries and strawberries are winners too. I made these for the cowboys in the wilderness and they loved them.

★   ★   ★   ★   ★   ★

Put all your batter ingredients into a large bowl and whisk until well mixed. Put a frying pan approximately 9 inches in diameter on a medium-high heat and add a small pat of butter. Move it around to help it melt and coat the bottom of the pan, then spoon in a ladleful of your batter.

Cook the pancakes, one at a time, for a few minutes until little bubbles begin to form on the top and the liquid batter has just set. Check underneath every now and then to make sure the pancake isn't burning, and flip it over once it's golden. It's an old saying that people often screw up with their first pancake, so don't worry if it doesn't look perfect, it will still be delicious. Usually the problem is that the pan is either too cold or too hot – see how it goes and then adjust the heat so you're ready to knock out the rest.

Once the pancake is cooked on both sides, move it to a plate and serve right away with a dollop of natural yogurt, a drizzle of honey, and a good pinch of cinnamon. Wipe out the pan with a ball of paper towels, add another pat of butter, and get on with the next pancake.

PS: Loretta had very kindly given me a jar of her homemade honey and it was delicious! I discovered that a nice added extra is to drizzle the cooked pancakes with a little honey on one side while still in the pan, then flip them back over so that the honey caramelizes the underside of the pancakes. Once golden brown, turn them out so they've got a really thin crispy topping. I love this and so do kids. Just make sure no one touches the pancakes for 30 seconds or so once they're done, as the caramel can burn.

BIG PANORAMAS AND CAMPFIRE MEALS
ARE THE GREAT REWARDS OF LIFE AS
A HARDWORKING RANCHER

Somewhere in Wyoming there's a confused horse running around that used to be called Redhead but is now called Oliver, thanks to my cowboy mate Hip renaming it after me. To return the favor, I'm naming this delicious old-school twist on Eve's pudding after him. It's a great dessert to have up your sleeve because it mostly uses store-bought ingredients. You can use canned peaches or apples instead of pears, and any soft fruit instead of huckleberries.

HIP'S PUDDING

★　　★　　★　　★　　★　　★

Serves 10

Get yourself a 12- to 14-inch (2 quart) round or oval earthenware baking dish or pan with high sides. Put the pears and the molasses or dark brown sugar into the dish and mix everything around with a spoon so the pears are well coated. Spread them out fairly evenly over the base of the dish.

Preheat your oven to 350°F while you make your batter. You can absolutely do this by hand, but it's quicker and easier if you use a food processor. Put the butter, light brown sugar, orange zest, vanilla seeds or extract, ground ginger, and a good pinch of sea salt into the processor and whiz until light and creamy. Run a spatula around the bowl to scrape the mixture back into the center and start whizzing again while you crack in your eggs, one by one. If the mixture starts to curdle, mix in a tablespoon of flour to bring it back. Once mixed, add the flour and the juice from your zested orange and whiz again until smooth. Spoon the batter over the pears, and use the back of a spoon to spread it right out to the edges. Don't worry if a few pears poke through.

Put a small handful of berries into a bowl with 1 tablespoon of brown sugar and scrunch them in your hands to release their juices. Toss through the rest of the berries until they're shiny and glossy. Sprinkle the berries and their juices over the batter and scatter over your remaining brown sugar. Cover with a lid or aluminum foil and bake in the hot oven for 45 minutes. After this time, remove the lid or foil and cook for a further 20 to 35 minutes, so the top turns golden. Stick a skewer into the center of the dish to check it's done – if it comes out clean, it's perfect. Great served warm with cream, ice cream, or yogurt. Enjoy!

PS: If you want to make sweet individual puddings, like I've done in the picture, the same principles apply. Just get 10 small ovenproof bowls (5 inches wide and 2½ inches deep is about right) and follow the recipe, dividing everything equally between the bowls. Cover each one with foil and bake at the same temperature for 20 minutes. Then remove the foil and return to the oven for another 20 minutes.

3 x 15-oz cans pear halves
or slices in juice, drained
3 tablespoons molasses
or dark brown sugar
2½ cups huckleberries, sour
blueberries, or blackcurrants
2 heaping tablespoons
light brown sugar
optional: good-quality vanilla ice
cream, cream, or yogurt, to serve

For the batter
2 sticks plus 2 tablespoons
softened unsalted butter
1⅓ cups (packed) light brown sugar
zest and juice of 1 orange
1 vanilla bean, halved lengthways and
seeds scraped out, or 1 tablespoon
good-quality vanilla extract
2 heaping teaspoons ground ginger
sea salt
4 large eggs, preferably
free-range or organic
2 cups plus 2 tablespoons
self-rising flour

Wine suggestion:
New Zealand white –
a late harvest Riesling

HONEY RICE

Rice pudding is a dessert that's loved all over the world, and this cowboy version is cheap, accessible, and easy to cook in a Dutch oven. The honey makes it wonderfully sweet, and I've also chosen to add some huckleberry jam and a delicious brittle topping for some lovely contrast and crunch. Mixing in chopped dried fruits or a few little chunks of chocolate just before serving would also make for a really nice surprise when eating it.

Serves 4–6

★　　★　　★　　★　　★　　★

optional: huckleberry, blueberry, or any good soft local jam or preserve, to serve

For the rice pudding
1¼ cups arborio or short-grain pudding rice
1½ quarts reduced-fat milk
scant ½ cup honey
1 vanilla bean, halved lengthways and seeds scraped out
sea salt

For the granola brittle topping
scant 1 cup mixed nuts and seeds, such as Brazil nuts, hazelnuts, almonds, pistachios, pumpkin or sesame seeds
2 tablespoons honey

Wine suggestion:
French sweet white – a good-quality Sauternes

Preheat your oven to 400°F. Put the rice, milk, honey, vanilla bean, and seeds and a good pinch of salt into a large saucepan. Give it a good stir, then put the pan on a very low heat for about 45 minutes, stirring occasionally, until the rice has absorbed most of the milk and is gorgeous and creamy.

While that's happening, make the granola brittle. Carefully chop the nuts and seeds into large pieces on a board. Scatter them over a sheet pan lined with parchment paper, drizzle over the honey, and mix around until everything is well coated. Smooth and flatten the mixture into one layer, then put into the oven for 10 to 15 minutes, until dark golden. Remove and leave to cool before breaking up into finer pieces.

By now, your rice should be thick and creamy. If you want to loosen the consistency, feel free to stir in a splash more milk. I like to serve the rice while it's hot, on a large platter or in individual bowls, with spoonfuls of the jam marbled into it and the crumbly brittle on top. This would make a cracking dessert for Christmas or Thanksgiving, with some sugar-stewed cranberries in place of the jam.

CINNAMON SWIRLS

Makes about 20

For the dough
1 x ¼-oz envelope active dry yeast
2½ cups warm water
1 tablespoon honey
8 cups bread flour
½ teaspoon salt
olive oil

For the filling
heaping ¾ cup almonds
heaping ¾ cup hazelnuts
1¾ sticks (14 tablespoons) unsalted butter
2 level teaspoons ground cinnamon, plus extra for sprinkling
5 tablespoons honey
heaping ½ cup turbinado sugar, plus extra for sprinkling

Wine suggestion:
a glass of ten-year-old Tawny Port, or a cup of tea

I baked these gorgeous cinnamon swirls with my cowboy mate Hip's lovely mum, Abbie. They can be eaten for breakfast, or as a sweet snack, and any leftovers can be used up in a bread pudding. Abbie likes to cook hers so the buns are just blondly golden. Some did come out of the oven slightly overcooked and dark golden, and I have to say I was a bigger fan of those, but each to their own. That's what cooking is all about.

★　　★　　★　　★　　★　　★

Dissolve the yeast in ¼ cup of the water and stir in the honey. Let stand 10 minutes, until starting to froth.

You can make the dough in a food processor, or in a bowl by hand. Just put your flour, yeast mixture, and salt into the bowl and gradually pulse or stir in your remaining water until the mixture becomes a soft, springy dough. Flours can vary, so if you feel it needs a little more water, add another splash. Dust a clean surface and your clean hands with flour and knead the dough for a few minutes. Lightly oil a bowl with some olive oil, then transfer the dough to the bowl, cover with a dish towel, and leave for at least 30 minutes in a warm place until doubled in size.

Preheat your oven to 350°F. Spread the nuts out over a sheet pan and pop them into the oven for 6 to 8 minutes until lightly golden. Meanwhile, mix 11 tablespoons of the butter with the cinnamon in a large bowl and put aside. When the nuts are lightly golden, remove them from the oven, wrap them in a clean dish towel, and bash them up with a rolling pin until fairly fine. Let them cool down completely, then mix them into the butter mixture and put aside.

Generously flour a clean surface and a rolling pin, and roll your dough into a large rectangle about ½ inch thick and approximately 20 x 24 inches, dusting with flour as you go. Dot the nutty butter mixture all around the dough, spreading it out as well as you can with the back of a spoon. Drizzle the honey evenly all over the mixture.

Carefully lift up the longest edge of the dough and roll it over. Keep rolling carefully until you have a thick sausage shape. Slice this across into rounds about 1¼ inches thick. Grease a deep 9 x 13-inch cake pan with your remaining 3 tablespoons of butter, then sprinkle the turbinado sugar all over the base. Lay your rounds of dough flat in the tray so they are nice and snug and you can see the swirls. Cover with a dish towel, then put them to one side to let them rise for 20 to 40 minutes, or until doubled in size. Sprinkle over a good coating of turbinado sugar and a little extra cinnamon, and bake in the oven for about 25 minutes, until lovely and golden. To serve, carefully run a knife around the sides of the pan, then turn it upside down over a board or platter so that all those lovely caramelized bottoms will be on show (don't be tempted to touch or taste at this point, though, as the hot caramel will burn you), and tuck in.

Even though it has a strong British heritage, America has embraced the apple pie to the point that it's now considered a quintessentially American dessert. American pies often look like the pies in cartoons and comics – big, robust, and full of attitude. The crumble-like topping sprinkled over my pie is an idea I've been playing about with, and I think it helps make it unique. Because huckleberries grow wild in Wyoming, I felt it was only right to use them, but feel free to use fresh or frozen blueberries in their place for equally delicious results. Assembling your pie is dead easy, and I'll talk you through it step by step, but if you'd like to see how it's done before you start, check out my website, www.jamieoliver.com/how-to, for a demonstration.

APPLE-BERRY PIE

Serves 10–12

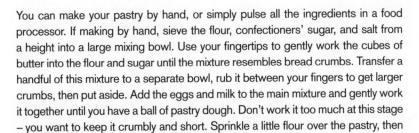

You can make your pastry by hand, or simply pulse all the ingredients in a food processor. If making by hand, sieve the flour, confectioners' sugar, and salt from a height into a large mixing bowl. Use your fingertips to gently work the cubes of butter into the flour and sugar until the mixture resembles bread crumbs. Transfer a handful of this mixture to a separate bowl, rub it between your fingers to get larger crumbs, then put aside. Add the eggs and milk to the main mixture and gently work it together until you have a ball of pastry dough. Don't work it too much at this stage – you want to keep it crumbly and short. Sprinkle a little flour over the pastry, then wrap it in plastic wrap and pop it into the refrigerator to rest for 1 hour.

Meanwhile, put the apples into a large saucepan with the zest and juice of 1 orange, a splash of water, and 5 tablespoons of sugar. Cover the pan and simmer on a medium heat for 10 minutes, until the apples have softened but still hold their shape. Remove from the heat and leave to cool. Scrunch a handful of berries in a bowl with the remaining sugar and the zest and juice of your remaining orange. Add the rest of the berries. Toss the cooled apples and their juices in a large bowl with the berries and the flour, then put aside.

Preheat your oven to 350°F. Take your ball of pastry out of the refrigerator and let it come up to room temperature. Get yourself a pie dish around 9 inches in diameter. Flour a clean surface and a rolling pin. Cut off a third of your pastry and put that piece to one side. Roll the rest into a circle just under ¼-inch thick, dusting with flour as you go. Roll the circle of pastry up over your rolling pin, then gently unroll it over the pie dish. Push it into the sides, letting any excess pastry hang over the edge. Tip in the fruit filling and brush all around the edge of the pastry with some of the beaten egg. Roll out the smaller ball of pastry just under ¼-inch thick and use your rolling pin to lay it over the top of the pie. Brush it all over with more beaten egg, reserving a little. Sprinkle over the reserved crumble mixture and the turbinado sugar.

Trim down the scruffy edges of pastry hanging over the sides to a 1-inch overhang, then fold the overhang back over the pie, sealing the edge by twisting or crimping it as you like. Brush these folded edges with your remaining beaten egg. Using a small, sharp knife, cut a cross into the middle of the pie. Place on the bottom of the oven and bake for 45 to 55 minutes, until golden and beautiful. Serve with ice cream, cream, or custard.

optional: good-quality vanilla ice cream, cream, or custard, to serve

For the pastry
4¼ cups all-purpose flour, plus extra for dusting
1 cup confectioners' sugar
a pinch of sea salt
2 sticks plus 2 tablespoons unsalted butter, chilled and cut into cubes
2 large eggs, preferably free-range or organic
a splash of milk

For the filling
10 small Granny Smith apples, peeled, cored, and halved, 3 sliced
juice and zest of 2 oranges
7 heaping tablespoons sugar
3½ cups huckleberries or blueberries
1 heaping tablespoon all-purpose flour
1 large egg, preferably free-range or organic, beaten
a small handful of turbinado sugar

Wine suggestion:
Italian sweet white – a Moscato d'Asti from Piemonte

Without a doubt this is the most epic book I've ever written in terms of logistics, costs, and area covered. There's no way I could have pulled it off without the help and support of *a lot* of very special people. I've done my best not to leave anyone out, but if I have, let me know and I'll get you into the reprint!

First and foremost, I had to give up a lot of family time to make this trip happen, so a very special personal thanks to my girls for all their love and support over the past year, and most especially to my beautiful wife, Jools, for allowing me to go on these trips even though she was pregnant with our third daughter. Thanks as well to Mum and Dad, Mrs N, and the inspirational Gennaro Contaldo.

I couldn't have done this without my wonderful food and editorial teams, especially the SAS Food Wonder Women who traveled with me this year. From the desert to cowboy country, they were my right hand and made each shoot an absolute pleasure: to Ginny Rolfe, Anna Jones, Sarah Tildesley, and Abigail "Scottish" Fawcett – thanks and much love. To the rest of my food team for doing such a great job for me: Pete Begg for his inspiration; the brilliant Claire Postans; lovely ladies Georgie Socratous, Bobby Sebire, Helen Martin, and Phillippa Spence. Thanks as well to the wonderful Laura Parr for keeping an eye on the nutrition of these recipes for me, and also to recipe testers Kate McCullough and Siobhan Boyle. Big thanks to my amazing and patient word girls: my editor, Katie Bosher, and editorial assistant, Rebecca (aka "Rubs") Walker, for all their hard work.

Love and thanks to David Loftus for the beautiful photography and collages you see in these pages. His consistent hard work, and his friendship, are appreciated by all. Thanks again to David Gleave (www.libertywines.co.uk) for the great wine suggestions, and also to my very good mate Adam Perry-Lang for giving me a jump start on American food.

Everyone at Penguin is always amazing. That's why I've been with them for ten years. First I have to big up John "Gunshot" Hamilton. He's really gone outside Penguin's normally exceptional standards

WITH THANKS...

to make this book come together as beautifully as it has – thanks so much, mate! The publishing date was forced forward a month (ages in publishing terms), so big thanks as well to Juliette Butler in production for making that happen. As ever, love and thanks to my good mate Tom Weldon; my wonderful editor at Penguin, Lindsey Evans; and the rest of the posse there: Keith Taylor, Clare Pollock, Chantal Noel, Kate Brotherhood, Elizabeth Smith, Jen Doyle, Anna Rafferty, Ana-Maria Rivera, Thomas Chicken, Zoe Caulfield, and the rest of the brilliant sales team. A big shout-out to freelance designer Chris Callard (www.beachstone.co.uk) and also to the lovely Annie Lee, for doing a brilliant job on yet another one of my books.

Fresh One is incredible, and the effort they put into this project was amazing. I've had the chance to work with some really wonderful producers, directors, and crew this past year. Huge thanks to my dear friends Zoe Collins, Jo Ralling, Roy Ackerman, and Simon Ford. Thanks to Tom McDonald, for keeping it together on a very bumpy flight, and for being an exceedingly special series producer. I was lucky enough to work with some of the best directors in the business: Kirsty Cunningham, Lana Salah, Pamela Gordon, and Tom Coveney – thanks, guys. And to the rest of the team, the producers, assistant producers, runners, and researchers – these really are the some of the hardest-working people in the industry and I'd be happy to work with you lot anytime: Chloe Huntly, Joanne Timoney, Katie Millard, Rosalind Malthouse, Simone O'Neill, Holly Wintgens, Amanda Sealey, Louise Dew, Isabel Davis, Emily Taylor, Georgina Crawford, Alex Buxton, and Lucy Gosling. Thanks as well to Frank Davis, who drove our supplies over all sorts of dodgy terrain from one coast to another! And to the crew I worked with: from camera, sound, and lighting, these guys are the best as far as I'm concerned. I'm honored to work with them and I'd share a sleeping bag with any of them any day: Luke Cardiff, Jon Sayers, Louis Caulfield, Geoff Price, Mike Sarah, James Goddard, and Mike Carling.

To my absolutely fantastic personal team for keeping everything running smoothly behind the scenes: the very lovely Louise Holland, Liz McMullan, Holly Adams and Saffron Greening, Beth Richardson, and Paul Rutherford. And of course big love to the rest of the hardworking gang at my office for their help and support in everything I do. Special thanks to my Web team, who've put together some really cool Web pages specifically to support this book (www.jamieoliver.com/jamies-america) – nice one, guys!

Massive thanks to Maggie Draycott at British Airways and to Niraj Sharma and Ammy Sandhu at United Airlines for helping to get us back and forth safely.

And lastly, to the wonderful Americans who appear in the photos and stories here; thanks so much for inviting me into your homes, being so lovely, and inspiring so many of these recipes. There were also many amazing people behind the scenes who contributed to making this experience a dream trip – so big thanks to all of you too: Jeff Richard, Donald Link, Marcelle Bienvenu, Sara Roahen, Coleen Rush, Lisa Latter, John Sharpe, Janos Wilder, Allan Werthen, Harry Tom, Teec-Nos-Pos School, Tim Rutherford, Damon Lee Fowler, Matthew Roher and team at Cha Bella, David Gelin, Craig Pascoe, Carolyn Wells, Sarah Solomon, the very lovely Cedric and Carla Horton, Robert Sietsema, Daniel Gritzer, Jeff Cicio, Mohammed Elsayed, Shannon Smith, Abelardo de la Peña Junior, Fabian and Maria Debora, Mario Tinoco, Claudia Wade, Marcella Tatarka, Steve "Scuba" Smith, Steve and Melody Singer, Paul Fees, and the Cody Nite Rodeo. Hopefully I'll be seeing you all again soon … *Yee haw!*

Finally, thanks to the Obamas for planting the first organic garden at the White House. Surely that can only mean good things for the food future of America!

INDEX